EXAM ESSENTIALS PRACTICE TESTS

Cambridge English: Advanced (CAE)

2

Tom Bradbury
Eunice Yeates

Australia • Brazil • Japan • Korea • Mexico • Singapore • Spain • United Kingdom • United States

ngl.cengage.com/eltexampreparation

PASSWORD examessentialsadvance!F6#2

Exam Essentials Practice Tests 2
Cambridge English: Advanced (CAE)
(without key)

Tom Bradbury and Eunice Yeates

Publisher: Gavin McLean

Publishing Consultant: Karen Spiller

Editorial Project Manager: Stephanie Parker

Development Editor: Diane Hall

Strategic Marketing Manager: Charlotte Ellis

Project Editor: Tom Relf

Manufacturing Buyer: Eyvett Davis

Cover design: Oliver Hutton

Compositor: Cenveo® Publisher Services

National Geographic Liaison: Wesley Della Volla

Audio: Martin Williamson,
    Prolingua Productions

DVD-ROM: Tom, Dick and Debbie Ltd

Contributing writer: Susan Yokes
    (video materials)

ISBN: 978-1-285-74509-1

National Geographic Learning
Cheriton House, North Way, Andover, Hampshire, SP10 5BE
United Kingdom

Cengage Learning is a leading provider of customized learning solutions with office locations around the globe, including Singapore, the United Kingdom, Australia, Mexico, Brazil and Japan. Locate your local office at: **international.cengage.com/region**

Cengage Learning products are represented in Canada by Nelson Education, Ltd.

Visit National Geographic Learning online at **ngl.cengage.com**

Visit our corporate website at **www.cengage.com**

Photos
169 t (Radius Images/Alamy), 169 c (1bestofphoto/Alamy), 169 b (Chris Whitehead/Getty Images), 170 t (Bambu Productions/Getty Images), 170 b (Ryan McVay/Getty Images), 170 c (RioPatuca Images/Fotolia), 172 t (Oleksandr Rupeta/Alamy), 172 c (dbimages/Alamy), 172 c (Ocean/Corbis UK Ltd), 172 b (Marka/Superstock Ltd.), 173 b (Deyan Georgiev/Alamy), 173 t (Richard Freeda/Getty Images), 175 c (Chris Ryan/Getty Images), 175 t (Pavel Losevsky/Fotolia), 175 b (Moodboard/Corbis UK Ltd), 176 c (BRIAN ANTHONY/Alamy), 176 t (Helen King/Corbis UK Ltd), 176 b (Jose Luis Pelaez Inc/Blend Ima/Corbis UK Ltd), 178 b (Denkou Images/Alamy), 178 c (SelectStock/Getty Images), 178 t (JGI/Jamie Grill/Blend Images/C/Corbis UK Ltd), 179 t (iMate/Fotolia), 179 c (Ghislain & Marie David de Lossy/Getty Images), 179 b (John Cumming/Getty Images), 181 t (Gijsbert Hanekroot/Alamy), 181 c (Carolyn Clarke/Alamy), 181 b (Ariel Skelley/Getty Images), 182 t (Marco Simoni/Robert Harding/Getty Images), 182 c (Cultura/Henn Photography/Getty Images), 182 b (Oliver Furrer/Getty Images), 184 c (Eric Nathan/Alamy), 184 t (Martin Barraud/Getty Images), 184 b (Bruce Ayres/Getty Images), 185 b (Mike Goldwater/Alamy), 185 t (Thomas Imo/Alamy), 185 c (Yoram Lehmann/Getty Images), 187 t (Christian Mueller/Shutterstock), 187 b (JMiks/Shutterstock), 187 c (Education Images/UIG/Getty Images), 188 b (Angela Hampton Picture Library/Alamy), 188 c (Hero Images/Hero Images/Corbis UK Ltd), 188 t (Rainer Elstermann/Getty Images), 190 c (Blend Images/Alamy), 190 b (Bubbles Photolibrary/Alamy), 190 c (Chabruken/Getty Images), 191 t (Dragon Images/Shutterstock), 191 c (imtmphoto/Shutterstock), 191 b (Voyagerix/Shutterstock)

Texts
Adapted from 'Caveman café brings Stone Age diet to the Berlin masses' by Tony Paterson, The Independent, 27 October 2011, copyright The Independent. Adapted from 'Birdwatching is the best training for animal behaviour' by Tim Birkhead, The Guardian, 24 February 2012, Copyright Guardian News & Media Ltd 2012. Adapted from 'Why the Maya Fell: Climate Change, Conflict - And a Trip to the Beach?' by Nicholas Mott, http://news.nationalgeographic.com/news/2012/11/121109-maya-civilization-climate-change-belize-science/, 9 November 2012. Adapted from Student Entrepreneurs by Laura Bridgestock, 27 March 2012, http://www.topuniversities.com/student-info/student-stories/student-entrepreneurs. Adapted from OSU Student Entrepreneur Talks Taking Risk, Embracing Failure, and Tasting the Business Life by OSU Startup Crew, http://oregonstate.startupweekend.org/2013/05/08/osu-student-entrepreneur-talks-taking-risk-embracing-failure-and-tasting-the-business-life/, with permission from Oregon State University Startup Crew. Adapted from 'The seductive phrase every publisher craves' by Robert McCrum, The Observer, 10 April 2011, Copyright Guardian News & Media Ltd 2011. Adapted from 'Ice Water Diver', Rhian Waller, National Geographic Magazine, http://ngm.nationalgeographic.com/125-exploration/risk-takers-gallery#/8, July 2013. Adapted from 'The long and short of what makes a leader' by Roger Dobson, The Independent, 10 February 2013, copyright The Independent. Adapted from 'The cycle path to happiness' by Simon Usborne, The Independent, 18 December 2012, copyright The Independent. Adapted from 'Care farms help people recover their better nature' by Bibi van der Zee, http://www.guardian.co.uk/society/2011/aug/02/care-farms-young-people-nature-benefit, Copyright Guardian News & Media Ltd 2011. Adapted from 'Why we build by Rowan Moore' review by Philippa Sockley, The Telegraph, 26 September 2012, © Telegraph Media Group Limited 2012. Adapted from 'The Architect's Home by Peter Gossel' review by Rowan Moore, The Observer, 21 April 2013, Copyright Guardian News & Media Ltd 2013. Adapted from '20th-Century World Architecture: The Phaidon Atlas by Phaidon editors; The Future of Architecture Since 1889 by Jean-Louis Cohen' review by Rowan Moore, The Observer, 28 October 2012, Copyright Guardian News & Media Ltd 2012. Adapted from 'Species Hunt' by A. R. Williams, National Geographic Magazine, http://ngm.nationalgeographic.com/2013/04/125-explore/seeking-new-species, April 2013. Adapted from 'The heart of Hemingway' by Sam Leith, The Spectator, 7 January 2012, http://www.spectator.co.uk/books/7545693/the-heart-of-hemingway/. Adapted from 'Have you got what it takes to be an Olympic athlete?' by Kate Carter, The Guardian, 28 January 2013, Copyright Guardian News & Media Ltd 2013. Adapted from 'What does it take to run a record label?' by Jack Oughton, http://careers.guardian.co.uk/what-does-it-take-to-run-a-record-label, Copyright Guardian News & Media Ltd 2013. Adapted from 'The Hook: Is it a good or bad time to start an indie label?' by Lars Brandle, http://www.themusicnetwork.com/music-features/industry/2013/04/02/the-hook-is-it-a-good-or-bad-time-to-start-an-indie-label/, 2 April 2013, with permission from The Music Network. Adapted from 'Celebrating Baby's 60th birthday and the start of the computer age' by Pat Hurst, Newsdesk, September 2013, with permission from The Press Association. Adapted from 'Hold the line - overheard phone calls more distracting than room full of people chatting' by Steve Connor, The Independent, 13 March 2013, copyright The Independent. Adapted from 'Australia's lost giants' by Joel Achenbach, National Geographic Magazine, http://ngm.nationalgeographic.com/2010/10/dreamtime-animals/achenbach-text, October 2010. Adapted from 'The artists' artist: modern composers' by Anna Tims, The Guardian, 4 August 2011, Copyright Guardian News & Media Ltd 2011. Adapted from 'Relics to Reefs' by Stephen Harrigan, National Geographic Magazine, http://ngm.nationalgeographic.com/2011/02/artificial-reefs/harrigan-text, February 2011. Adapted from 'Have you considered History of Art?' by Laura Shand, The Independent, 1 October 2102, copyright The Independent. Adapted from Museum careers, http://www.museumsassociation.org/careers - nos 9921/9922/9924/9925, with permission from Museums Association, www.museumsassociation.org. Adapted from 'Forest Giant' by David Quammen, National Geographic Magazine, http://ngm.nationalgeographic.com/2012/12/sequoias/quammen-text, December 2012. Adapted from http://www.spiked-online.com/index.php?/inspired/ articles 1386/1398/1458/1384, with permission from spiked Ltd. Adapted from 'Why you will never sleep on a plane if a baby is crying' by Nick Collins, The Telegraph, 17 October 2012, © Telegraph Media Group Limited 2012. Adapted from 'The enduring myth of music and maths' by Tim Gowers, The Independent, 6 July 2011, copyright The Independent. Adapted from 'The Truth About Chimps' by Joshu

Although every effort has been made to contact copyright holders before publication, this has not always been possible. If notified, the publisher will undertake to rectify any errors or omissions at the earliest opportunity. Note that the sample answer sheets in the Practice tests are not the updated official answer sheets provided by Cambridge as these were not available at the time of publication.

Printed in Greece by Bakis SA
Print Number: 04   Print Year: 2018

Contents

CAMBRIDGE ENGLISH: ADVANCED

Paper 1: READING AND USE OF ENGLISH (1 hour 30 minutes)

Part	Task type and focus	Number of questions	Task format
1	**Multiple-choice cloze** Task focus: vocabulary	8	A multiple-choice cloze text with eight gaps, followed by eight four-option questions.
2	**Open cloze** Task focus: grammar and some vocabulary	8	A modified cloze text with eight gaps which you fill with the appropriate word.
3	**Word formation** Task focus: vocabulary	8	A text with eight gaps. You are asked to complete the text by making an appropriate word from the word prompt you are given for each gap.
4	**Key word transformations** Task focus: grammar and vocabulary	6	This task consists of six discrete key word transformations. You are asked to complete a sentence which means the same as the given sentence using the key word.
5	**Multiple choice** Task focus: reading for detailed understanding of a text, gist, opinion, attitude, tone, purpose, main idea, meaning from context, implication, text organisation features	6	You answer six four-option multiple-choice questions on a text.
6	**Short texts** Task focus: reading to understand meaning across different texts.	4	You read four short texts by different writers on a similar topic, and with a similar purpose. Reading across the texts, you identify similarities and differences in the themes and opinions of the writers.
7	**Missing paragraphs** Task focus: close reading of a text, identifying references and meanings across discourse.	6	You read a text from which six paragraphs have been removed. There is one extra paragraph. You decide which paragraphs complete each gap in the text.
8	**Multiple matching** Task focus: reading for specific information in a text, detail, opinion, attitude	10	You match ten questions to different texts or different sections of a text.

Paper 2: WRITING (1 hour 30 minutes)

Part	Task type and focus	Number of questions	Task format
1	**Question 1** Essay	Part 1 is compulsory. 220–260 words	You write an essay based on a given title and accompanying ideas, including one of your own.
2	**Questions 2–4** may include an email/a letter, a report, a review or a proposal	You have a choice from three tasks. 220–260 words	You carry out a writing task, using the appropriate style and format.

Paper 3: LISTENING (40 minutes approximately)

Part	Task type and focus	Number of questions	Task format
1	**Multiple choice** Task focus: understanding gist, detail, function, purpose, feeling, attitude, opinion, genre, agreement, etc.	6	A series of short unrelated extracts, from monologues or exchanges between interacting speakers. There is one three-option question for each extract.
2	**Sentence completion** Task focus: detail, specific information, stated opinion	8	A monologue. The task consists of eight gapped sentences.
3	**Multiple choice** Task focus: understanding attitude and opinion, main idea, specific information and gist	6	A listening text involving interacting speakers. You have six four-option multiple-choice questions, and need to decide what the correct answer is.
4	**Multiple matching** Task focus: understanding mood and attitude, main ideas, specific information and context	10	Five short monologues, all on a similar theme. You listen once and match each speaker to information from two separate lists.

Paper 4: SPEAKING (15 minutes approximately)

Part	Task type and focus	Input	Task format
1 **Interview** (2 mins)	The interlocutor asks each candidate to say a little about themselves.	Verbal questions	You must be able to • give personal information. • talk about present circumstances / past experiences. • talk about future plans.
2 **Individual long turn** (4 mins)	Each candidate talks about a pair of photographs for 1 minute, followed by a 30-second response from the second candidate.	Visual stimuli, with verbal and written instructions	You must be able to • give information. • express your opinions. • relate photos to yourself and your own experience.
3 **Two-way collaborative task** (4 mins)	The interlocutor asks candidates to carry out a task based on written prompts.	A written question with written stimuli and verbal instructions	You must be able to • exchange information and opinions. • express and justify opinions. • agree, disagree or partly agree. • suggest and speculate.
4 **Discussion** (5 mins)	The interlocutor asks candidates general opinion questions related to the topic covered in Part 3.	Verbal prompts	You must be able to • exchange information and opinions. • express and justify opinions. • agree, disagree or partly agree.

Exam Essentials Practice Tests is a series of materials published by National Geographic Learning for students preparing for the major EFL/ESL examinations: Cambridge English: First (FCE); Cambridge English: Advanced (CAE); and International English Language Testing System (IELTS). The series is characterised by the close attention each component pays to developing a detailed knowledge of the skills and strategies needed for success in each paper or part of the exams.

Cambridge English: Advanced (CAE) Practice Tests helps learners become aware of the Cambridge English: Advanced (CAE) exam requirements, offers details about the format and language in the exam, and helps learners develop exam skills necessary for success. The book also provides extensive practice in all parts of the exam, using the actual test format.

Taking the Exam

Cambridge English: Advanced is one of a series of five Cambridge English exams corresponding to different levels of the Common European Framework of Reference for Languages (CEFR):

• Cambridge English: Key (KET) CEFR Level A2

• Cambridge English: Preliminary (PET) CEFR Level B1

• Cambridge English: First (FCE) CEFR Level B2

• Cambridge English: Advanced (CAE) CEFR Level C1

• Cambridge English: Proficiency (CPE) CEFR Level C2

Cambridge English: Advanced is widely recognised by universities and similar educational institutions, and in commerce and industry, as proof that the holder of this qualification can take a course of study in English at university level, and also carry out managerial and professional work effectively. It can also be used as proof of English skills when applying for employment in English-speaking environments.

The exam can be taken on many dates during a year, and can be taken on paper or on a computer. It consists of four Papers.

Paper 1 Reading and Use of English (1 hour 30 minutes)

• Part 1 is a multiple-choice cloze task. You read a text with eight gaps. This is followed by eight four-option multiple-choice questions. You need to complete each gap with the correct option. Part 1 tests your knowledge of vocabulary, including idioms, fixed phrases, phrasal verbs, collocations and shades of meaning.

• Part 2 is an open cloze task. You read a text with eight gaps. You need to complete each gap with an appropriate word. Part 2 tests your knowledge of the structure of the language – grammar and some vocabulary.

• Part 3 is a word formation task. You read a short text with eight gaps. You need to complete each gap with an appropriate word formed from a prompt word in capitals that appears to the right of the text on the same line as the gap. Part 3 tests your knowledge of how words are formed from other words.

• Part 4 consists of six sentences, each of which is followed by a word and a gapped sentence. You need to complete the gapped sentence so that its meaning is the same as the first sentence using three to six words, including the word given. Part 4 tests your knowledge of vocabulary and grammar.

• Part 5 consists of a long text with six four-option multiple-choice questions. Part 5 tests your ability to read for detail, gist, opinion, attitude, purpose, implication and text organisation features such as reference and comparison.

• Part 6 consists of four short texts written by four different people about the same subject, together with four questions. The questions test your ability to understand the opinions and attitudes expressed in the texts and to identify when writers agree and disagree with each other.

• Part 7 consists of a long text from which six paragraphs have been removed and placed in jumbled order after the text. You have to decide from where in the text the paragraphs have been removed. Part 7 tests your understanding of how a text is structured.

• Part 8 consists of a long text with several sections or several short texts. There are 10 questions which require you to decide which section of the long text or which short text each one refers to. Part 8 tests your ability to read for specific information, detail, opinion and attitude.

Paper 2 Writing (1 hour 30 minutes)

- Part 1 is compulsory. You are required to write an essay in 220–260 words. Before you write your answer, you must read the instructions as well as an input text or texts. Part 1 focuses on your ability to evaluate, express opinions, hypothesise, etc. Persuasion is always an important element in your writing in Part 1.

- There are three questions to choose from in Part 2. For questions 2–4, you are required to write an email/letter, a proposal, a report or a review in 220–260 words. Part 2 focuses on your ability to give opinions, persuade, justify, give advice, compare, etc.

- Both parts of the Writing Paper test your ability to write a text according to instructions in an appropriate style and register for a given purpose and target reader. Effective text organisation, accuracy and a good range of vocabulary are also important.

Paper 3 Listening (approximately 40 minutes)

- Part 1 consists of three short monologues or texts involving interacting speakers. You are required to answer two three-option multiple-choice questions for each extract. Part 1 tests your ability to understand feeling, attitude, opinion, purpose, function, agreement, course of action, general gist, detail, etc.

- Part 2 consists of a long monologue. You are required to complete eight gapped sentences with information you hear on the recording. Each gap is completed by one, two or three words or a number. Part 2 tests your ability to understand specific information and stated opinion.

- Part 3 consists of a text involving interacting speakers. You are required to answer six four-option multiple-choice questions. Part 3 tests your ability to understand attitude and opinion.

- Part 4 consists of five short monologues on a related theme. There are two tasks in this part. Both tasks require you choose from a list of options the opinion that each speaker expresses. Part 4 tests your ability to understand gist, attitude and main point and to interpret context.

Paper 4 Speaking (approximately 15 minutes)

The Speaking Paper generally involves two candidates and two examiners.

- In Part 1 you have a brief conversation with the examiner. Part 1 tests your ability to give personal information and use social and interactional language.

- In Part 2 the examiner gives you and the other candidate visual and written prompts. Each candidate is required to use the prompts he/she is given to talk for a minute. He/She is also required to answer a question based on the other candidate's prompts in 30 seconds. Part 2 tests your ability to organise a larger unit of discourse to compare, describe, express opinions and speculate.

- In Part 3 the examiner gives you and the other candidate visual and written prompts. You are required to use the prompts to have a conversation with the other candidate. Part 3 tests your ability to sustain an interaction, exchange ideas, express and justify opinions, agree and/or disagree, suggest, evaluate, reach a decision through negotiation, etc.

- In Part 4 the examiner asks you questions based on the topics you talked about in Part 3. You are required to have a three-way discussion with the examiner and the other candidate. Part 4 tests your ability to exchange information, express and justify opinions, agree and/or disagree.

Preparing for the exam

In preparing for the four Papers, the following points should be taken into account.

Reading and Use of English

To prepare for the **Use of English** (Parts 1, 2, 3 and 4), you need to develop your awareness and use of both grammatical structures and vocabulary. You need to know how structures such as verb forms, modal and auxiliary verbs, pronouns, prepositions, conjunctions, modifiers and determiners are used correctly in a variety of different types of text. You also need a good knowledge of vocabulary, so learn whole phrases rather than single words in isolation, how words and phrases are used in combination with other words, how words can have different meanings and uses, and how different words can be formed from a root. It helps to read widely and to pay attention to grammar and vocabulary as you read. Make use of dictionaries and grammar books (except when doing the tests), and develop an efficient system for recording the new vocabulary and grammar you encounter.

To prepare for the **Reading** (Parts 5, 6, 7 and 8), you should read from a range of material: newspapers, magazines, journals, novels, leaflets, brochures, etc. When you read, pay attention to text organisation features, train yourself to recognise the author's purpose in writing and his or her tone, and learn to read between the lines for what is implied rather than stated explicitly. It is important to practise different reading strategies that can be used for different parts of the Reading Paper, for example skimming for the main idea and gist, scanning to locate specific information or reading closely to determine the writer's precise meaning.

Writing

You need to be familiar with all the text types you may be required to write in the exam. You should also be aware of the criteria that will be used in marking your texts.

• Has the candidate achieved the purpose stated in the instructions?
• Does the text have a positive general effect on the target reader?
• Does the text cover all the content points?
• Is the text organised effectively and are ideas linked appropriately?
• Has language been used accurately?
• Does the text have a good range of vocabulary and grammatical features?
• Is the register appropriate for the task?
• Is the layout appropriate?

Listening

You should practise listening to a wide variety of spoken English: announcements, speeches, lectures, talks, radio broadcasts, anecdotes, radio interviews, discussions, etc. You should also practise listening for different purposes: to understand gist, identify context or attitude or find specific information.

Speaking

You should practise speaking English as much as possible. It is important to master conversational skills such as turn taking and the appropriate way to participate in a discussion, giving full but natural answers to questions and requesting clarification.

Further information can be obtained from the Cambridge English website: www.cambridgeenglish.org

Practice Tests: contents

Cambridge English: Advanced (CAE) in the *Exam Essentials Practice Tests* series prepares candidates for the Cambridge English: Advanced examination by providing **eight full practice tests,** which accurately reflect the latest exam specifications.

There are **three guided tests** at the beginning, which feature **essential tips** to practise exam strategy. These tips offer guidance and general strategies for approaching each task. Other tips offer advice relevant to specific questions in the guided tests. These guided tests will help students prepare for each paper, while the following five **tests (without guidance)** will offer students thorough practice at a realistic exam level.

The **DVD-ROM** accompanying the book includes the audio materials for all the Listening Papers. These accurately reflect the exam in both style and content. Moreover, the audio materials for Tests 1 and 2 have been recorded with the repetitions and full pauses, exactly as in the exam itself.

A **writing bank** includes **sample answers** for the kinds of tasks that occur in Paper 2 (Writing), writing tips in the form of notes and **useful phrases** for the different task types. Varied **visual materials** for Paper 4 (Speaking) have also been included, while a **language bank** supplies useful phrases and expressions for use in the Speaking Paper.

There is also a **glossary** for each test, explaining vocabulary that is likely to be unfamiliar to students.

Clear and straightforward design simplifies use of the book. **Exam overview** tables ensure that key information is readily accessible, while a specially designed menu makes it easy to navigate through the different parts and papers of each practice test.

You will find **sample exam answer sheets** on pages 166–168 which you can photocopy and use to note down your answers. These will help you practise using the answer sheets you will be given in the real exam.

For more practice, there is also an additional book of tests for this exam: *Exam Essentials Practice Tests 1 Cambridge English: Advanced (CAE).*

Practice Tests: principles

In writing this book, three guiding principles have been observed.

Firstly, that it should be useful for teachers, students sitting the Cambridge English: Advanced exam for the first time or re-sitting the exam, whether they are working alone or in a class. Students approaching the exam for the first time would be best advised to work through the book linearly, developing their skills and confidence; those re-sitting the exam can consult the Exam overview tables to concentrate on particular areas for targeted revision. The **without key** edition can be used by students working in a class, while the **with key** edition includes a detailed **answer key and all the audio scripts,** ensuring that students working alone can benefit from support while attempting these tests.

The second principle is that the questions should accurately reflect the range of questions found in the Cambridge English: Advanced exam. Thus students obtain guidance concerning the general content and the best way of approaching the tasks from the questions themselves. Seeing the questions in this light – as instructions to the candidate from the examiner rather than intimidating challenges – also helps students feel less daunted by the whole experience of sitting a major exam like this.

The third principle is that the texts used in the practice tests should be not only representative of those used in the exam, but also varied and interesting. Everyone finds it easier to learn if the subject matter is relevant to his or her lifestyle and interests. In choosing, editing and creating the texts here, we have done our utmost to ensure that the experience of working with this book is as stimulating and rewarding as possible.

This edition of *Exam Essentials* for students of Cambridge English: Advanced (CAE) includes a brand new DVD-ROM which focuses on the Speaking test component of the Cambridge English: Advanced examination. The DVD-ROM includes two videos:

• a complete Cambridge English: Advanced Speaking test.
• a short clip giving valuable advice about the Cambridge English: Advanced Speaking test.

To maximise learning from the complete Cambridge English: Advanced Speaking test, the following PDFs are also available on the DVD-ROM:

• a worksheet for individual or class use.
• an answer key for the worksheet.
• the complete script of the Speaking test.

A complete Speaking test

A full Cambridge English: Advanced Speaking test interview is approximately 15 minutes in length. Please note that the interview shown on this DVD-ROM is a slightly extended version of the Speaking test. This allows for a wide range of language and types of response to be included. This interview also features high-level candidates whose performance would achieve a good pass in the exam. The video therefore provides a good model to follow. Don't worry if you feel you may not perform to this high standard in every area of the test. You will need to demonstrate a good level, but you will not need to use every structure or item of vocabulary perfectly in order to pass the test.

The video clearly details:

• the role of the examiners.
• the timings of the test.
• the four parts of the test and what is involved in each one.

The role of the examiners

There are two examiners in the test room. Examiner 1 (the interlocutor) asks the candidates questions and handles the tasks. He or she has to keep to very strict timings and has a script to follow. Unscripted conversation or questions are therefore not possible. This is to ensure that each candidate receives equal treatment. Examiner 2 (the assessor) does not usually speak in the test, except to greet the candidates. However, Examiner 2 will make notes. Both examiners give marks to the candidates.

The timings of the test

Part 1: Interview – 2 minutes (3 minutes for groups of three)

Part 2: Individual long turn – 4 minutes (6 minutes for groups of three)

Part 3: Collaborative task – 4 minutes (6 minutes for groups of three)

Part 4: Discussion – 5 minutes (8 minutes for groups of three)

The four parts of the test

Part 1: Interview – this includes greeting the candidates, introducing the examiners and general questions about yourself.

Part 2: Individual long turn – this involves talking about two out of three pictures and briefly answering a question about your partner's pictures after he/she has spoken.

Part 3: Collaborative task – this is where both candidates talk about prompts on a diagram, and reach a decision through negotiation.

Part 4: Discussion – the interlocutor leads a discussion by asking candidates questions. Candidates exchange information and opinions related to the topic in Part 3.

How each part of the test should be answered

The video offers tips for improving candidates' performance in each of the four parts. In Part 1, candidates need to give personal information, talk about their present circumstances, talk about past experiences and future plans as well as express opinions. In Part 2, candidates need to express their opinions through comparing, hypothesising and speculating on the pictures given. In Part 3, candidates need to work together to exchange ideas and opinions, agree or disagree, suggest, speculate, evaluate and reach a decision through negotiation. In Part 4, candidates express and justify their opinions and agree and disagree.

Tips and advice

Following the Speaking test, there is a short clip to supplement the speaking tips given in the book. In this section, which is about five minutes long, an examiner gives some tips and advice about how to do well in the Cambridge English: Advanced Speaking test.

The worksheet

This printable worksheet accompanies the complete Cambridge English: Advanced Speaking test. Although primarily designed for self-study, the worksheet can also be used in the classroom. It provides in-depth information about the Speaking test and focuses on the language each candidate uses in the video.

The worksheet is divided into four sections which relate to each part of the Speaking test. It includes activities which:

• draw students' attention to key features of the candidate's response.
• relate these features to the marking criteria used by the examiners.
• give the student practice in developing their own answers for similar questions.

A separate answer key and a full video script are also provided.

PAPER 1 Reading and ▶ Part 1
Use of English | Part 2
PAPER 2 Writing | Part 3
| Part 4
PAPER 3 Listening | Part 5
PAPER 4 Speaking | Part 6
| Part 7
| Part 8

For questions **1–8**, read the text below and decide which answer (**A**, **B**, **C** or **D**) best fits each gap. There is an example at the beginning (**0**).

Mark your answers **on the separate answer sheet**.

Example:

0 **A** scan **B** glance **C** view **D** spot

```
0  A   B   C   D
```

Essential tips

▶ Part 1 of the Reading and Use of English paper tests your awareness of vocabulary.

▶ Read the whole text to get a general idea of the subject.

▶ There is only one correct answer for each question, and it must fit in the sentence and also the meaning of the whole text.

▶ The gapped word may be part of a collocation (two words that are frequently combined – e.g. *make progress*), a phrasal verb or an expression, or it may just be the only suitable word for the specific context.

▶ Look carefully at the words before and after each gap. For example, sometimes only one option is correct because of a preposition that follows the gap.

Question 2: All four options fit the gap in terms of their meaning but only one option is followed by the preposition *on*.

Question 4: This is an example of a collocation. Only one option goes with *forbidden*.

Question 5: Which of these phrasal verbs means 'to cause something new to happen'?

Question 8: This is an example of an item where the answer depends on the grammatical structure that comes after. Only one of the options can be followed by an infinitive – *to have lost* – in this sentence.

A Stone-Age restaurant

At first (**0**) …….., Berlin's Sauvage restaurant looks much like many other fashionable eateries. But look closely and you'll discover that it offers an unusual experience (**1**) …….. Paleolithic (or Stone-Age) food.

Diners sit at candle-lit tables and eat meals (**2**) …….. on the dietary habits of our prehistoric (**3**) …….. who lived between two million and 200,000 years ago. The food includes unprocessed fruit, vegetables, meat, fish, eggs, nuts and seeds, but sugar, bread, rice and dairy products are (**4**) …….. forbidden, as they were unavailable to Stone Age hunter-gatherers.

The restaurant's owners insist that the 'Paleo diet' (**5**) …….. greater energy levels, increased muscle mass and clearer skin. 'Many people think this diet is just a passing fashion, but it's a world-wide (**6**) ……..,' says one. It is probably strongest in the USA where thousands of people have apparently gone 'Paleo'. One of the best-known people to (**7**) …….. the caveman cuisine is the veteran pop singer, Tom Jones, who (**8**) …….. to have lost more than ten kilos after switching to it.

1	**A** consisting	**B** starring	**C** highlighting	**D** featuring
2	**A** based	**B** linked	**C** derived	**D** inspired
3	**A** founders	**B** originators	**C** ancestors	**D** pioneers
4	**A** tightly	**B** precisely	**C** extremely	**D** strictly
5	**A** brings about	**B** sets up	**C** pulls out	**D** follows with
6	**A** situation	**B** phenomenon	**C** circumstance	**D** incident
7	**A** enter	**B** adopt	**C** assume	**D** exert
8	**A** asserts	**B** maintains	**C** claims	**D** states

For questions **9–16**, read the text below and think of the word which best fits each gap. Use only one word in each gap. There is an example at the beginning (**0**).

Write your answers **IN CAPITAL LETTERS on the separate answer sheet**.

Example: | 0 | O | F | | | | | | | | | | | | | | | | | | | | | | |

Body language – do we really understand it?

Newspapers accuse a well-known footballer (**0**) .... anti-social behaviour in a night club. His manager makes a public statement in (**9**) .... he asserts that the young man is innocent. When asked (**10**) .... makes him so sure, the manager says 'he looked me straight in the eye when he told me.'

Can we really know (**11**) .... or not someone is telling the truth just by looking in their eyes? Psychologist Robert James is far (**12**) .... convinced. '(**13**) .... and large, maintaining eye contact is something liars do because eye movements are fairly easy to control.'

Communications expert Becky Rhodes shares his scepticism. 'Body language clues are never precise (**14**) .... to rely on with absolute confidence,' she says. She illustrates this by describing the 'Othello error', named (**15**) .... Shakespeare's tragic character who claims his wife has been deceiving him and then interprets her shocked reaction (**16**) .... guilt. 'Personally, the minute I see a security guard watching me in a shop, I start looking guilty, so my body language definitely doesn't reflect the truth about me.'

Essential tips

▶ Part 2 of the Reading and Use of English paper tests your awareness of grammar and common expressions, and your ability to use these words correctly.

▶ Read the whole text to get a general idea of the subject.

▶ Most of the gaps need grammatical words. Decide which type of word each gap needs. These could include: prepositions (e.g. *of, in*), articles (*a, the*), pronouns (*they, it, them*), relative pronouns (*who, which*), conjunctions (*and, so*), parts of verbs (*be, been*), modal verbs (*might, must*), particles of phrasal verbs (*look **through**, look **into***), parts of phrases (*in **order** to*).

▶ The gap will probably not need a topic word. For example, in the phrase *she might have known*, *known* would not be gapped, but *she* or *might* or *have* could be.

▶ Sometimes more than one answer is possible. For example, if *may* is possible, *might* and *could* are often possible too. So, don't worry if you can think of more than one answer, just choose one.

▶ The word you choose must fit the meaning of the text as a whole. So, when you complete the task, read the whole text to see if it all makes sense.

Question 9: A relative pronoun is needed here. Which one can follow a preposition?

Question 11: Look at the whole sentence, and particularly at this part of the question: *can we know ... or not someone is telling the truth?* Which word often follows *know* in questions?

Question 12: Look at the whole of the second paragraph. The psychologist does not believe the manager was right. Which word fits *far ... convinced* to express this idea?

Question 13: This is a linking phrase which means 'in general'. You need a preposition to complete it.

PAPER 1	Reading and ▸	Part 1
	Use of English	Part 2
PAPER 2	Writing	**Part 3**
		Part 4
PAPER 3	Listening	Part 5
PAPER 4	Speaking	Part 6
		Part 7
		Part 8

For questions **17–24**, read the text below. Use the word given in capitals at the end of some of the lines to form a word that fits in the gap **in the same line**. There is an example at the beginning (**0**).

Write your answers **IN CAPITAL LETTERS on the separate answer sheet**.

Example: 0 S H O R T A G E S

Fog catchers – a way of getting water into the desert

In the Atacama Desert of northern Chile, water (**0**) ....   **SHORT**

are nothing new. In one of the driest places on earth,

some local (**17**) .... have never seen a drop of rain.   **RESIDE**

(**18**) ...., water supplies for the few remote settlements   **HISTORY**

have been trucked in. In the last 20 years, however,

some communities have turned to 'fog catchers' as an

alternative source of water and a means of (**19**) .... the   **VITAL**

arid land.

Although it never rains, a heavy (**20**) .... fog often rolls off   **COAST**

the Pacific Ocean and across the desert. As it reaches the rocky

foothills of the Andes mountains, (**21**) .... is captured in large,   **MOIST**

specially designed nets. Droplets run down the nets into pipes,

and then into (**22**) .... tanks. This water is fresh enough to drink,   **STORE**

but enough is also collected for other uses like washing

and farming.

This simple and (**23**) .... technology is relatively cheap and easy   **INVENT**

to manage, which is why 'fog catchers' are now being tried out in

other parts of the world where (**24**) .... of desertification is   **REVERSE**

a high priority.

Essential tips

▸ Part 3 of the Reading and Use of English paper tests your knowledge of vocabulary, in particular your ability to build words from a basic root using prefixes and suffixes and making other kinds of changes.

▸ Read the whole text to get a general idea of the subject.

▸ Think about which type of word is needed for each gap. Is it a verb, noun, adjective or adverb? Try writing V (for verb), N (for noun), ADJ (for adjective) or ADV (for adverb) by the gaps to remind yourself of the word type required.

▸ Look at the whole sentence, not just the line with the gap in it.

▸ Look at the word in capital letters to the right of the gap. You will need to alter the form of this word by adding a prefix or suffix or by making some other change.

▸ Some words will need more than one change.

▸ When you've finished the task, read through it again and check that it all makes sense.

▸ As you read it again, check the spelling, and, also, whether words should be singular or plural.

Question 17: Look at the words before and after the gap to check whether the word should be singular or plural.

Question 18: An adverb is often needed at the start of a sentence. First, think about how to form an adjective from *history*. Then, think how this adjective can become an adverb. Also, check the spelling.

Question 19: A verb meaning 'giving new life to' is needed here. You will need to add a prefix and a suffix.

Question 20: Sometimes you may think that no change is needed. Here, for example, you may think that *coast fog* is possible. However, you will always need to make some change to the word in capital letters. In this case, you need to change *coast* in some way to make it an adjective.

Essential tips

▸ Part 4 of the Reading and Use of English paper tests your knowledge of grammar, vocabulary and sentence structure, and your ability to use these in an accurate way.

▸ For each question, read both sentences carefully. The second sentence must have the same meaning as the first, but in different words.

▸ You must not change the key word in any way.

▸ You may need to change the word order. Think about words that may need to change, for example, an adjective to an adverb, or the other way round.

▸ You may need to change the sentence from negative to positive or from active to passive, or the other way round.

▸ You must use between three and six words. Contracted words count as two words, e.g. *don't* = *do not*.

Question 25: Which phrase means 'knew nothing at all'? How can *whose* be used to mean 'who the folder belonged to'?

Question 26: What pattern of words comes after *encourage*? What phrase beginning *make a ...* means the same as *complain*? How should *formally* be changed?

Question 27: Can you change *demolish* to make a noun? Can you think of a phrase including *place* that means 'happened'?

Question 30: What passive structure beginning with *have* means 'get someone to service your car'? If the structure is passive, you do not need to mention who serviced the car – i.e. the mechanic. Notice that the first sentence begins with *wanted* in the past; make sure the changes you make express this meaning.

For questions **25–30**, complete the second sentence so that it has a similar meaning to the first sentence, using the word given. **Do not change the word given.** You must use between **three** and **six** words, including the word given. Here is an example (**0**).

Example:

0 Chloe would only eat a pizza if she could have a mushroom topping.

ON

Chloe .... a mushroom topping when she had a pizza.

The gap can be filled with the words 'insisted on having', so you write:

Example: | **0** | INSISTED ON HAVING |

Write **only** the missing words **IN CAPITAL LETTERS on the separate answer sheet.**

---

25 Paula knew nothing at all about who the folder belonged to and why it appeared on her desk.

WHOSE

Paula had absolutely .... and why it appeared on her desk.

26 Naomi said Michael should formally complain about the service they'd had at the hotel.

MAKE

Naomi encouraged .... about the service they'd had at the hotel.

27 The stadium was demolished in 2003, and there are still no plans to build a new one.

PLACE

The .... in 2003, and there are still no plans to build a new one.

28 Jenny's achievements impress me much less than her sister's do.

NEARLY

I don't think Jenny's achievements are .... her sister.

29 Unless someone comes late, we should be able to get through all the points in today's meeting.

TURNS

As .... on time, we should be able to get through all the points in today's meeting.

30 I wanted to get a mechanic to service my car before I went on holiday, but I didn't have time.

HAVE

I would like .... before I went on holiday, but I didn't have time.

PAPER 1 Reading and	Part 1
Use of English	Part 2
PAPER 2 Writing	Part 3
	Part 4
PAPER 3 Listening	**Part 5**
PAPER 4 Speaking	Part 6
	Part 7
	Part 8

You are going to read a newspaper article. For questions **31–36**, choose the answer (**A**, **B**, **C** or **D**) which you think fits best according to the text.

Mark your answers **on the separate answer sheet**.

Birdwatching

Bird expert Tim Birkhead looks at the fascinating subject of what we know or can know about birds.

The sight of two lovebirds nibbling each other's necks is enough of a cliché that we barely give it a second thought. These small parrots are called lovebirds because their closeness and mutual preening resemble human affection. But what do they feel when they behave like that? Indeed, do they feel anything at all? Even asking the question seems wrong somehow, especially if you consider yourself an ethologist, a student of animal behaviour. The Nobel Prize winner, Niko Tinbergen, warned fellow ethologists to steer well clear of feelings. 'This is not the method we shall follow in our study of animal behaviour,' he announced in 1951. Like most ethologists, through much of my career I have hardly deviated from this hard-nosed approach. But every so often, I have seen something that simply wouldn't sit easily with it.

When my boyhood birdwatching became an obsession rather than simply a hobby, my despairing father warned me that I'd never make a career out of it, but luckily I did. Birdwatching is the best possible training for studying animal behaviour; to study birds well, you have to almost think like a bird. I spent years on various remote islands watching those great seabirds, guillemots. Intensely social, guillemots live shoulder-to-shoulder in huge city-like colonies. Like us they form friendships and long-term pair bonds and, like lovebirds, they show their affection for their partners through mutual preening and striking greeting ceremonies.

Once as I watched, an incubating guillemot stood up from its egg and roared out its greeting – apparently to no one. I was perplexed, but on looking out to sea – hundreds of metres away – there was a guillemot flying towards the colony. A few seconds later, it landed beside its partner. Guillemots were never quite the same for me after this. They can see so much better than I can, and they have some kind of guillemot-recognition system in their brain. The moment eventually inspired me to explore and write about the way birds use vision, hearing, touch, smell, taste and feelings to experience the world.

While it was relatively straightforward to describe how much better or worse a bird sees, hears, smells or touches than we do, trying to understand – scientifically – how a bird feels is fraught with difficulties. As the philosopher Thomas Nagel pointed out in his 1974 essay 'What is it like to be a bat?', we cannot know what it is like to be another person, let alone another species. He chose bats because they are mammals and we share a lot of physiology and neurobiology with them, and because bats possess a sense most of us don't have: echolocation (listening for echoes to locate things). I suspect Nagel thought that no human can echolocate, but in fact some blind people do so extremely well. Nagel's point, however, is this: because it is impossible to know what it is like to be another person, trying to imagine what non-humans feel is a waste of time.

It isn't. The behavioural thinking that I have followed all these years has served me, and other scientists like me, well. But it's also a kind of trap. Anything that doesn't fit gets ignored because the intellectual framework doesn't permit one to say something different for fear of being labelled unprofessional. But ways of thinking come and go. As our knowledge of animal behaviour has increased, and with it the realisation that so many behaviours we once considered uniquely human, like tool use and language, aren't, the boundaries are changing.

It's all very well to study the survival value of long-term pair bonds or mutual preening, but without knowing anything about the sensory bases for these behaviours, our understanding is always going to be incomplete. A few years ago, behaviourial zoologists discovered 'symmetry', and assumed that symmetry (for example, in a perfectly proportioned human face or a peacock's tail) constituted beauty and quality, and was therefore the basis for the selection of partners. Few researchers bothered to test whether animals could assess symmetry in the same way as we can. One who did checked whether female starlings could distinguish males based on the symmetry of their feathers. These highly social birds couldn't. Their senses weren't up to it. Any study that had assessed starling partner choice on the basis of symmetry without knowing this would have reached false conclusions. In contrast, the sense of vision in starlings (and most other birds) is far better than our own: they can discriminate many more colours than we can, and they use this to assess potential partners.

31 What does the writer suggest about birds in the first paragraph?
   A   The names commonly given to them can be inappropriate.
   B   People are often too subjective in the way they think about them.
   C   Insufficient attention is paid to the way they behave towards each other.
   D   Most serious research on them ignores the idea they might have emotions.

32 What does the writer say about himself in the second paragraph?
   A   His personal sympathies lie with particular species of birds.
   B   He has managed to achieve what was expected of him.
   C   He recognised early on how unusual his interests were.
   D   His understanding of birds stems from lengthy observation.

33 The writer describes a particular incident in the third paragraph to explain
   A   what originally attracted him to guillemots.
   B   what led him to investigate birds' senses.
   C   the challenges that birdwatchers encounter.
   D   the sophistication of guillemot communication.

34 Why does the writer refer to an idea put forward by Thomas Nagel?
   A   to underline the differences between birds and mammals
   B   to explain scientists' neglect of an aspect of animal research
   C   to emphasise the significance of the subject he is studying
   D   to draw attention to advances in scientific knowledge

35 What point does the writer make in the fifth paragraph?
   A   The way animals behave may have changed over time.
   B   Scientific debate has become more and more competitive.
   C   Research has shown the limitations of certain ideas about animals.
   D   The cautious approach he adopted in his work is a source of regret to him.

36 The writer discusses the study of 'symmetry' to illustrate
   A   the danger of ignoring birds' senses as a subject of study.
   B   the fact that birds tend to have better eyesight than humans.
   C   the idea that theories in science are disproved on a regular basis.
   D   the error in regarding beauty as a key factor in birds' choice of partners.

PAPER 1	Reading and ▸	Part 1
	Use of English	Part 2
PAPER 2	Writing	Part 3
		Part 4
PAPER 3	Listening	Part 5
PAPER 4	Speaking	**Part 6**
		Part 7
		Part 8

You are going to read four contributions to a debate on whether entry to museums should be free of charge. For questions **37–40**, choose from the contributions **A–D**. The contributions may be chosen more than once.

Mark your answers **on the separate answer sheet**.

Should entry to museums be free of charge?

The views of four speakers at a conference on museum funding are summarised here.

A

In the late 1990s, the then UK government decided to end admission charges to a number of leading museums and art galleries in the country, and within a few years visitor numbers to these institutions had almost doubled; one report estimated an increase from 27 to 42 million visitors within a year. This is the clearest possible evidence for the popularity of free museum admission, with both local citizens and tourists. It is no coincidence that the UK saw an impressive growth in tourism to the country in the same period, and there is no need to go into detail here about the implications of this for employment and general prosperity. Add to this the contribution that museums make in communicating culture, knowledge and inspiration to visitors, particularly younger ones, and it becomes obvious that the state investment required to fund free entry to museums pays off handsomely.

B

It is hardly surprising that surveys show most people favour free museum admission. Why would anyone spurn a free chance to see a collection of beautiful paintings or some fascinating historical objects? The fact is, however, that although visitor numbers generally go up when admission is free, more detailed analysis of the figures reveals some complex issues. For example, it is far from certain that free museum access automatically brings in the tourists. Most market research indicates that they want quality and will pay for it if necessary. Moreover, the evidence suggests that people who run museums which rely on the state for their funding have little incentive to make their collections more exciting and imaginatively displayed in order to boost visitor numbers; the fee, or absence of one, does their work for them. The need to attract paying customers, on the other hand, tends to concentrate the minds of museum and gallery directors.

C

Free admission to museums and galleries usually causes attendance to rise and, with effective marketing, stimulates growth in the tourist industry. However, studies have also found that, by and large, increased entries are accounted for by tourists, who do not pay local income taxes, and more frequent visits by local people who already go to museums, rather than a wider spread of the population. In other words, all taxpayers subsidise museum access for tourists and a limited local largely middle-class demographic who could afford to pay for museum admission. Therefore, the claim that free museums make the wider population more knowledgeable and cultured is questionable at best. The fact is, the majority have little interest in museums and are resentful when they learn how much they are paying for them. They would be even more perturbed to hear that state-funded museums, free of the need to compete to survive, tend to be complacent and unenterprising.

D

Museums have a crucial role to play in preserving and transmitting a nation's history and heritage, and in broadening intellectual and cultural horizons, among the younger generation in particular. Opinion polls show that most people understand this and, for this reason, favour free access. They also show people understand that free museum admission requires state funding, which in turn depends on taxation. While most of us dislike paying taxes, we know what they are for. People can also appreciate that government funding gives those who run museums a certain level of security which allows them to plan for the longer-term. This tends to lift the quality of museum collections and the way they are displayed and explained to visitors. Great museums which have free access also help to boost tourism, which is so central to the economic well-being of many countries nowadays.

Which contributor

shares A's view regarding the role of museums in education?

37 ___

has a different opinion from the others about the possible impact of the cost of entry to museums on tourism?

38 ___

has the same opinion as C on the way state funding affects the development of museums?

39 ___

takes a different view from the others regarding public attitudes towards the cost of entry to museums?

40 ___

Essential tips

▶ Part 6 of the Reading and Use of English paper tests your ability to understand opinions and attitudes expressed in different texts and to decide whether different writers have similar or different opinions. There are always four short texts by different writers about the same subject.

▶ Read the title and the texts quickly to get a general idea of what they are about. Don't worry if there are words or phrases you don't understand.

▶ Look carefully at the four questions and highlight the key words relating to the topic in each.

▶ Read the first text and highlight the parts of the text that refer to each of the questions. Write the relevant question numbers next to the text. Then do the same for the other three texts.

▶ Go through the questions again and highlight the part asking you to differentiate somehow between texts (usually at the beginning of the question).

▶ Then look at the parts of each text that are relevant to Question 37. Compare them carefully and decide which have similar views and which have different views.

Question 37: The key words in this question are *role of museums in education*. The relevant part of text A is '... the contribution that museums make in communicating culture, knowledge and inspiration to visitors, particularly younger ones ...' Now look at the other three texts and highlight references to education. As in text A, the word *education* may be paraphrased. The question asks which contributor shares A's view, so you need to work out which text expresses a similar view to A's.

Question 38: The key words in this sentence are *impact of the cost of entry ... on tourism* and you are asked to find a different opinion from the others, so you need to find three views that are similar and one that is different. The relevant part of text A is '... the clearest possible evidence for the popularity of free museum admission, with both local citizens and tourists. It is no coincidence that the UK saw an impressive growth in tourism.' So, writer A says free museum entry increased tourism. The relevant part of text B is 'It is far from certain that free museum access automatically brings in the tourists.' Is this similar or different from the view expressed in A? Now, go through the same process with texts C and D.

PAPER 1 Reading and ▸   Part 1
          Use of English   Part 2

PAPER 2 Writing   Part 3
                             Part 4
PAPER 3 Listening   Part 5

PAPER 4 Speaking   Part 6
                             Part 7
                             Part 8

You are going to read a magazine article about the ancient Maya civilisation in Central America. Six paragraphs have been removed from the article. Choose from the paragraphs **A–G** the one which fits each gap (**41–46**). There is one extra paragraph which you do not need to use.

Mark your answers **on the separate answer sheet.**

The rise and fall of the ancient Maya civilisation

No civilisation has fallen quite like the Maya, seemingly swallowed by the jungle after centuries of urban, cultural and agricultural evolution. What went wrong? Recent discoveries point not to a cataclysmic eruption, earthquake or plague but rather to climate change. But first came the boom years, roughly AD300 to 660. At the beginning of the so-called Classic Maya period, some 60 Maya cities sprang up across much of modern-day Guatemala, Belize and Mexico's Yucatán Peninsula.

41

But then came the bust, a decline that lasted at least two centuries. By 1100, the residents of once thriving Maya cities seem to have just disappeared. In the nineteenth century, when explorers began discovering the overgrown ruins of 'lost cities', theorists imagined an immense volcanic eruption or earthquake — or maybe an empire-wide pandemic.

42

One study of stalagmites in a cavern in Belize links swings in weather patterns to both the rise and fall of the empire. Formed by water and minerals dripping from above, stalagmites grow more quickly in rainier years, giving scientists a reliable record of historical rainfall trends. 'The early Classic Maya period was unusually wet,' according to lead researcher Douglas Kennett. And during this time, he says, 'the population proliferated, aided by a surge in agriculture.'

43

But the long wet spell turned out to be an anomaly. When the climate pendulum swung back, hard times followed. 'Mayan systems were founded on those high rainfall patterns,' Kennett said. 'They could not support themselves when patterns changed.'

The following centuries were characterised by repeated and, at times extreme, drought. Agriculture declined and, not coincidentally, social conflict rose.

44

But times would get even harder. The stalagmite record suggests that between 1020 and 1100 the region suffered its longest dry spell of the last 2,000 years. With it, the study suggests, came crop failure, famine, mass migration and death. By the time Spanish conquistadors arrived in the sixteenth century, inland Maya populations had decreased by 90 per cent, and urban centres and farms had been abandoned and reclaimed by forest.

45

According to climate scientist, Benjamin Cook, this widespread deforestation reduced the flow of moisture from the ground to the atmosphere, interrupting the natural rain cycle and in turn reducing rainfall. Computer simulations that Cook ran for one study show that localised drying decreased atmospheric moisture by five to 15 per cent annually. 'Even a ten per cent decrease is considered an environmental catastrophe,' he says.

46

But, according to Professor of Environment and Society B.L. Turner, 'that's the kind of oversimplification we're trying to get away from. The Mayan situation is not applicable today — our society is just so radically different.' In his own study, Turner concludes that the natural environment recovered rather quickly after the dry centuries. What happened to the Maya, he suggests, is that in order to escape starvation and wars inland, many moved to coastal areas where life was comparatively easier. And once there, they may simply have forgotten their great cities.

A To some extent, however, the Maya may have shaped their own decline. At the height of the civilisation, the area had a population of tens of millions, and vast numbers of trees would have been cut down to make space for cities and farms, and to provide fuel.

B Indeed, it was during the rainiest decades of this era, from AD440 to 660, that the cities sprouted. In fact, all the hallmarks of Maya civilisation — sophisticated political systems, monumental architecture, complex religion — came into full flower during this era.

C One common misconception is that the Maya completely vanished after the arrival of the Spanish in the sixteenth century. There are, in fact, Mayan people still in the area today, with their own culture and traditions. The mystery, historically, is why their cities were abandoned and never reclaimed.

D With their pyramids, squares, ball courts and government buildings, they were where the urban Maya discussed philosophy, developed an accurate solar-year calendar and relished the world's first hot chocolate. Farmers, too, were riding high, turning hillsides into terraced fields to feed the fast-growing population.

E Add this to the broader trend and the situation becomes dire — a cautionary tale for the modern world, some warn. The fear is that, as more and more forestland is turned into farms and cities, and as global temperatures continue to rise, we may risk the same fate that befell the Maya.

F The Maya religious and political system was based on the belief that rulers were in direct communication with the gods. When these divine connections failed to produce rainfall and good harvests, tensions probably developed. In only 25 years between 750 and 775, for example, 39 rulers commissioned the same number of stone monuments — evidence of 'rivalry, war, and strategic alliances,' according to Kennett's study.

G Today, however, scientists generally agree that the Maya collapse has many roots, all intertwined — overpopulation, warfare, famine, drought. And one of the hottest fields of inquiry in recent years has centred on climate change, perhaps of the Maya's own doing.

Essential tips

▶ Part 7 of the Cambridge English: Advanced Reading and Use of English exam tests your understanding of the organisation of a text, in particular the way paragraphs are connected with each other.

▶ Read the main text quickly to get a general idea of what it is about and how it is organised. Do not worry about the gaps or any words you do not know at this point.

▶ Then, carefully read each paragraph in the main text. Make sure you know what the main idea in each paragraph is.

▶ Read the gapped paragraphs A–G, and make sure you know what the main idea in each is.

▶ Look for links between the main text and the gapped paragraph. The gapped paragraph may have links to the paragraph before it, or the paragraph after it, or to both.

▶ The links between paragraphs might be: connected ideas; related vocabulary – e.g. *wolves and bears* in one paragraph and *these animals* in the other; reference words like *this, there, she, her*; linking words and phrases such as *firstly, secondly, however, that's why, on the other hand*.

▶ There is one extra gapped paragraph which will not fit any gap.

▶ Once you have finished, re-read the completed text and make sure that it makes sense.

Question 41: The last sentence in the previous paragraph is about the growth of the Mayan cities. Several gapped paragraphs refer to the cities. Look for one that gives some extra details about the cities, and which contains pronouns referring to the cities.

Question 42: The last sentence of the previous paragraph refers to nineteenth-century theories about the disappearance of the Maya civilisation. Look for a gapped paragraph which contrasts this with more modern theories.

Question 43: The following paragraph starts 'But the long wet spell turned out to be an anomaly.' Can you find a gapped paragraph which refers to a 'wet spell'?

Question 45: The following paragraph starts with a sentence about the effect of 'this deforestation'. Which gapped paragraph refers to deforestation?

You are going to read a magazine article about four students who have started their own businesses. For questions **47–56**, choose from the students (**A–D**). The students may be chosen more than once.

Mark your answers **on the separate answer sheet**.

Which student

acknowledges the value of taking expert advice?	**47**
is unconcerned about the possibility of failure?	**48**
is surprised at the lack of competition for her business?	**49**
has established a precedent in her university?	**50**
accepts that her business may have had a negative impact on her studies?	**51**
has created a business which has exceeded her expectations?	**52**
believes her personality has changed through working on her business?	**53**
regrets missing out on certain aspects of student life?	**54**
thinks that entrepreneurs like her should follow their instincts?	**55**
claims to have benefited from skills acquired while taking part in an unrelated activity?	**56**

Essential tips

▶ In this part of the exam you are required to read one text or a number of short texts to find specific information, which may include an opinion or the expression of an attitude.

▶ Read the instructions, the title and the questions.

▶ Skim through the texts quickly to get a general idea of what they are about. Don't worry if there are words or phrases you don't understand.

▶ Read each question again and make sure you understand what it is asking. Underline the key words in the question (the words that show you what you should look for in the text).

▶ Scan the text for ideas or words that relate to the question. Read the relevant part of the text carefully.

▶ Remember that the part of the text that gives the answer for each question will almost certainly not use the same words; instead, it will express the idea in a different way.

▶ All the texts are about the same topic, so similar points may be made in two or three texts. When you match a question with a text, make sure it reflects exactly what is in that text.

Question 47: The word *expert* is in the question. Look for other words in the texts that express a similar idea. Then check that the part of the text you find also expresses the idea of acknowledging the value of taking advice.

Question 48: Think of other words or phrases that express the same idea as 'failure'. Then scan the texts for references to this. Make sure the one you choose contains the idea that the writer is unconcerned about the possibility of failure.

Question 49: What other words or phrases could express the idea of 'competition' for a business? Look through the texts quickly to see if you can find an expression of surprise with regard to competition.

Students who start businesses

Meet some enterprising students who have started their own businesses while at university.

A Lisa James

As she's doing business studies, it may not be surprising that Lisa James has set up her own company, but it's happened on a much greater scale than she'd envisaged. The idea for Carefree Flowers came from a visit to a friend who was in hospital. Real flowers were banned, so instead, Lisa created an arrangement of origami paper ones, each containing an individualised message. Before long, Lisa and her mother, Maria, had set up Carefree Flowers to cater for the demand.

Lisa handles the marketing and design. 'Mum does the rest, so I can do my coursework, though not much else – I don't go to parties, for example.' She's also good at managing her time. 'It's something I got used to at school – I did competitive athletics and had to fit it around schoolwork.'

Lisa plans to continue developing the business, but she can't look too far ahead. 'Someone else might see the potential in it and take our trade away. That'd hurt, but if it happened, I guess I'd start another business.'

B Joanna Payne

Joanna Payne is in her final year of a computer science degree. Her university offers 'sandwich' courses, meaning that students can spend year three of a four-year degree working for a business. When Joanna proposed devoting the year to setting up her own business, her lecturers were hesitant but agreed. Joanna launched Buccaneer Productions, specialising in creating games for smart phones. The three games she's released so far have impressed the university so much that it's now policy to encourage sandwich-year entrepreneurship. Joanna's sandwich year was busy, but her life is even more hectic now as she has to juggle lectures and a dissertation with running the business. 'I'd love to go out at weekends like my course mates do, but I can't afford the time,' she says. 'The apps market is really fast-moving and tough, and you've got to keep on top of it, otherwise it can all come crashing down.' The upside, of course, is that Joanna now has a pretty good idea of what it takes to set up an apps business.

C Alexis Taylor

When Alexis Taylor graduates in psychology, she will leave university with a well-established business, Taylor Tutors. The company offers one-to-one tutoring for high school students. All the tutors are students with recent experience of school. Alexis came up with the idea in her first year. 'It seemed an obvious way to earn some money,' says Alexis. 'I set up a database of students from my university, did some marketing in local schools, and it pretty much evolved as I'd imagined. I don't know why no one else has done it. I worry they might do actually.' She thinks she was fortunate to have chanced upon a mentor, John Martino, an older businessman who kept her on track at times.

Her business and the degree are both relatively flexible, but Alexis admits to having missed classes and deadlines in her hectic lifestyle. 'Also, I probably haven't done as much reading as I should've – psychology's a heavy subject in that sense.' But she's convinced she's done enough, and her entrepreneurial experience will stand her in good stead.

D Zoe Roberts

Two months after Zoe started her art degree, her bicycle was stolen. 'It was a real shock and I immediately wanted to do something,' she says. With the help of a lecturer, she designed a 'cycle wrapper', a cover to reduce bike theft and protect bikes from the weather.

Eighteen months later, it's still just a prototype. Zoe has set up a company, filed a patent, talked to potential investors and manufacturers, and even persuaded the university authorities that the 'wrapper' could bear the university name. But a product launch still seems a distant concept. 'I had no idea it would take so long,' she says. 'I've spent as much time on this project as on my degree. Sometimes I wonder whether it's been worth it. But it's transformed me. I'm much tougher than I used to be. People have told me to give up. They say the 'wrapper' will never work. But a gut feeling tells me it'll come good and I need to stick with it. As a poor student, I've got nothing to lose really, so that's what I'll do.'

Essential tips

▶ Paper 2 consists of two parts. Part 1 of the Writing paper is compulsory for everyone. You will be asked to produce an essay in which you must develop and support an argument on a supplied topic. The essay should always be between 220 and 260 words.

▶ In Part 2 there are three writing tasks. You must choose one of the three to answer. The types of text you can choose to write will include: an email or letter (formal or informal), a proposal, a report or a review.

▶ You should practise producing each text type that appears in the test.

▶ The information you will need in order to plan and produce each written piece in the test is called the input text. This input text might take the form of a bulleted list, an advertisement, a notice, an announcement, etc. Always read the input text carefully to make sure you understand exactly what you are being asked to write.

▶ Pay particular attention to the purpose of each written piece and its target reader.

▶ It is very important to write each item in the appropriate register. Think about whether the language you use should be formal or informal. Ask yourself whether you need to sound neutral or persuasive.

▶ Be aware of the structure you will need to use for each item you write. For example, how should you organise the paragraphs in your essay and what must each one contain? In your report, should you use headings and lists?

▶ Plan before you write, but don't spend too much time drafting a rough version; you won't have time to rewrite it properly. Use your own words as far as possible.

▶ Get into the habit of learning what 220–260 words look like in the various forms required for the test. Try to ensure that your handwriting is clear. You may lose points if the examiner cannot read what you have written.

▶ Allow a few minutes before the end of the test to quickly read through your work, checking your spelling and punctuation.

▶ See the Writing bank on pp. 193–205 for examples of the different types of writing required for this test.

PAPER 1 Reading and
Use of English

PAPER 2 Writing ▶ **Part 1**

PAPER 3 Listening Part 2

PAPER 4 Speaking

Essential tips

▶ Read the instructions carefully. Note how many benefits you are asked to address.

▶ What can you learn from the input text? Does everyone who attended the public meeting feel the same about the proposal?

▶ When referring to the points made at the meeting, try to use your own words. Don't copy the information from the input text.

▶ What is the standard structure of an essay? What should you include in each part of it?

▶ Who is going to read the essay? What is the appropriate register you should use here?

▶ Are you required to simply report what happened at the meeting, or are you being asked to express your own opinion?

You **must** answer this question. Write your answer in **220–260** words in an appropriate style on the separate answer sheet.

1 Your class has attended a public meeting on a proposal to build a bypass around your town (a road that avoids the town). You have made the notes below.

> **Local politicians point out the following benefits of the bypass:**
>
> - a welcome reduction in pollution and noise
> - improved transport links
> - less traffic congestion in the town centre

> **Some opinions expressed in the meeting:**
>
> "Traders in the town will suffer economically."
>
> "Land will have to be cleared, and we are concerned about the impact on the environment."
>
> "What about loss of revenue when tourists no longer visit sites of historical interest in the town?"

Write an essay for your tutor discussing **two** of the benefits in your notes. You should **explain whether you think the advantages of the bypass outweigh the disadvantages** and **provide reasons** to support your opinion.

You may, if you wish, make use of the opinions expressed in the meeting, but you should use your own words as far as possible.

PAPER 1 Reading and
          Use of English

PAPER 2 Writing ▶ Part 1
                         Part 2

PAPER 3 Listening

PAPER 4 Speaking

Essential tips

▶ In this part of the test, you will have the opportunity to express yourself more imaginatively and creatively.

▶ Remember, you only need to choose one task in Part 2 of the Writing paper.

▶ Read each of the three questions carefully. Choose the one that you are most comfortable with.

Question 2

▶ Read the input text carefully. Who is the email from?

▶ How will you organise and structure your proposal? Remember, it is important to show that you have understood what you need to do here, and to present your proposal in a clear way.

▶ What idea could you propose? Don't spend too much time trying to think of the best possible idea. However, make sure that your idea directly relates to improving the employees' working experience.

▶ What is the appropriate register to use here?

▶ Plan before you begin writing. Do you have enough points to make in order to meet the required word count of 220–260?

Question 3

▶ What sort of letter do you think is called for here: formal, semi-formal or informal?

▶ Check that you remember how to set out a letter in English.

▶ As always, pay attention to the instructions and don't leave anything out. Note, for

Write an answer to **one** of the questions **2–4** in this part. Write your answer in **220–260** words in an appropriate style on the separate answer sheet. Put the question number in the box at the top of the page.

2 You have received the following email from the Managing Director at your place of work.

> Dear Colleagues,
>
> I am pleased to announce that a generous budget of £3,000 has been set aside to improve the working experience of everyone at the company. I invite all employees to submit a proposal outlining how they feel this money would best be spent. Please illustrate exactly how you believe your proposal will positively impact everyday life at the company. The most popular proposal will be implemented.
>
> Good luck!
>
> Margaret Wheeler
>
> CEO

Write your **proposal**.

3 In your local newspaper, you have just read an article heavily criticising students' behaviour in the town, outside of school hours. Write a letter to the editor and include the following information:

- your overall reaction to the article
- specific points that you agree or disagree with, and why
- a suggestion for a follow-up article.

Write your **letter**.

4 You see this ad on a community noticeboard.

> New Book Group
>
> We need your help to compile a reading list of book titles for our new book group! So far, we have 20 members; men and women ranging in age from 17 to 58. Please send us your review of a novel that you think will appeal to our group members, giving reasons for your choice. Thank you.

Write your **review**.

example, that one of the bullet points asks you to mention specific points which you agree or disagree with, giving your reasons why.

▶ What key phrases are you likely to need for expressing agreement, disagreement and opinions?

Question 4

▶ Read the ad carefully. Who is the book review for?

▶ Note that you are not necessarily required to write about a book that you like; the objective is to recommend

a novel that will appeal to the group members.

▶ Mention the genre of the novel. For example, is it crime fiction, a romantic novel, a thriller, etc.?

▶ Stick to the structure of a book review, outlining the plot and demonstrating a clear understanding of the themes and the main characters.

▶ Balanced book reviews tend to be more effective than reviews which are entirely positive or entirely negative.

Track 1

You will hear three different extracts. For questions **1–6**, choose the answer (**A**, **B** or **C**) which fits best according to what you hear. There are two questions for each extract.

Extract One

You overhear two friends discussing an incident that happened with another friend.

1 The woman did not challenge the friend because she
- **A** feels her friend is aggressive.
- **B** doesn't believe it would help.
- **C** thinks her friend would be hurt.

2 What does the man think the woman should do?
- **A** Say something immediately.
- **B** Back down and just let it go.
- **C** Discuss the issue rationally.

Extract Two

You hear two people discussing the British winter.

3 The woman says she dislikes the British winter because she
- **A** comes from the Mediterranean.
- **B** doesn't have the right clothes.
- **C** finds it much too cold and dark.

4 From the man's point of view, the British winter is
- **A** just long enough.
- **B** not long enough.
- **C** a little too long.

Extract Three

You hear a couple disagreeing about Valentine's Day.

5 What is the man's main complaint about the event?
- **A** He is upset because he can't afford it.
- **B** He is annoyed by the selfishness of it all.
- **C** He hates champagne and chocolates.

6 What point are the couple in agreement on?
- **A** that Valentine's Day is really a money-making scheme
- **B** that they should go to a restaurant on Valentine's Day
- **C** that Valentine's Day is an important, romantic occasion

Essential tips

▶ Read carefully through each question before the recording is played. Think about what you are going to hear. Practising the strategy of prediction will increase your chances of successful listening.

▶ One of the objectives in this part of the test is identifying how the speaker feels. Remember to listen for adjectives that describe feelings and attitudes. You should also pay attention to the speaker's tone of voice, which will provide you with clues as to how he or she feels.

▶ Remember that the questions and answer options may be paraphrased, that is, they may use different words from the ones used by the speakers. Pay close attention to the meaning expressed rather than waiting to hear the same words and expressions in the recording.

Question 1: It is clear that the woman did not challenge her friend, but what was the reason for this? How would you describe her attitude to the whole situation?

Question 2: Pay close attention to the language used in the answer options. Can you find the same meaning, perhaps expressed using different words, anywhere in the recording?

Question 6: Note that you need to look for a point of agreement here. Does the man or woman mention anything about agreeing with the other one?

PAPER 1 Reading and
Use of English

PAPER 2 Writing

PAPER 3 Listening ▶
Part 1
Part 2
Part 3
Part 4

PAPER 4 Speaking

Essential tips

▶ Always read the instructions carefully.

▶ One focus of this part of the test is listening for specific information. Look at the sentences and pay attention to their structure. This will help you to identify the parts of speech you may need to complete each one.

▶ Remember that each gap may be completed by a number, a word, or a phrase.

▶ The subject of the recording is provided in a heading at the top of the page. By reading it, you can make predictions about what you are going to hear, and begin to think about all the vocabulary you know related to that topic.

▶ The recording will be played twice. Try to complete each sentence the first time, and confirm your answers the second time.

Question 8: What does Tara say about her own experience of studying media or journalism at university?

Question 10: The word *to* appears before the gap. What part of speech do you need here? Don't forget that you may need more than one word. Pay attention to see if a phrasal verb is used by the speaker.

Question 11: What could, potentially, have been a discouraging aspect of the work experience programme at the radio station (but wasn't for Tara)?

Question 13: What does Tara say about moving to London and the job she is in now?

🎧 **Track 2**

You will hear a radio producer describing how she got into her career. For questions **7–14**, complete the sentences with a word or short phrase.

BECOMING A RADIO PRODUCER

Tara Blackshaw was asked to talk to the audience about her

(**7**) ....

Tara explains that studying media or journalism at university

was not (**8**) .... she took.

She doesn't necessarily think it's a bad idea to do a

(**9**) ...., but it's not a requirement.

Finding and pursuing a career in an area they are passionate about

is the one thing Tara wants the audience members to

(**10**) .... from the talk.

Tara was not discouraged by the fact that the training programme at her local radio

station was (**11**) ....

She describes how certain she was that she had found her ideal job as soon as she

(**12**) .... in the studio.

Fifteen years before, Tara had relocated to London and was

(**13**) .... for her current job.

Tara describes the work as a (**14**) ....

because it can be challenging and difficult, but also very rewarding.

PAPER 1 Reading and Use of English

PAPER 2 Writing

PAPER 3 Listening ▶
- Part 1
- Part 2
- **Part 3**
- Part 4

PAPER 4 Speaking

Essential tips

▶ One of the things you will be asked in this part of the exam is to identify attitude and opinion. As always, listen carefully to what the speakers say, but pay attention to how they say it as well.

▶ The questions here are multiple-choice with four answer options. Remember, you may hear items from all four options mentioned in the recording, but listen carefully to identify the one that answers the question correctly.

▶ The instructions will tell you the topic of the recording. Take a minute to think about any vocabulary you know related to that topic.

Question 16: This question asks you about Fiona's attitude at the beginning of the conversation. How does she sound to you? Which of the options best matches her tone of voice?

Question 18: Without listening to the recording, any of these options could be possible, but remember to listen for what the speaker specifically states.

Question 20: You already know from the question that Nick describes how making ski films affects him. Only one of the options is correct, and he may express this idea using different words. What does he say about how the process makes him feel?

🎧 **Track 3**

You will hear two friends, Fiona and Matthew, discussing an interview which featured an American skier and filmmaker called Nick Waggoner. For questions **15–20**, choose the answer (**A**, **B**, **C** or **D**) which fits best according to what you hear.

15 What is Matthew doing when Fiona arrives at the coffee shop?
  A He has started reading the interview.
  B He is in the middle of reading the interview.
  C He has finished reading the interview.
  D He is thinking about reading the interview.

16 What is Fiona's reaction to the topic, at first?
  A genuinely curious about it
  B completely bored with it
  C totally fascinated by it
  D not that interested in it

17 What made Nick Waggoner choose the location for his film *Solitaire*?
  A It was suitable for using a helicopter.
  B He liked the challenge it would provide.
  C It had the most dramatic landscapes.
  D The snow conditions were perfect there.

18 What was the impact of Arne Backstrom's death on Nick and Zac?
  A It was OK as they didn't know Arne well.
  B It affected Nick and Zac very deeply.
  C They decided to abandon the project.
  D They were not entirely surprised by it.

19 What did Nick and Zac do after Arne's death?
  A They learned how to fly a plane.
  B They connected with other colleagues.
  C They moved the film dates forward.
  D They learned how to paraglide.

20 How does Nick describe the effect that making ski films has on him?
  A He says it energises him.
  B He says it bores him.
  C He says he doesn't like it.
  D He says it frightens him.

PAPER 1 Reading and
          Use of English

PAPER 2 Writing

PAPER 3 Listening ▶

PAPER 4 Speaking

Part 1
Part 2
Part 3
Part 4

Essential tips

▸ Part 4 of the Listening paper is a matching exercise. There are three additional options that you will not need.

▸ You are required to do two tasks at the same time in this part of the test. Read the instructions and make sure you understand exactly what you will need to listen for in each task.

▸ The five speakers will speak on the same theme. Pay attention to the main points and attitudes they express.

▸ Remember, the options do not appear in the order in which they are heard on the recording.

Questions 21–25:

Option A: If someone avoids writing, what kinds of words might they use to express this?

Option D: Who, if anyone, mentions their own opinion of their writing?

Option H: For this option to be correct, someone must mention how often they write. What sorts of words should you listen for here?

Questions 26–30:

Option B: This option mentions 'enthusiasm', which may or may not be the exact word used in the recording. Does any speaker use words or phrases with the same meaning to describe their experience in the writers' group?

Option F: What kind of tone of voice do you think someone would use if they felt the writing group members were 'harsh critics'?

Option G: This option provides you with two clues before you listen. You know you need to identify a speaker who mentions the feedback they get in the writers' group and the amount they get. What does 'constructive' mean? Does anyone express this idea?

🎧 **Track 4**

You will hear five short extracts in which people talk about being in writers' groups.

While you listen you must complete both tasks.

TASK ONE

For questions **21–25**, choose from the list (**A–H**) what each speaker says about their own writing.

A	tends to avoid writing		
B	panics under pressure	Speaker 1	21
C	finds the process isolating	Speaker 2	22
D	is satisfied with their own work	Speaker 3	23
E	feels it's a waste of time	Speaker 4	24
F	had been out of practice	Speaker 5	25
G	never finishes anything		
H	writes every day		

TASK TWO

For questions **26–30**, choose from the list (**A–H**) what each speaker says about their experience of being in a writer's group.

A	enjoys the positive feedback		
B	gets the enthusiasm they need	Speaker 1	26
C	looks forward to the social aspect	Speaker 2	27
D	doesn't like the group leader	Speaker 3	28
E	finds the motivation to keep writing	Speaker 4	29
F	thinks the members are harsh critics	Speaker 5	30
G	minds the lack of constructive feedback		
H	struggles to find time to attend		

PAPER 1   Reading and
          Use of English

PAPER 2   Writing

PAPER 3   Listening

PAPER 4   Speaking

Essential tips

Part 1

▶ This part of the test has two phases. In the first phase, the examiner will ask you a couple of basic things about yourself. In the second phase, you will be asked broader types of questions about your life and your opinions.

▶ Listen carefully to what you are being asked. If you didn't understand or hear the question clearly, don't be afraid to ask the examiner to repeat it.

▶ The objective of Part 1 is to show that you can interact socially. Don't go off the point in order to talk about something you have already prepared. Keep your answers relevant to the questions.

▶ Don't panic if you are caught off guard by a question and find it difficult to think of the answer, e.g. 'What is your happiest memory?' You can supply any happy memory, or you can even make one up.

Part 4

▶ This focus here is on expressing and justifying opinions. Remember, you can hold any opinion you want, but you must support your ideas with examples.

▶ Be respectful of your partner's views and remember to be polite.

▶ You can practise using appropriate expressions, such as *I see what you're saying, but ...*, *That's an interesting point; however, ...*, *From my own point of view ...* and so on.

Part 1 (2 minutes)

The examiner will ask you a few questions about yourself and about a general topic. For example, the examiner may ask you:

• **How long have you been studying English?**
• **What do you enjoy most about learning English?**
• **What is your happiest memory?**

Part 2 (4 minutes)

You will each be asked to talk on your own for about a minute. You will each be given three different pictures to talk about. After your partner has finished speaking, you will be asked a brief question connected with your partner's photographs.

> **Audiences** (compare, contrast and speculate)

Turn to pictures 1–3 on page **169**, which show people in different audiences.

(*Candidate A*), it's your turn first. Here are your pictures. They show **audiences in different situations**.

I'd like you to compare **two** of the pictures and say **what kind of event the people are attending, and describe how they appear to be responding to it**.

(*Candidate B*), **which of these audiences do you relate to the most? Why?**

> **Job types** (compare, contrast and speculate)

Turn to pictures 1–3 on page **170**, which show people doing different jobs.

Now, (*Candidate B*), here are your pictures. They show **people doing different jobs**.

I'd like you to compare two of the pictures and say **what kind of person would choose this job type and what challenges the job might present**.

(*Candidate A*), **which of these jobs would you least like to do? Why?**

Part 3 (4 minutes)

Look at page **171,** which shows some potential benefits of teenagers learning to save money.

> **Teenage savings** (discuss, evaluate and negotiate)

Here are some ways in which teenagers might benefit from developing the habit of saving money and a question for you to discuss. First, you have some time to look at the task.

(*Pause 15 seconds*)

Now talk to each other about **how important these benefits may or may not be**.

Now you have a minute to decide **which benefit is the most important for teenagers**.

Part 4 (5 minutes)

The examiner will encourage you to develop the topic of your discussion in Part 3 by asking questions such as:

• Is it more important for teenagers to save money or just to enjoy 'the best years of their lives'? Why?

• Do you think that financial responsibility should be limited to adults? Why (not)?

• It has been said that setting and managing a budget can be of benefit to a teenager. Do you agree?

For questions **1–8**, read the text below and decide which answer (**A**, **B**, **C** or **D**) best fits each gap. There is an example at the beginning (**0**).

Mark your answers **on the separate answer sheet**.

Example:

| **0** | **A** presents | **B** appears | **C** springs | **D** lands |

| **0** | A | **B** | C | D |

Essential tips

▸ Read through the text first for general understanding.

▸ Remember that the gapped word or words will often be part of a collocation or a fixed phrase.

▸ Check the words on each side of the gap carefully. Often, the options have very similar meanings but only one is correct because of a word (e.g. a particular verb) before the gap or another word (e.g. a preposition) after it.

▸ Remember to read the whole text through again when you have completed the task to check whether it makes sense.

Question 1: Which verb often goes with *it* to mean 'be successful'?

Question 3: The idiom *to go to any ... to do something* means to make a big effort to achieve something, including taking extreme or unusual steps. Which word completes the idiom?

Question 5: All four words can form phrases with *in*. However, three of them express the idea of a series of things, but only one expresses the idea of the result of a series of things. The result here is boosted sales.

Question 7: We often use one of these adjectives to describe something abstract like an aim or an idea which is difficult to define or achieve. This is the meaning here. The other words are used to describe places that are hard to reach or things that are hard to see.

Word-of-mouth success – what publishers dream of

'Word of mouth', a phrase that first (**0**) …….. in Shakespeare's play *Twelfth Night*, is the kind of publicity all publishers want for their books. Positive reviews are useful, but it's only when lots of people start talking about a book that it really (**1**) …….. it sales-wise. Word of mouth is what (**2**) …….. behind the initial success of JK Rowling's Harry Potter books, for example.

Some publishers will go to any (**3**) …….. to stimulate the phenomenon. Years ago, one company paid its own staff to read books published by the company whenever they travelled on public transport. The thinking was that the bright yellow covers would (**4**) …….. and become the subject of casual conversations among passengers, which would in (**5**) …….. boost sales.

With the (**6**) …….. of social networking, creating word of mouth has almost become a science. However, despite Twitter, Facebook and the rest, publishers still find it as difficult as ever to generate that (**7**) …….. thing, a viral conversation about a new book that persuades lots of people to buy it. It still seems to be unclear what the (**8**) …….. to achieving word of mouth is.

1	**A** pushes	**B** hits	**C** makes	**D** gets
2	**A** formed	**B** ran	**C** rested	**D** lay
3	**A** lengths	**B** extents	**C** terms	**D** measures
4	**A** show off	**B** stick up	**C** stand out	**D** shine on
5	**A** order	**B** turn	**C** line	**D** sequence
6	**A** advent	**B** entrance	**C** outset	**D** opening
7	**A** remote	**B** isolated	**C** hidden	**D** elusive
8	**A** root	**B** key	**C** base	**D** guide

PAPER 1	Reading and Use of English	▶	Part 1
			Part 2
PAPER 2	Writing		Part 3
			Part 4
PAPER 3	Listening		Part 5
PAPER 4	Speaking		Part 6
			Part 7
			Part 8

For questions **9–16**, read the text below and think of the word which best fits each gap. Use only one word in each gap. There is an example at the beginning (**0**).

Write your answers **IN CAPITAL LETTERS on the separate answer sheet**.

Example: | 0 | I | N | | | | | | | | | | | | | | | | | | | | |

Ice water diver

Rhian Waller is a marine biologist with a special interest (**0**) .... deep-sea corals. She admits that, as (**9**) ...., little is known about these corals because they are very hard to reach, 1000 metres below the ocean's surface. However, (**10**) .... is known is that they are being damaged by fishing nets, and research is needed to support conservation work.

(**11**) .... recently, Rhian had only been able to study the corals through film sent from robotic submarines, but then some were discovered in Alaskan fjords that were shallow (**12**) .... to dive in. This was a wonderful opportunity, but two problems faced Rhian initially: (**13**) .... only was the water in the fjords scarcely above freezing, but she had never actually dived before.

She describes the experience as 'intense'. Within five minutes (**14**) .... being in the water, her head and hands were completely numb, and she often had (**15**) .... poor visibility she couldn't even see her own elbow. Despite the extreme conditions, however, Rhian's team were able to gather data on the corals of a kind that is (**16**) .... but impossible in the deep ocean.

Essential tips

▶ Read the text quickly for general meaning.

▶ Remember that the gapped words will be structural items like articles, pronouns, prepositions and linkers. A few may form part of common expressions.

▶ Read the whole sentence to see whether the word you need is part of a longer or parallel structure like *either ... or* or *on the one hand ... on the other hand*.

▶ Remember that there could be more than one correct answer. But you should write one word only in the gap.

Question 9: From the whole text, we learn that our knowledge of deep-sea corals is still limited, but scientists are trying to find out more about them. Can you think of a two-word phrase *as ...*, which means 'so far' or 'up to this point in time'?

Question 11: Gaps at the beginning of sentences can often look difficult to fill. The best approach is to look carefully at the previous sentence or the whole sentence that follows the gap, or both. In this case, look carefully at what comes after it. The text tells us that previously Rhian could only study the corals using robotic submarines, but now she is able to dive in the Alaskan fjords. Which word can go with *recently* to give the idea of 'previously'?

Question 13: This is an example of a longer, parallel structure: *... only, ... but ...*

Question 16: Can you think of a common structural word to complete an expression that means 'almost impossible'?

PAPER 1	Reading and	▸	Part 1
	Use of English		Part 2
PAPER 2	Writing		**Part 3**
			Part 4
PAPER 3	Listening		Part 5
			Part 6
PAPER 4	Speaking		Part 7
			Part 8

For questions **17–24**, read the text below. Use the word given in capitals at the end of some of the lines to form a word that fits in the gap **in the same line**. There is an example at the beginning (**0**).

Write your answers **IN CAPITAL LETTERS on the separate answer sheet**.

Example: | **0** | P | R | E | S | I | D | E | N | T | I | A | L | | | | | | |

Essential tips

‣ Read through the text for general understanding.

‣ Remember to think about the type of word that should go in each gap – a verb, noun, adjective or adverb?

‣ Remember that some words will need more than one change – a prefix and a suffix.

‣ If the word needed is a noun, check whether it should be singular or plural.

‣ When you've finished the task, read through it again and check that it all makes sense.

Question 17: A noun is needed here. Be careful with the spelling.

Question 18: If the gap is the first word in a sentence and it is followed by a comma, what type of word is it likely to be?

Question 19: *Facial* is an adjective, so the gapped word here will be a noun. Should it be singular or plural?

Question 20: The word needed here is a noun. But does it refer to people or a more abstract idea? Read the whole paragraph before deciding.

Leaders with long faces

In most (**0**) …….. elections in the USA in the twentieth century, the taller of the two candidates won. This association of (**17**) …….. with success is something that has been widely accepted. (**18**) …….., some recent research suggests that people's confidence in a potential leader can also be influenced by how long that person's face is.

According to Daniel Re, one of the main researchers, our natural attraction to facial (**19**) …….. that suggest tallness, as long faces do, is thought to have evolved long ago when the (**20**) …….. of a community depended on choosing the right leader. 'Especially when we're faced with a (**21**) …….. situation, we seem to prefer the most dominant-looking people for leadership,' he says.

In the study, (**22**) …….. were asked to manipulate faces on a computer screen in order to make them look like people they would want as national leaders. A significant number chose to (**23**) …….. the faces, particularly for male leaders in difficult times.

As Dr Re noted, the implication is that 'leadership choices are affected by physical features that are (**24**) …….. to political expertise.'

PRESIDENT

HIGH

INTEREST

CHARACTER

SURVIVE

THREAT

VOLUNTARY

LONG

RELEVANT

PAPER 1	Reading and Use of English	▶	Part 1
			Part 2
			Part 3
PAPER 2	Writing		Part 4
PAPER 3	Listening		Part 5
PAPER 4	Speaking		Part 6
			Part 7
			Part 8

Essential tips

▶ Remember to read both sentences carefully in each question. The second sentence must have the same meaning as the first.

▶ Remember that you must not change the key word in any way, and that you must use between three and six words.

▶ You can use contractions, e.g. *can't*, *wouldn't*, but remember that they count as two words. Make sure you count the number of words you write in the gap carefully.

▶ When you have completed a question, read through it again and check that the meaning is the same and the spelling is correct.

Question 25: The first sentence is all in the past simple. Is the second sentence also past simple? What structure is needed in the second sentence?

Question 26: Be careful with the tense. Also, you need to change *misunderstood* to a noun.

Question 27: Which phrase with the word *stand* means 'no way' or 'no possibility'?

Question 29: You need a passive structure to introduce the information here. Also, *handed* in this context needs a preposition after it.

For questions **25–30**, complete the second sentence so that it has a similar meaning to the first sentence, using the word given. **Do not change the word given.** You must use between **three** and **six** words, including the word given. Here is an example (**0**).

Example:

0 Chloe would only eat a pizza if she could have a mushroom topping.

ON

Chloe .... a mushroom topping when she had a pizza.

The gap can be filled with the words 'insisted on having', so you write:

Example: | 0 | INSISTED ON HAVING

Write **only** the missing words **IN CAPITAL LETTERS on the separate answer sheet**.

---

25 I only watched that film because you recommended it to me.

NEVER

I would .... you hadn't recommended it to me.

26 It seems as if we misunderstood what the aims of the course were.

BEEN

There seems .... what the aims of the course were.

27 The traffic was so bad that there was obviously no way we would get to the theatre on time, so we went home.

STAND

The traffic was so bad that we obviously didn't .... to the theatre on time, so we went home.

28 Michelle's brother talks a lot more than she does.

NOWHERE

Michelle is .... her brother.

29 There's a rumour that Jordi Marse, the Barcelona manager, has resigned this morning.

HANDED

Jordi Marse, the Barcelona manager, ... his resignation this morning.

30 I'm sure people will object to the idea of building a new runway at the city airport.

BOUND

There .... the idea of building a new runway at the city airport.

PAPER 1	Reading and ▸	Part 1
	Use of English	Part 2
PAPER 2 Writing		Part 3
		Part 4
PAPER 3 Listening		**Part 5**
PAPER 4 Speaking		Part 6
		Part 7
		Part 8

You are going to read a newspaper article. For questions **31–36**, choose the answer (**A**, **B**, **C** or **D**) which you think fits best according to the text.

Mark your answers **on the separate answer sheet**.

Cycling

Keen cyclist Simon Usborne looks at some research on cycling.

You need only look at a professional cyclist to appreciate the potential effects of cycling on the body. But what about the mind? It's a question that has long challenged psychologists, neurologists and anyone who has wondered how, sometimes, riding a bike can induce what feels close to a state of meditation.

I'm usually incapable of emptying my mind but there have been occasions on my bike when I realise I have no recollection of the preceding kilometres. Whether riding along country lanes in spring, or doing city commutes, time can pass unnoticed in a blissful blur of rhythm and rolling, and I'm not alone in feeling this.

But what do we really know about how cycling affects us? Danish scientists who set out to measure the benefits of breakfast and lunch for academic achievement among children found diet helped, but that the way pupils travelled to school was far more significant. Those who cycled or walked did better than those who travelled by car or public transport. Another study by the University of California showed that old people who were most active, including those who cycled, had five per cent more grey matter than those who were least active.

But what is it about cycling that makes us believe it has a special effect? Psychiatrist John Ratey thinks cycling increases 'the chemistry in your brain that makes you feel calm,' but also that carrying out multiple operations, like negotiating a junction or jostling for space in a race, can be an effective therapy. He is currently leading a study in which more than 20 pupils with attention deficit hyperactivity disorder (ADHD), a condition affecting the ability to apply one's mind to something, are expected to show improved symptoms after a course of cycling. The link between cycling and ADHD is well-established. It's 'like taking a little bit of Ritalin,' Dr Ratey says, Ritalin being a stimulant commonly used to treat ADHD. Exercise can achieve the same effect as prescribed medicine, but not all exercise is equal, as shown in a German study involving 115 students, half of whom did activities such as cycling that involved complex coordinated movements, while the rest performed more straightforward exercises with the same aerobic demands. Both groups did better than they previously had in concentration tests, but the 'complex' group did a lot better.

There have been other interesting findings too. In 2003, neuroscientist Dr Jay Alberts rode a tandem bicycle across the American state of Ohio with a friend who has Parkinson's disease (a condition affecting the nervous system). The idea was to raise awareness of the disease, but to the surprise of both riders, the patient showed significant improvements. Dr Alberts then scanned the brains of 26 Parkinson's patients during and after an eight-week exercise programme using stationary bikes. Half the patients were allowed to ride at their own pace, while the others were pushed incrementally harder, just as the scientist's tandem companion had been. All patients improved, and the 'tandem' group showed particularly significant increases in connectivity between areas of grey matter responsible for functions such as walking and picking things up. Cycling, and cycling harder, was helping to heal their brains.

line 37 We don't know how this happens, but there is more startling evidence of the link between Parkinson's and cycling. A video on the internet features a 58-year-old Dutchman with severe Parkinson's. At first, we watch the patient trying to walk along a hospital ward. He can barely stand and his hands shake uncontrollably. Cut to the car park, where we find the man on a bicycle being supported by staff. With a push, he's off, cycling past cars with perfect balance and coordination. After a loop, he comes to a stop and hops to the ground, where he is immediately immobile again. Doctors don't fully understand this discrepancy either, but say the bicycle's rotating pedals may act as some sort of visual cue that aided the patient's brain.

The science of cycling is evidently incomplete, but perhaps the most remarkable thing about it for the everyday rider, its effects on hyperactive children notwithstanding, is that it can require no conscious focus at all. The apparent mindlessness of pedalling can not only make us happier, but also leave room for other thoughts. On the seat of my bike, I've solved problems at work, made life decisions and reflected usefully on emotional troubles, as, I'm sure, have countless others.

▶ Remember that in this part of the test, you need to understand various things about a text: detailed meaning, the writer's opinions and attitudes, the purpose of the whole text or of one paragraph, how the text is organised and how different words and phrases relate to each other. Sometimes the meaning is suggested or implied rather than stated explicitly, and you need to understand this.

▶ Read through the text for overall understanding and to see how it is organised. Don't worry if there are words or phrases you don't understand.

▶ Read each question and highlight the key words. Highlight the piece of text where this question is answered.

▶ Look in the text for the answer to the question. One of the options will express the same idea, but probably not in the same words as in the text.

▶ Check that the three other options are definitely incorrect. Sometimes you will be able to find the answer by eliminating each wrong option in turn.

Question 31: This is an example of a question about the writer's 'purpose'. What is the main point of the second paragraph? Read the paragraph again and also look at what comes before and after the paragraph. Then go through each option carefully. Option A: he gives some personal information but is that the point of this paragraph? Option B: is he introducing a new subject here? Option C: is he expressing an opinion in this paragraph? Option D: is he illustrating a point? If so, what is the point?

31 What is the writer's main intention in the second paragraph?
    A to give some personal information
    B to introduce a new subject
    C to express his opinion
    D to illustrate a point

32 According to the third paragraph, what do certain studies show?
    A Cyclists tend to live longer than non-cyclists.
    B Cycling seems to be the healthiest form of exercise.
    C Intellectual performance appears to be boosted by cycling.
    D Older people appreciate the value of exercise more than young people do.

33 What do the studies described in the fourth paragraph suggest?
    A Cycling has as much impact on physical fitness as simpler physical activities.
    B The variety of tasks involved in cycling can be hard for some children to cope with.
    C Children suffer from ADHD because they are deprived of physical exercise like cycling.
    D The act of cycling can improve the ability to focus attention on a task.

34 Studies of people with Parkinson's disease reveal that
    A cycling on ordinary bikes is better than cycling on stationary bikes.
    B the social aspects of cycling are important for people with Parkinson's.
    C the more effort Parkinson's sufferers put into cycling the more good it does them.
    D not every person who suffers from Parkinson's will benefit from cycling.

35 What does 'this discrepancy' in line 37 refer to?
    A how cycling could be incorporated into treatment for Parkinson's
    B why someone with Parkinson's can cycle but not walk
    C why Parkinson's affects some people and not others
    D how a link between cycling and Parkinson's was discovered

36 With the phrase 'its effects on hyperactive children notwithstanding', the writer is referring to the fact that cycling
    A is more life-enhancing to adults than younger people.
    B enables people to think more effectively.
    C can be both complex and mindless.
    D is not yet fully understood.

Question 35: Even if you are not sure what the word *discrepancy* means, you should be able to work out the answer here. The word *either* just after *discrepancy* refers back to the beginning of the paragraph – 'we don't know how this happens' – which is about what's described in the previous paragraph. This tells you that 'this discrepancy' is about something said in this paragraph. What is the main topic of this paragraph?

Question 36: Even if you are not sure about the meaning of the word *notwithstanding*, you can still work out what is meant here. Look back at the part of the text which mentions 'hyperactive children'. According to the text, what makes cycling good for 'hyperactive' children? According to the final paragraph, what makes cycling good for people referred to here?

PAPER 1 Reading and
         Use of English ▶
PAPER 2 Writing
PAPER 3 Listening
PAPER 4 Speaking

Part 1
Part 2
Part 3
Part 4
Part 5
Part 6
Part 7
Part 8

You are going to read four comments in a debate about zoos. For questions **37–40**, choose from the comments **A–D**. The comments may be chosen more than once.

Mark your answers **on the separate answer sheet.**

Zoos

Zoos are notable tourist attractions as well as being centres of research and conservation. However, there is a long-running debate about whether it is right to keep wild animals in captivity, particularly in urban locations. Here are four contributions to a recent online discussion about the subject.

A

With the destruction of natural habitats in so many parts of the world, zoos play an increasingly important role in conservation. Without their intervention, many more of the world's surviving species would become extinct. Zoos are able to intervene because of their expertise, which is developed through long-term, sustained studies at the zoos themselves, but also in support of field work in the wild. One advantage of having this scientific work done in zoos is that it becomes more easily accessible to the wider public. Zoos are great vehicles for informing people of all ages, though particularly younger ones, in a direct and memorable way, about the proper treatment of animals, and how crucial they are to the world's different ecosystems. This has not always been the case, but modern zoos look after animals well and, as such, present a valuable model to the wider population.

B

There have been many bad zoos in the past, but zoo animals today are well-fed and cared for in spacious surroundings. Zoologists and animal psychologists are brought in to design species-appropriate enclosures and activities. Studies of animals in zoos provide information that would be very hard to obtain in the wild. A study of gorillas at zoos in the UK and the USA, for example, discovered that happiness can increase the primates' lives by up to 11 years, and findings of this kind are useful for zoologists in both zoos and the wild. Sadly, zoos' efforts to breed animals that are close to extinction have mostly failed. The issue here is that the odds against reviving a species from a tiny captive community are very high. But generally, as institutions of scientific endeavour, zoos are crucial in the wider dissemination of knowledge, skills and values with regard to wildlife.

C

Care of wild animals in captivity tends to be much more humane than it was in the past, but the fact is that zoos are for commerce and entertainment. Most visitors go to zoos to be diverted by weird and wonderful creatures rather than to learn. One zoo study found that visitors spent less than eight seconds per snake and one minute per lion. What could possibly be learned from that? It is also widely acknowledged that, despite the best intentions of scientists, most zoo-based attempts to breed species in order to stave off extinction have been strikingly unsuccessful. Captive breeding programmes will only ever work in large nature reserves. Moreover, claims that zoos are ideal locations for studying animal behaviour conveniently ignore the point that environments affect behaviour, and so studies of animals in zoos may only tell us about captive populations and provide little data about animals in their natural habitats.

D

However well intentioned zoo-keepers may be, zoos can never replicate the natural habitats of most wild animals. As a result, zoo animals are psychologically affected and often display abnormal, even self-destructive, behaviour. Attempts to use zoos for breeding threatened species are also well intentioned, but, with rare exceptions, they fail to bear fruit. The key factor again is probably that zoos are nothing like nature, and wild animals simply do not breed well in confinement. The notion that zoos can be places of learning, enlightening the population about wildlife, is also well meant, but how much can visitors really discover about wild animals from seeing them in cages and small enclosures? The only way to understand an animal properly is to see it in its natural environment, and, if that is not possible, then film and books will give a more accurate picture than the artificial and misleading context of a zoo.

Which writer

takes a similar view to D regarding the role zoos play in educating the public?	37
has a different opinion from the others about the well-being of animals kept in zoos?	38
takes a different view from the others regarding zoos and endangered species in zoos?	39
shares A's opinion of zoos as centres of research?	40

Essential tips

- Remember: in this part of the exam you have to decide whether four different writers have similar or different opinions about a particular subject.

- Read the title and the texts quickly for general understanding.

- Highlight the key words in each question.

- Read the first text and highlight the sections that relate to each question. Remember to write the question numbers in the relevant places. Do the same for each text.

- Then look across the four texts and compare the parts of the texts that refer to each question. Read the opinions carefully and decide which ones are similar and which are different.

Question 37: The key words here are *the role zoos play in educating the public*. Look at this part of text D: 'The notion that zoos can be places of learning, enlightening the population about wildlife, is also well-meant, but how much can visitors really discover about wild animals from seeing them in cages and small enclosures?' In D's view, are zoos effective at educating the public or not? When you have decided what D thinks, look through the other texts for a similar view.

Question 38: The key words here are *the well-being of animals kept in zoos*. *Well-being* can refer to both physical and mental health. You are asked to find one writer expressing a different opinion on this point from the other three. A says this: 'This has not always been the case, but modern zoos look after animals well and, as such, present a valuable model to the wider population.' So A says zoo animals are well cared for and implies that, as a result, their health is good. B says 'zoo animals today are well-fed and cared for in spacious surroundings. Zoologists and animal psychologists are brought in to design species-appropriate enclosures and activities.' So, B says the care is good and the implication is that the animals are healthy. So, now we know that either C or D expresses a different view. Which one is it?

PAPER 1	Reading and ▸	Part 1
	Use of English	Part 2
PAPER 2	Writing	Part 3
		Part 4
PAPER 3	Listening	Part 5
PAPER 4	Speaking	Part 6
		Part 7
		Part 8

You are going to read a newspaper article about a special farm which provides help to teenagers with behavioural problems. Six paragraphs have been removed from the article. Choose from the paragraphs **A–G** the one which fits each gap (**41–46**). There is one extra paragraph which you do not need to use.

Mark your answers **on the separate answer sheet**.

Care farms

Before breakfast, two young people head down to the woods, struggling a little with the heavy bag of food for the pigs. 'Scatter them in different piles,' says the farm staff member. 'If you put them in one place, the smaller pigs won't be able to get anything.' The pigs, which are enormous, surge towards us, and their new feeders step backwards. 'I'm not doing that,' says 15-year-old Daniel firmly.

41

The teenagers are part of a group from a London secondary school who are staying at Jamie Fielden's farm, one of a number of 'care farms' providing a type of eco-therapy. The pupils brought here have been chosen by their teachers: 14 year-old Sofia, for example, has a difficult home life, Georgia, 14, is extremely quiet, and Sam, 13, has challenging behaviour.

42

Besides farmwork, the young people have group sessions with the farm psychotherapist who teaches them techniques for calming down, or for dealing with difficult situations. They can do 'horse-whispering' with her, one-to-one therapy making use of one of the farm horses. Phones and sweets are banned, as part of the focus on creating a calm, supportive atmosphere and reducing over-stimulation.

43

And the young people seem to be thriving. Aaron, a 12-year-old with serious attendance issues, is clearly taken with the horse whispering: 'I feel as though the horse is calm and I'm calm. I had to work out how to speak calmly to make her do what I wanted.'

44

And this is what Fielden aims to provide. Trained as a teacher, he wants to 'give young people a chance to have the experiences that I had as a kid growing up on a farm'. He set up the farm with a couple of other teachers and his mother, a psychotherapist, a few years ago. The farm's main source of income is the fees schools pay to send pupils there, and since opening, more than 700 children have attended.

45

Care farms first appeared over a decade ago in the UK. Now, there are more than 80, and they have their own association called Care Farm UK. Founder member Ian Egginton-Metters says: 'There is evidence that 'green care' works. Charities give funding for our eco-therapy projects, which are focused around taking people out of institutions and putting them in the natural environment.'

46

Whatever the reasons, however, there is clearly an impact. A week after the pupils arrive back at school in west London from Jamie's Farm, teachers report on a difference in behaviour. Georgia gave a talk to her class about her experiences, Sofia's participation in class is better than it has ever been, and Sam says he wants to go back to the farm next year. There is no doubt amongst the teachers that they will continue to send troubled pupils to the farm in years to come.

A A classmate, Hasan, describes a similar sense of tranquillity. 'I expected to be really annoyed and bored here, but as soon as we arrived it was fantastic. There's so much space. You don't get stressed out. There's time to think.' Like his peers, he has a complicated home life and needs support.

B Along with this, the teachers accompanying them are encouraged to form closer bonds with their charges and to observe the way that farm staff interact with the young people, and the methods they use to get the behaviour they want.

C This expansion of the sector is evident, but there are differing explanations as to why care farming makes a difference, ranging from those pointing to the therapeutic aspect of the physical labour and the contact with plants and animals, to others claiming it is all to do with taking people away from their problems at home.

D Before coming here he was sceptical, but no longer. 'There's something about coming here, from very chaotic environments, as most of

these young people do, that does them good. You have to work hard, take responsibility, and you're a valued member of the community.'

E Sofia, however, who is a good head shorter than her fellow pupil, moves forward, methodically pouring out a dozen small heaps under the trees. 'She's a natural,' says her supervisor admiringly. Sofia does not look up, but a little smile flickers across her young face.

F An impressive figure, but isn't it an expensive option for schools? Fielden believes the results justify the cost. Eight out of ten children who stay at the farm show a persistent improvement in behaviour. 'Head teachers tell me they're rebooking because they're no longer seeing those children in trouble. That's what we want.'

G Most of them, they soon tell me, have never been to the countryside before. For five days, they get up early, eat wholesome food and do various chores dependent on the season. It is summer and they are pulling up coriander from the vegetable beds, feeding animals and helping with the harvest.

Essential tips

▸ Remember that in this part of the test you need to understand the organisation of a text – how the paragraphs work together.

▸ Read through the main text first for a general understanding of its subject and organisation.

▸ Then read the gapped paragraphs A–G, and make sure you know what each one is about.

▸ Look for links between the main text and the gapped paragraphs. Remember that a gapped paragraph may have links to the paragraph before it, or the paragraph after it, or to both.

▸ The links may be connected ideas, related vocabulary, pronouns, linking adverbs and expressions and so on.

▸ Sometimes more than one of the paragraphs A–G look possible for a gap, but there is only one correct answer. If you look carefully, you will find reasons to exclude all attractive-looking paragraphs except the correct one.

▸ Don't forget to read through the completed text to check that it makes sense.

Question 41: The first main text paragraph mentions two young people, a member of the farm staff, pigs and Daniel who is one of the two young people. If you look quickly these gapped paragraphs all look possible: A, D, E and G. In paragraph A, Hasan could be Daniel's classmate, but does the rest of the first sentence in A fit? In paragraph D, the first sentence seems to follow from the previous paragraph, but does the rest of D follow? In paragraph E, Sofia could be Daniel's fellow pupil – does the rest of E fit? In paragraph G, *they* could refer to Sofia and Daniel, but does *most of them* make sense after the first main paragraph?

Question 42: The previous paragraph refers to a group of children from a school in London. Which gapped paragraph could also refer to this group?

Question 43: The previous paragraph describes what the therapy for the young people consists of. Which paragraph gives more information about what happens to this group?

Question 44: The first sentence of the following paragraph is: 'And this is what Fielden aims to provide.' What could *this* refer to?

Essential tips

▶ Remember that in this part of the test you read one long text or a few short texts to find specific information, which may include an opinion or the expression of an attitude.

▶ Read the instructions and the title.

▶ Then, either skim read the text first before you read the questions, or read the questions first before you skim read the text. Experiment and see which way works better for you.

▶ When you read the questions, highlight the key words that show you what you should look for in the text.

▶ Remember that the part of the text that gives the answer to a question will almost certainly not use the same words, and the meaning may be implied rather than stated clearly.

▶ Also, similar points may be made in two or three texts, so when you match a question with a text, make sure they have exactly the same meaning.

Question 47: A key word here is *function*. Which review refers to what the book might be used for?

Question 48: The key ideas here are *the style of writing* and *difficult to read*. You are unlikely to find these exact words in the reviews, but can you find any paraphrases of them?

Question 49: The expression *of note* means important or well known. Two of the reviews refer to architects or buildings that have been left out of the books. Which review says that very few important ones have been left out?

You are going to read reviews of books about architecture. For questions **47–56**, choose from the reviews (**A–D**). The reviews may be chosen more than once.

Mark your answers **on the separate answer sheet**.

About which book is the following stated?

The exact function of the book is difficult to determine.	**47**
Sometimes the style of writing can be difficult to read.	**48**
Very few architects or buildings of note are left out of it.	**49**
It contains examples of well-directed humour.	**50**
Useful references to little-known architectural work are included.	**51**
It is based on other writing by the same author.	**52**
It provides evidence that one view of architects is false.	**53**
It gives a more accurate account than previous books on the same subject.	**54**
The size of it is misleading.	**55**
The author is rightly critical of architecture from a particular period.	**56**

Reviews of books about architecture

A *The Meaning of Home* by Edwin Heathcote

This book is so slim and whimsical-looking you could easily mistake it for 'bookshop candy' – those cute, little tomes perched around cash registers – but don't be fooled. While entertaining enough, it also draws on the work of such heavy-hitting intellectuals as Ludwig Wittgenstein, Walter Benjamin and Carl Jung. It grew from Heathcote's popular series of newspaper columns but here he expands on those pieces with each of the 34 chapters focussing on an individual household room or a discrete building component (floor, ceiling, roof, etc.). Each chapter is a densely packed mixture of observations and curiosities, delivered in an almost stream-of-consciousness narrative, drawing on tidbits of history, folklore, mythology, philosophy, architectural innovation, scientific research, symbols, rituals and literature, plus cinema and other areas of popular culture.

Many of the ideas are fascinating, though some rooms get far more interesting treatment than others – and certain observations (such as the notion that traditional cellars in legend, movies, and real life are often dark, creepy places, harbouring unknowns) state the obvious. Nonetheless, what comes across overall is how passionately Heathcote has reconsidered the home and how broadly he has read and observed.

B *Why We Build* by Rowan Moore

Rowan Moore, a trained architect and architecture critic for *The Observer* newspaper, has produced a thought-provoking, philosophical look at the relationship between people and buildings, from the often power-crazed planners and architects to those who come later, and work and live in them. One could say there are almost two books here: partly a biography of the brilliant Brazilian architect, Lina Bo Bardi, it is also a much wider exploration of the impetuses behind modern architecture. Moore takes us from the extraordinary artificial Palm Islands in Dubai to the Dome in London, via many buildings, periodically returning to descriptions of Bo Bardi's poetic and humane work. Justifiably hard-hitting in his treatment of many of the skyscrapers that have gone up in London in the last two decades, his elegant, sharp wit is regularly put to good use, revealing the waste, vanity and muddled-thinking associated with many of the larger construction projects.

C *The Architect's Home* by Peter Gossel

A favourite fiction about modern architects is that they don't live in their own creations but favour elegant historical houses while condemning others to their concrete monstrosities. The 480 pages devoted to 100 projects by European architects, mostly from the past 100 years, in Peter Gossel's book amply refute this charge. Beautifully produced, with well-chosen images and prose that is informative if not always very digestible, *The Architect's Home* shows how absolutely wonderful modern architecture can be.

We have the fabulous creations of some of the twentieth century architectural greats such as Le Corbusier, Gropius and Aalto, but alongside them Gossel has unearthed a number of unfamiliar gems such as Charlotte Perriand's house in the Savoie mountains of France and the black-painted studio of the Swede, Sigurd Lewerentz. There are a fair number of strange omissions such as Konstantin Melnikov's amazing house in Moscow, but, on the whole, the demonstration that, when given the chance, modern architects do in fact build adventurous and imaginative homes for themselves is very welcome.

D *20th Century World Architecture* by Phaidon editors

In the middle of the last century, writers such as Nikolaus Pevsner tried to define the architecture of their epoch. It was about the inevitable progression to an architecture suitable to the machine age. This so-called 'modern movement' was led by a small number of masters – Walter Gropius, Le Corbusier and Mies van der Rohe – and its advance was marked out by a few canonical works, such as villas, exhibition pavilions and factories. When the inevitable reaction came, and traditionalists called for a return of decoration and historical styles, the distilled version of modern architecture promoted by Pevsner and others became a useful caricature.

The reality was more complicated, and now the publishers Phaidon have produced this huge book to put the record straight. They have largely succeeded. Setting architecture in wider geographical and cultural contexts, the book's range is highly impressive. It is hard to quibble with any inclusions or exclusions of either people or their constructions. My only reservation is that it suffers from some uncertainty of purpose. Clearly not a guidebook – with 3800 photographs of 757 buildings it is almost too heavy to lift – it's not quite an encyclopedia either.

Essential tips

▶ Part 1 is always an essay in response to a proposition of some kind, made, for example, in a seminar or lecture or panel discussion. Your task is to develop and support an argument on the particular topic supplied. You cannot predict what the topic will be, but you can learn to identify the advantages and disadvantages of various propositions and how to present them in an organised way.

▶ You should practise working on 'for and against' essays and familiarise yourself with the correct structure: an introduction, main body (usually two paragraphs) and a conclusion.

▶ Use formal language in the Part 1 essay and present your argument clearly. State the topic, then provide the key points for and against the proposal, supporting these ideas, where possible, with examples or justifications.

▶ If you happen to feel strongly about the topic, be sure to remain objective. Don't use emotional language and don't express your own opinion until the final paragraph of the essay.

▶ Practise using appropriate linking words and phrases to introduce points, to add points, to contrast points and to conclude the essay.

▶ Read carefully through questions 2, 3 and 4 in Part 2 before deciding which item you will write. Make sure you know how to structure the text type you choose and that you know the appropriate vocabulary to use.

▶ Remember that all questions in Part 2 could require formal or informal writing. The question will not specify which register you should use; you will need to figure this out from the input text. To determine this, pay close attention to the style and tone of the input text, and who the target reader of the piece will be.

▶ Read as many letters, reports, proposals and reviews as possible. You can find a wide range of professional reviews, for example, online. (Ensure these are on reputable and professional websites.) Pay attention to how they are structured and the language that they use.

▶ In the test, there will be blank pages in the question booklet where you can jot down some notes if you wish. Don't spend too long planning at the expense of completing your written piece.

▶ Resist the temptation to reuse any points provided in the input text. You can certainly refer to them, but do so in your own words rather than reproducing them exactly as they appear in the test. It is important to demonstrate your own range of language.

▶ You will not be allowed to use a dictionary during the test.

PAPER 1 Reading and
Use of English
PAPER 2 Writing ▶ **Part 1**
Part 2
PAPER 3 Listening
PAPER 4 Speaking

You **must** answer this question. Write your answer in **220–260** words in an appropriate style on the separate answer sheet.

1   One of your professors is a committed vegetarian. In a recent lecture, she proposed that all meat dishes be removed from the menu in the cafeteria. You have made the notes below.

> **Why we should ban meat from our cafeteria**
>
> • healthier for everyone
> • what about animals' rights?
> • better environment if no meat consumption

> **Other students expressed these opinions during the lecture:**
>
> "Eating meat is natural and normal and always has been."
>
> "But where does all this stop? Should we also ban milk, cheese and eggs?"
>
> "What about personal choice and people's right to eat whatever they want?"

Write an essay for your professor discussing **two** of the points she made. You should **explain whether or not you think banning meat from the canteen is the best choice for everyone** and **provide reasons** to support your opinions.

You may, if you wish, make use of the opinions expressed in the lecture, but you should use your own words as far as possible.

Essential tips

▶ Decide which two points you are going to focus on. Then think about how you can expand on and develop each one.

▶ Be sure to stick to the point and keep the essay on track. Avoid repeating yourself.

▶ Remember, this is an academic essay and the register should be formal. Don't use slang or other informal language.

▶ Think about the words and phrases you could use to present each point.

▶ You can argue for or against the proposal, but do so objectively. Try not to let your personal feelings come through as you write the essay. Remember, you may state your own opinion in the conclusion, but it shows skill if you can maintain a distance and present the facts clearly. You can also argue both sides of the proposal and write a balanced, objective argument overall.

▶ Use examples to support each advantage or disadvantage that you mention. Remember, for the purposes of this exercise, the examples do not have to be real or true.

Write an answer to **one** of the questions **2–4** in this part. Write your answer in **220–260** words in an appropriate style on the separate answer sheet. Put the question number in the box at the top of the page.

Essential tips

▸ Not all possible Part 2 task types appear on every paper. For example, you could be asked to produce a letter (formal or informal), or you could be asked to write an email.

▸ The review question could be based on a book or a film, but you might also be asked to review a product or service, or an event or performance. You may invent any of these items if you wish.

Question 2

▸ What is the style of the input text? What register should you use?

▸ Don't make the mistake of thinking that an email does not require the same attention to detail as a letter; organisation and layout are equally important here.

▸ What can you learn from the instructions and from Dan's email? Underline the information that will be important to consider in your reply.

▸ Remember, you can also come up with other points not featured in the input text.

Question 3

▸ As you consider answering this question, ask yourself whether you have an adequate range of vocabulary on the topic of transport.

▸ Structure in all text types is very important, but in a report it is vital that the information is presented in an organised way, making it easy for the reader to follow and understand. It is a good idea to use headings in a report.

2   A couple of years ago you did a *Volunteering Abroad* programme in South Africa. Your 17-year-old cousin, Dan, is thinking of doing the same thing and has written to you asking about it.

Read the extract from Dan's email.

> The animal conservation work you did sounds interesting – can you tell me a bit more about it, for example, which animals did you work with? I definitely hope to do a lot of travelling while I'm there too. Can you suggest anywhere I can visit? I suppose what I'm wondering more than anything is whether you think I'll enjoy it.
>
> Thanks, Paul!
>
> Dan

Write your **email**.

3   You see this post on a community website:

Your local council is compiling a web page about public transport options in your town. They would like local people to send in reports about the public transport services they use. In your report, you should:

- mention which services you use and how often you use them
- describe the quality of the service including factors such as cost and reliability
- recommend or suggest any services and facilities that you think are missing.

Write your **report**.

4   You receive this flyer from a local arts group.

> Film Event
>
> On the grounds of City Hall every Friday this summer we will screen a film free of charge. We would like you to suggest suitable titles, but we specifically want films that are socially relevant today. The screenings will begin at 9.00 p.m. each Friday. Please send us your review of a film that you think would be suitable, giving reasons for your choice.

Write your **review.**

▸ Pay attention to the areas mentioned in the input text and don't leave any of them out.

▸ Notice that you are also required to include some suggestions or recommendations in your report.

Question 4

▸ Be careful not to rush in and write a review of any film you happen to like very much. In this case, it must be socially relevant.

▸ What does *socially relevant* mean? You need to demonstrate in your review that your chosen film has social relevance.

▸ Bear in mind that this will be a public screening. Will the event mainly be for adults? How can you tell?

▸ The film you write about does not have to be real; you can make one up to suit this purpose. The important thing is that you provide a proper assessment of the film and show how it would be a suitable choice for the event.

Essential tips

▶ Make sure you listen to the entire extract before choosing your answer.

▶ Always try to choose your answer after the first listening, and confirm it after the second.

▶ Don't panic if you hear any words you don't recognise. Listen carefully and think about the context of what is being said.

▶ Listen for any stressed words. These often contain important information, either for specific details or for letting you know how the speaker feels.

Question 2: You need to identify something that surprised the man, something unusual, something he hadn't expected. What word in the extract signals this idea?

Question 3: In order to identify the woman's attitude, you need to listen to the points she makes, but also to her tone of voice. Read the answer options carefully. Which one best describes her attitude?

Question 4: Don't hurriedly choose an answer option just because you recognise a key word in the extract. Ensure that the full idea expressed in the answer you choose can be heard in the extract.

Question 6: You need to find out whether there is agreement between the speakers. Listen for language that indicates agreement or disagreement.

Track 5

You will hear three different extracts. For questions **1–6**, choose the answer (**A**, **B** or **C**) which fits best according to what you hear. There are two questions for each extract.

Extract One

You hear a man making a phone call to deliver some good news.

1 Is the woman busy when her friend phones her?
   A   She is very busy.
   B   She is not busy at all.
   C   She is a little busy.

2 What surprised the man?
   A   that he had actually passed the driving test
   B   that he had felt so nervous before the test
   C   that his friend was nervous before her test

Extract Two

You hear a woman telling a friend about her experience at a careers fair.

3 What is the woman's attitude?
   A   pessimistic
   B   bored
   C   angry

4 What does the man advise the woman to do?
   A   speak to her parents
   B   become an accountant
   C   make a focused plan

Extract Three

You hear a woman discussing plans for her cousin's visit with a friend.

5 What is the man's criticism of the woman's plan?
   A   There won't be enough time to visit all the places.
   B   He is concerned that it might be too boring.
   C   Her cousin doesn't like museums or galleries.

6 Does the woman agree with the man's suggestion?
   A   Yes, she does.
   B   No, she doesn't.
   C   She is undecided.

PAPER 1   Reading and
          Use of English
PAPER 2   Writing
PAPER 3   Listening   Part 1
                               Part 2
PAPER 4   Speaking   Part 3
                               Part 4

Essential tips

▸ Practise for this part of the test by listening to podcasts of lectures or presentations.

▸ Make the most of the time before the recording is first played by reading carefully through the rubric, the title and the set of statements. These will help you to think about the type of information you need.

▸ In this part of the test, all correct answers are the exact words or phrases as they are used in the recording. The statements may be paraphrased, but the missing words are not.

▸ If you are really not sure, you should make your best guess rather than leaving a blank space. No marks are deducted for getting an answer wrong, and you may have understood more than you realise.

Question 7: What does the speaker like doing when she travels? What part of speech follows *for*? What other words can you think of for *sleep*?

Question 9: Listen for a reference to the idea of travel being extended or stopping. This is where you will find the missing word or phrase.

Question 10: The use of the word *more* suggests that the speaker makes a comparison, and you know from the sentence structure that you need an adjective here. What adjective does she use?

Question 13: There is a reference to a trend here. What trend does the woman mention? Remember, she may use a term other than 'trend'.

🎧 **Track 6**

You will hear a travel writer describing her relationship with sleep. For questions **7–14**, complete the sentences with a word or short phrase.

___

SLEEP, WONDERFUL SLEEP

The woman's guilty secret is that she schedules time for

(**7**) .... on her trips.

According to the woman, a (**8**) ....

of travelling is sleeping better.

The woman believes that our travel experience is extended when we sleep; it isn't a

(**9**) .... from it.

She comments that the sleep we experience when travelling tends to be significantly

more (**10**) ....

For the speaker, getting over long-distance travel is particularly affected by

(**11**) .... adjustments.

She finds that sleep while travelling is more (**12**) ....

than what we experience at home.

The speaker refers to a trend called (**13**) ...., which

involves not rushing journeys.

In the end the speaker thinks she might (**14**) .... to her

fellow travellers how much she actually sleeps when she's on the road.

PAPER 1 Reading and
            Use of English

PAPER 2 Writing

PAPER 3 Listening ▶

PAPER 4 Speaking

Part 1
Part 2
Part 3
Part 4

🎧 **Track 7**

You will hear a radio interview about the challenges which first-year college students often face. For questions **15–20**, choose the answer (**A**, **B**, **C** or **D**) which fits best according to what you hear.

15 What does Martin Ferguson say about his job as an Information and Advice Officer?
    A His professional background is working in customer service.
    B He recruits students and enrols them at Stanmere College.
    C He helps students before and after they begin their course.
    D He works exclusively with the first year university students.

16 Martin says that, overall, the most common difficulty for students starting college is
    A the new environment.
    B the volume of work.
    C too much freedom.
    D time management.

17 What does Martin emphasise to students?
    A that there isn't any shame in being weak
    B that how they're feeling is very common
    C that all of their friends are struggling too
    D that it's important to show their feelings

18 Regarding finances, what does Martin give his students?
    A a course in financial management
    B tricks for saving their money
    C a pre-made budget for students
    D tips on how to spend less money

19 Primarily, according to Martin, additional difficulties include students'
    A physical and psychological well-being.
    B concerns about failing their exams.
    C anxieties about their family back home.
    D lack of meaningful friendships.

20 Who does Martin recommend study groups to?
    A students who are worried about exams
    B students who like clubs and societies
    C students who are not very outgoing
    D students who might be depressed

Essential tips

▸ This is the longest part of the Listening paper. Practise listening to recordings of this length so that you don't lose your focus before the end of the recording in the test.

▸ Pay attention to the question stem and listen for 'trigger' words. For example, if the question asks *How long ...?* listen for time frames.

▸ Remember, the questions appear in the same order as the information in the recording.

▸ Unlike Part 2, the answers in Part 3 may be paraphrased from the recording, so listen carefully for the key ideas.

Question 16: Notice the word *overall* in the question. Martin might mention various difficulties, but this tells you that you need to identify an overall, or main, problem.

Question 17: As always, pay close attention to how the question is phrased. Note that it doesn't ask what Martin says to the students, but what he emphasises to them.

Question 20: Pay attention to the pronoun *who* and listen for any mention of study groups. What does Martin say about them?

🎧 **Track 8**

You will hear five short extracts in which people talk about the things they do to reduce stress.

While you listen you must complete both tasks.

TASK ONE

For questions **21–25**, choose from the list (**A–H**) what each speaker says about what brought them to this particular practice.

A	was worried about taxes	
B	was busy relocating	Speaker 1 [**21**]
C	takes on too much	Speaker 2 [**22**]
D	had left a busy job	Speaker 3 [**23**]
E	lost a family member	Speaker 4 [**24**]
F	does it for free at the gym	Speaker 5 [**25**]
G	lacked a healthy balance	
H	has a very physical job	

TASK TWO

For questions **26–30**, choose from the list (**A–H**) what each speaker says about the effect the practice has on them.

A	gets a tranquil feeling	
B	sleeps more often	Speaker 1 [**26**]
C	feels a burden lifted	Speaker 2 [**27**]
D	gained some weight	Speaker 3 [**28**]
E	feels their mind has cleared	Speaker 4 [**29**]
F	is totally relaxed	Speaker 5 [**30**]
G	no longer has nightmares	
H	thinks life seems less hectic	

Essential tips

▸ As this part of the test focuses on gist and attitude, a good way to practise for it is to study the kind of vocabulary that expresses feelings and attitudes.

▸ The series of five short recordings will be played through once and then replayed. Unlike in Part 1, they will not be played and replayed one at a time.

▸ Practise working on two tasks at once.

▸ The instructions will tell you what the common theme is. Take a moment to try and predict what you might hear in the recording.

▸ Even though the speakers may mention practices you have never heard of before, don't worry. You won't be asked questions about the practices themselves, only how the speaker started doing them and how they feel afterwards.

Questions 21–25:

Option B: What does *relocating* mean? Do any of the speakers talk about this?

Option E: *Lost a family member* is another way of saying what? Does anyone make reference to this?

Option F: Does anyone mention the gym and, importantly, do they say anything about not paying fees?

Questions 26–30:

Option A: What is another way of saying *tranquil*? Who, if anyone, makes specific reference to this?

Option B: Be sure to consider the entire phrase in each option. Does anyone mention sleep and, if so, do they say they sleep more often now?

Option H: More than one speaker may describe their life as being hectic, but does anyone specifically say the effect of the practice is that their life now feels less crazy?

Essential tips

Part 1

▶ In this part of the test, the examiner (or interlocutor) will not direct you to interact with your partner, but it's fine if you do.

▶ Remember to speak clearly. It's understandable that you may feel nervous but try not to rush what you are saying.

▶ Always give complete answers rather than a brief *yes* or *no*. Make a habit of repeating part of the question, which will ensure that you address what you are being asked, e.g. *What are your hobbies? My hobbies are …*

▶ Wherever possible, try to offer additional information, for example, include a brief reason for the answer you have just given.

Part 2

▶ In this part of the test, you have to talk on a subject for about a minute. This is a long time, so make sure that you prepare for the test by practising talking for this amount of time.

▶ The examiner could ask you to compare or contrast pictures, identify things in them or to speculate about them. You will be given three pictures and you have to talk about two of them.

▶ There will probably be two parts to the question that you are asked about the pictures, so make sure you answer both parts. If you can't think of anything to say, make time to think by using hesitation phrases, e.g. *let me see, I'm not sure about that, let me think about that for a moment.*

▶ Listen carefully while the other candidate is talking as the examiner will ask you an extra question related to what the other candidate has been talking about. You should answer in about 30 seconds.

Part 1 (2 minutes)

The examiner will ask you a few questions about yourself and about a general topic. For example, the examiner may ask you:

- **What are your hobbies?**
- **Do you like watching films in English?**
- **What kind of career interests you the most?**

Part 2 (4 minutes)

You will each be asked to talk on your own for about a minute. You will each be given three different pictures to talk about. After your partner has finished speaking, you will be asked a brief question connected with your partner's photographs.

Restaurants (compare, contrast and speculate)

Turn to pictures 1–3 on page **172**, which show different restaurants.

(*Candidate A*), it's your turn first. Here are your pictures. They show **different types of restaurant.**

I'd like you to compare **two** of the pictures and say **what kinds of dishes are probably served in each one and who might typically dine** in these restaurants.

(*Candidate B*), **which of these restaurants appeals to you the most? Why?**

Collector items (compare, contrast and speculate)

Turn to pictures 1–3 on page **173**, which show different collector items.

Now, (*Candidate B*), here are your pictures. They show **various items that people collect.**

I'd like you to compare **two** of the pictures and describe **what kind of person would collect these items and why people collect things.**

(*Candidate A*), **which of these collections do you think is the most interesting? Why?**

Part 3 (4 minutes)

Look at page **174,** which shows some potential benefits of online learning.

Online learning (discuss, evaluate and negotiate)

Here are some benefits of online learning and a question for you to discuss.

First, you have some time to look at the task.

(*Pause 15 seconds*)

Now talk to each other about **ways in which students can benefit from online learning and how relevant you feel these benefits are.**

Now you have a minute to decide **what you feel is the main *disadvantage* of online learning, and why.**

Part 4 (5 minutes)

The examiner will encourage you to develop the topic of your discussion in Part 3 by asking questions such as:

- Which do you prefer between online learning and learning in the traditional classroom? Why?

- With online learning, is it possible to have interaction with other learners?

- In the near future, do you think people will only study online? Why (not)?

PAPER 1 Reading and ▸ Part 1
      Use of English   Part 2
PAPER 2 Writing   Part 3
              Part 4
PAPER 3 Listening   Part 5
PAPER 4 Speaking   Part 6
              Part 7
              Part 8

For questions **1–8**, read the text below and decide which answer (**A**, **B**, **C** or **D**) best fits each gap. There is an example at the beginning (**0**).

Mark your answers **on the separate answer sheet**.

Example:

0 **A** view   **B** survey   **C** outline   **D** inquiry

0	A	B	C	D

Essential tips

▸ Read through the text quickly first.

▸ Remember that only one option is correct for each gap. It needs to fit in the sentence and also with the meaning of the whole text.

▸ Look carefully at the words before and after each gap. For example, sometimes only one option is correct because of a preposition that follows the gap.

▸ When you have completed all the gaps, read through the text again to check that it makes sense.

Question 1: This is a phrase which means 'just about to do something'.

Question 2: Look at the words following the gap. Which adverb is likely to collocate with *long*?

Question 3: Which of these phrasal verbs means 'it was discovered that'?

Question 4: All four options could be used to start a sentence. However, three of them either have the wrong meaning or need to be followed by a preposition.

Finding new species

A group of scientists recently conducted a biodiversity (**0**) …….. of a tropical forest in Suriname, Latin America. One day, a local guide caught a large catfish, and was on the (**1**) …….. of cutting it up for cooking when two of the scientists intervened. They had noticed that the creature had (**2**) …….. long spines, probably to protect it from predators. It (**3**) …….. out to be an undiscovered species. (**4**) …….. any catfish in reference books, the as yet unnamed fish was one of 46 candidates for new species status that the scientists found during their visit.

In the 1730s, Swedish botanist Carl Linnaeus (**5**) …….. rules for classifying species, the most basic biological (**6**) ……..: since then, scientists have catalogued more than 1.7 million species, but it is thought that there may be as many as 8.7 million on earth. Figures for different groups of animals have been (**7**) …….. and most mammal, birds and reptiles are believed to have been discovered. Fish, shellfish and spiders, however, are a different story, and literally millions of species of insects (**8**) …….. for future generations to discover.

1	**A** edge	**B** line	**C** verge	**D** border
2	**A** intensely	**B** utterly	**C** highly	**D** exceptionally
3	**A** turned	**B** came	**C** carried	**D** gave
4	**A** Opposite	**B** Unlike	**C** Contrary	**D** Distinct
5	**A** laid on	**B** set out	**C** fixed up	**D** put through
6	**A** category	**B** section	**C** department	**D** version
7	**A** accounted	**B** composed	**C** compiled	**D** joined
8	**A** stay	**B** endure	**C** persist	**D** remain

For questions **9–16**, read the text below and think of the word which best fits each gap. Use only one word in each gap. There is an example at the beginning (**0**).

Write your answers **IN CAPITAL LETTERS on the separate answer sheet**.

Example: | 0 | T | H | E | | | | | | | | | | | | | | | | | | |

Why you forgot what you came into the room for

The brain may be (**0**) …….. least understood organ in the human body. It guides everything we do, but every (**9**) …….. often it lets us down. One annoying, if (**10**) …….. exactly life-threatening, example of this is when you walk into a room, (**11**) …….. to realise you have forgotten what your reason for going there was. Why is (**12**) …….. an incredibly powerful organ as the brain unable to remind us of something that simple?

(**13**) …….. spent many years investigating the brain, scientist Gabriel Radvansky thinks he has an answer. He has conducted numerous experiments in (**14**) …….. participants' memories were tested after crossing a room or exiting through a doorway. Invariably, passing through a doorway resulted (**15**) …….. more memory errors. Radvansky refers to what happens as an 'event boundary' in the brain. As (**16**) …….. as the brain is concerned, a doorway is a boundary between one event, or experience, and another. The brain files away all information about the first event, and focuses on the second, the new room; this makes it hard to recall a decision made in a previous room.

Essential tips

▶ Read the whole text quickly.

▶ Most of the gaps need grammatical words. Decide which type of word each gap needs. These could include: prepositions (e.g. *of*, *in*), articles (e.g. *a*, *the*), pronouns (e.g. *they*, *it*, *them*, *theirs*), relative pronouns (e.g. *who*, *which*), conjunctions (e.g. *and*, *so*), parts of verbs (e.g. *be*, *been*), modal verbs (e.g. *might*, *must*), particles of phrasal verbs (e.g. *look* **through**, *look* **into**), parts of phrases (e.g. *in* **order** *to*).

▶ The gap will probably not need a topic word. For example, in the phrase *if only he had known about*, *known* would not be gapped, but *if*, *only*, *he*, *had* or *about* could be.

▶ Remember that the word you choose must fit the meaning of the whole text, not just a few words before and after a gap. Read the complete text to see if it makes sense.

Question 10: Look at the whole sentence here. Is it 'life-threatening' to forget why you have entered a room? Thinking about this question should lead you to the missing word.

Question 11: This is a phrase, *… to do something*, used to describe something that happens immediately afterwards and causes surprise or disappointment.

Question 12: Look carefully at the structure of the whole sentence following the gap. Why is the word *as* there?

Question 13: If you can't think of a suitable word here, it may help to try thinking of a phrase that makes sense. In this case, *Because he has* would fit the sentence. In written English, phrases like *because he has*, *after he had*, *when he had* are often replaced by a particular form of an auxiliary verb before a past participle – auxiliary verb + *spent*.

PAPER 1 Reading and
Use of English

PAPER 2 Writing

PAPER 3 Listening

PAPER 4 Speaking

Part 1
Part 2
Part 3
Part 4
Part 5
Part 6
Part 7
Part 8

For questions **17–24**, read the text below. Use the word given in capitals at the end of some of the lines to form a word that fits in the gap **in the same line**. There is an example at the beginning (**0**).

Write your answers **IN CAPITAL LETTERS on the separate answer sheet**.

Example: | 0 | I | N | D | U | S | T | R | I | A | L | | | | | | | |

Essential tips

▶ Read the whole text for general understanding first.

▶ When you decide which type of word is needed for a gap, note it down next to the gap – noun, verb, adjective or adverb. Only these four types of word are tested in this part of the exam.

▶ Remember that some words will probably need more than one change.

▶ Be careful with spelling.

▶ Check whether nouns should be singular or plural.

▶ When you complete the task, read through the text again. Does it all make sense?

Question 18: What type of word is *advances*? So, what type of word is needed for the gap?

Question 19: You need to form a noun here. It can be either singular or plural.

Question 20: The noun required here refers to a process of simulating something that happened in the past.

Question 21: What kind of word can often come before an adjective, modifying the adjective?

Early human development and climate change

According to recent research, it was in times of wetter weather that early human beings in southern Africa made the greatest (**0**) ....   **INDUSTRY**

and cultural leaps forward. (**17**) .... of modern humans is   **EMERGE**

thought to have taken place in Africa over 200,000 years ago,

but two eras of (**18**) .... advances have been identified in   **INNOVATE**

southern Africa about 71,500 and 64,000 to 59,000 years ago,

which saw the development of personal (**19**) .... in the form   **ADORN**

of shell jewellery, also of bone tools and probably of language.

In a computer-based (**20**) .... of climate change over the last   **CONSTRUCT**

100,000 years, scientists discovered that these two periods were

characterised by (**21**) .... heavy rainfall in southern Africa,   **NOTE**

whilst the rest of the continent experienced long-term drought.

The researchers believe their (**22**) .... support the view that   **FIND**

there was significant movement of ancient humans to the more

hospitable conditions of southern Africa. This would have

resulted in population (**23**) ...., competition for resources and   **GROW**

exchange of ideas, which in turn fuelled progress. So, these

distant ancestors of ours may well have benefited (**24**) ....   **TECHNOLOGY**

from climate change.

Essential tips

▶ Part 4 tests a wide range of grammatical structures and vocabulary items. However, certain things are often required: changing the word order, replacing ordinary verbs with phrasal verbs, changing verbs to nouns and vice versa.

▶ Don't forget: you must not change the key word and you have to use between three and six words. Remember also that contractions count as two words (e.g. *don't* = two words).

▶ Remember that each question usually tests two different points. For example, changing an active to a passive structure, plus changing a verb to a noun.

▶ When you have completed a question, read through it again and make sure that you have not changed the meaning.

Question 25: *Must* expresses the idea of 'sure'. Because 'he wasn't lying' is about the past, what structure needs to follow *must*? And which verb collocates with *truth*?

Question 26: What phrase including *it* and *long* expresses the idea that something 'soon' happened? Which phrasal verb with *on* means 'acquire' or 'accept'?

Question 27: The first part of this question tests a structure used to give emphasis; it means 'although something is / was …'. In the second part of the question, you will need to change a verb to a noun.

Question 28: You need a passive structure here. You also need a phrasal verb meaning 'to challenge someone'.

For questions **25–30**, complete the second sentence so that it has a similar meaning to the first sentence, using the word given. **Do not change the word given.** You must use between **three** and **six** words, including the word given. Here is an example (**0**).

Example:

0 Chloe would only eat a pizza if she could have a mushroom topping.

   ON

   Chloe .... a mushroom topping when she had a pizza.

The gap can be filled with the words 'insisted on having', so you write:

Example: | **0** | INSISTED ON HAVING |

Write **only** the missing words **IN CAPITAL LETTERS on the separate answer sheet.**

---

25 We've talked a lot about Peter's description of what happened that day at the beach and I'm sure he wasn't lying.

   MUST

   We've talked a lot about Peter's description of what happened that day at the beach and he .... truth.

26 Once Catherine moved to the Finance Department, she soon acquired more responsibilities than she had ever had in her previous job.

   LONG

   Once Catherine moved to the Finance Department, it .... on more responsibilities than she had ever had in her previous job.

27 Radford has contributed in a useful way this season but the team would probably be fine without him.

   THOUGH

   Useful .... this season, the team would probably be fine without him.

28 We could always rely on Maria to challenge our supervisor whenever he became too bossy and demanding.

   STAND

   Maria could always .... to our supervisor whenever he became too bossy and demanding.

29 Everyone in the office was really surprised when the manager decided to cancel the meeting.

   OFF

   The manager's decision to .... as a real surprise to everyone in the office.

30 John said that he wouldn't hesitate to recommend Elaine for the coaching job at Darnell Sports Centre.

   HAVE

   John said that he .... Elaine for the coaching job at Darnell Sports Centre.

PAPER 1 Reading and ▶
          Use of English
    Part 1
    Part 2
    Part 3
    Part 4
    Part 5
    Part 6
    Part 7
    Part 8

PAPER 2 Writing

PAPER 3 Listening

PAPER 4 Speaking

You are going to read a book review. For questions **31–36**, choose the answer (**A**, **B**, **C** or **D**) which you think fits best according to the text.

Mark your answers **on the separate answer sheet**.

Hemingway's Boat

Sam Leith reviews a biography of the great American novelist and short story writer, Ernest Hemingway:
Hemingway's Boat: Everything He Loved in Life, And Lost, 1934–1961, by Paul Hendrickson.

In *Hemingway's Boat*, Hendrickson takes the idea that writing about Hemingway's boat *Pilar* is a way of getting at deep things about the man. *Pilar* was there all the second half of his life and fishing was more than a recreation for Hemingway: it was at the centre, this book plausibly suggests, of his being in the world. Paul Hendrickson duly set about getting to the core of Hemingway's relationship with *Pilar*. And how!

He hasn't just interviewed Hemingway's sons and surviving former friends and helpers. He has investigated the history of the company that built Hemingway's boat, and visited the muddy waterway in which she first floated. If a journalist published a news report on Hemingway's arrival in Cuba, where he lived for many years, Hendrickson will have studied his subsequent career. If Hemingway fished a particular stream on one occasion in his teens, Hendrickson will have fished it too. This is the total immersion school of – well, biography isn't quite the word. It's a sort of mental home invasion.

The narrative loops around in time – describing the acquisition of the boat, and going forward and back to his childhood, zipping into his legacy, and closing in on his death. As well as the *Pilar* story, it describes, at some length, a trio of others. There's Arnold Samuelson, a well-educated wanderer who ended up crewing his boat; there's Walter Houk, a junior diplomat, whose wife worked as Hemingway's secretary and who was similarly taken up; and there's Hemingway's youngest son, Gregory ('Gigi'). The author interviewed the latter two, and extensively researched the first, telling their previously under-examined stories fully and sympathetically in the hope that, in the overlap between them, we'd get somewhere close to Hemingway. It works.

This book places you formidably deep in Hemingway's world and life. It takes you down to the insertions and deletions in manuscripts, and shows you how the sentences were formed; with what agony and then excitement he wrote. Not that it cuts corners on the wild, action-man stuff either. Hemingway was insanely competitive, and behaved with infantile petulance when a guest out-hunted or out-fished him. At one point the author remarks drily, when Hemingway shoots himself in the leg on board *Pilar*: 'Perhaps if the fisherman hadn't been trying to land the fish and gaff it and shoot it in the head all at once, the accident would never have occurred.' And he sure did love shooting. Here we meet Hemingway shooting at bottles, shooting his initials into the top of a shark's head, blowing away seabirds with a shotgun, and so on.

But here, too, is the Hemingway who knew what a monster he could be, and regretted it. This was a man who was capable of great acts of kindness and generosity, and of remorse. There are some killingly poignant quotes – long, wonderful letters written to the sick children of friends, for instance, and the interviews with his beloved but tragic son Gigi. It gathers to a really moving end. There is so much in this long book which is interesting and enlightening that it defies any attempt to reduce it to a neat outline.

So I regret that I do have some reservations. *Hemingway's Boat* has received praise, not only for its research, but for its prose; it's in a style that strikes some people as literary. To my mind, however, it's showily overwritten. Besides the tricksy devices like sudden switches to the present tense, it abounds with pompous turns of phrase – sometimes clumsily repeated, among the crazy level of descriptive detail, with at least three chapters containing the words 'Amid so much ruin, still the beauty'. Which brings to mind all the irritating verbless sentences.

The problem is, he's doing several things: this is not just a book about Hemingway, it's also a memoir of writing a book about Hemingway, and, in some sense, it's a novelisation of the author's worshipful and faintly competitive relationship with his literary master. He bosses the reader about ('take another look at the photograph') and lets what he takes to be Hemingway-style confidence drift into his prose. It's as if someone has told Hendrickson that this is literary writing, and that it will make the difference between a good book and an astonishing one. I don't think Hemingway – who, as Hendrickson admits, is much harder to imitate than he looks – would have agreed. I'm sure it's just Hendrickson. The fact is, though, this book would have been astonishing without it.

31 The reviewer's main intention in the second paragraph is to illustrate
- **A** how difficult it was for Hendrickson to write about Hemingway.
- **B** how detailed Hendrickson's research on Hemingway was.
- **C** how important boats and fishing were to Hemingway.
- **D** how much variety there was in Hemingway's life.

32 According to the reviewer, why did Hendrickson devote so much of his book to Samuelson, Houk and Gregory Hemingway?
- **A** They had never been written about before by biographers of Hemingway.
- **B** They were the most important people in Hemingway's life.
- **C** They provided clues to Hemingway's true character.
- **D** They all spent time with Hemingway on his boat.

33 What does the reviewer suggest about Hendrickson's biography in the fourth paragraph?
- **A** It enhances Hemingway's reputation as a writer.
- **B** It goes into too much detail about certain aspects of Hemingway's behaviour.
- **C** It underlines the influence Hemingway's lifestyle had on his writing.
- **D** It gives a balanced picture of Hemingway as a writer and as a man.

34 What point does the reviewer make about Hendrickson's biography in the fifth paragraph?
- **A** It is difficult to summarise.
- **B** It gets worse as it goes along.
- **C** It can be too sentimental in places.
- **D** It is best when showing Hemingway's good side.

35 The reviewer quotes the words 'Amid so much ruin, still the beauty' to exemplify
- **A** a tricksy device.
- **B** a pompous turn of phrase.
- **C** a crazy level of descriptive detail.
- **D** a verbless sentence.

36 What point does the reviewer make in the final paragraph?
- **A** Hendrickson makes some of the same mistakes as Hemingway did in his writing.
- **B** Hendrickson's biography would have met Hemingway's approval.
- **C** Hendrickson's book is excellent in spite of the way he writes.
- **D** Hendrickson has taken notice of some bad advice.

Essential tips

▶ Make sure you read the title and the byline just underneath it. This should be a helpful introduction to the subject of the text you are going to read.

▶ Read the text quickly for general understanding. Try to get an idea of the way it is organised.

▶ Read each question and highlight the key words. Find and mark the relevant piece of text for each question.

▶ Look at the options for the first question and highlight the key words in them. Then look at the relevant piece of text and highlight words that relate to each option, before deciding which option best reflects the text.

▶ If you find it difficult to decide which option is best, try eliminating options that you feel confident are wrong. Narrowing your choice down like this should help you find the answer.

Question 31: This is an example of a question about the writer's 'purpose' in one part of the text. What is the main point of the second paragraph? Look at the options carefully. Options A and B are about the way Hendrickson worked, while Options C and D are about Hemingway. Is the main focus of the second paragraph on what Hendrickson did or on what Hemingway did? Often with 'purpose' questions, it helps to look at the previous paragraph too.

Question 32: Find and mark the section in which Samuelson, Houk and Gregory are mentioned. Then examine each option in turn. Option A: we are told that Hendrickson describes these three people 'at some length', but does the text suggest that biographers had never written about them before? Option B: all three people featured in Hemingway's life, but does the text say they were the most important people in his life? Option C: all three seem to have been close to Hemingway and so would know something about the novelist's character, but does the text suggest they 'provided clues' about it? Option D: the text says that Samuelson and Houk spent time on Hemingway's boat, and we could assume that his son would have done too. But does the text say this is why Hendrickson wrote about them 'at some length'?

Question 35: Mark the relevant part of the text. Then highlight or underline in the text where the quote in the question stem and each of the options are referred to. You may not know what every word or phrase in the options means, but by looking carefully at the structure of the sentences in the text, you should be able to work out what the phrase refers to.

PAPER 1 Reading and ▸   Part 1
Use of English   Part 2
                  Part 3
PAPER 2 Writing   Part 4
                          Part 5
PAPER 3 Listening   **Part 6**
                          Part 7
PAPER 4 Speaking   Part 8

You are going to read four reviews of a book about maps. For questions **37–40**, choose from the reviews **A–D**. The reviews may be chosen more than once.

Mark your answers **on the separate answer sheet**.

On The Map by Simon Garfield

Four reviews of Simon Garfield's book about the long and varied history of map-making.

A

On The Map offers a chronological history of maps, atlases, charts and globes from Ancient Egypt to contemporary digital cartography, and along the way provides a wealth of facts and anecdotes, all delivered with the expansive liveliness of an expert story-teller. Simon Garfield acknowledges he is neither a cartographer nor a professional historian, but his painstaking research and enthusiasm more than compensate for any omissions – there is very little on maps of Asia, for example – or for the lack of a rigorous guiding principle of the kind expected in books with more academic pretensions. Garfield, justifiably, is as enthralled by the beautiful, often factually erroneous drawings of the distant past as he is by today's GPS, video-game landscapes and social-media-based graphics. Given Garfield's descriptive intensity, it seems particularly strange that the black-and-white map illustrations that feature throughout are often reduced in scale to an extent that they become practically illegible.

B

Perhaps because Simon Garfield is a journalist rather than a historian, his understanding of the average reader's attention span is mercifully realistic. In this eminently readable history of map-making, Garfield rarely offers a train of thought that is not rounded off with a fascinating anecdote or neat piece of cartographic trivia. The fact that the book, which covers a lot of ground in over 400 pages, tends to wander unpredictably or gloss over certain important subjects, only adds to its appeal for the non-specialist. Regrettably, the visual presentation of maps – too many compressed, hard to decipher images – fails to match the standard of the text. Also, some of Garfield's observations on contemporary achievements in map-making like GPS – 'a loss to geography, history, navigation … and the sense of being connected to the world around us' – seem overly critical. On the whole, however, this is a fine introduction to the subject.

C

Simon Garfield clearly has a gift for digging up intriguing facts and stories, and this wide-ranging history of map-making, from Ptolemy in Ancient Alexandria to the interactive, digital images of today, generously illustrated with well-chosen historical treasures, is entertaining in many respects. Its best chapters tend to be those built around controversies such as the debate over the authenticity of a map claimed to depict sea voyages to America by the Norse hundreds of years before Columbus, but, overall, it suffers from a lack of a clear focus. Ironically, for a book about maps, the reader all too easily gets lost in all the vivid detail and anecdotes. One is also distracted by some awkward phrasing and surprisingly imprecise language. On the whole, however, the book does the job as a lively guide for those who are interested in maps but do not necessarily know much about them.

D

All surveys are, by nature, selective, and it is hardly surprising that a book such as *On The Map*, which attempts to cover over 2,000 years of map-making in an accessible way for readers who know little about the field, should skip or just sample certain subjects – for example, the methods and tools map-makers have used through history are barely touched on. Harder to accept or rationalise is the apparent lack of a guiding principle, besides that of cramming in as many fascinating facts as possible, and making it all fun. Garfield has a talent for communicating a telling detail or a curious turn of events, and he is particularly strong on certain periods of history, including the modern era. His chapter on such achievements as satellite navigation systems and mapping structures in computer games shows an admirably open-minded curiosity.

Which reviewer

shares C's opinion about the way the book is organised?

[37]

has a different opinion from the others about the quality of writing in the book?

[38]

takes a similar view to A regarding the reproduction of maps in the book?

[39]

shares D's view on the way the book's author deals with recent developments in map-making?

[40]

Essential tips

- ▶ Remember that you need to decide whether four different writers have similar or different views on the same subject.

- ▶ Read the title and the texts quickly to familiarise yourself with the subject.

- ▶ Highlight the key words in the questions.

- ▶ Go through each text carefully in turn, highlighting the sections relating to each question. Write the question numbers next to parts you highlight. Remember that the ideas in the question may be expressed differently in the texts, for example by using synonyms or changing the way a concept is expressed grammatically, e.g. *education* could be expressed as 'the way people learn'.

- ▶ Remember that a question will ask you to identify a writer's view on a subject and compare it with other people's views. The question tells you what the subject is, but not what any of the writers' views are. For example, if you are asked who shares writer A's view on the 'significance of something', you are not told whether A thinks it is significant or not – that is for you to work out.

Question 37: The key words here are *the way the book is organised*. You are asked who shares C's opinion about this. C says that 'overall, it suffers from a lack of a clear focus. Ironically, for a book about maps, the reader all too easily gets lost in all the vivid detail and anecdotes.' So, C thinks the 'lack of clear focus' is a problem with the way the book is organised. B's view of the book is that 'The fact that the book, which covers a lot of ground in over 400 pages, tends to wander unpredictably ... only adds to its appeal for the non-specialist.' 'Tends to wander unpredictably' tells us that B also thinks the book lacks a 'clear focus', but B regards this as positive – it 'only adds to its appeal for the non-specialist.' So, B does not fully share C's opinion. Now look at what A and D say. Which one, like C, has a critical view of the book's organisation?

Question 38: The key words here are *the quality of writing in the book*, and you are asked to identify which reviewer has *a different opinion* from the other three about this. A says the books is 'all delivered with the expansive liveliness of an expert story-teller.' So, A thinks the writing is very good. B refers to 'this eminently readable history of map-making.' So, B thinks the writing is of high quality too. Now we know that either C or D must have a different opinion about the quality of the writing. Which one is it?

You are going to read a newspaper article about fitness tests for athletes. Six paragraphs have been removed from the article. Choose from the paragraphs **A–G** the one which fits each gap (**41–46**). There is one extra paragraph which you do not need to use.

Mark your answers **on the separate answer sheet**.

Have you got what it takes to be a top athlete?

Journalist Kate Carter tries out some advanced tests for sports people
at Loughborough University's Sports Science Institute

Not so long ago, identifying a potential sports star was a matter of seeing how well they could sprint around a track, or kick a football. Now, sports scientists use advanced tests to determine fitness, agility, body composition, reaction times and much more. But how does an average recreational athlete compare? A recent convert to running, I'm at the Sports Science Institute lab at Loughborough University, which gathers statistics on athletes from a range of sports, to find out my potential. Dr James Carter, head of the institute, starts by getting my standard physical measurements.

41

I am made to sit in a device called a BodPod, and given a scan to examine bone density and create a picture of my internal body fat. After that, it's on to the treadmill for the VO2 max test, which measures fitness. This consists of running at increasing speed on an ever steeper incline while puffing into a large mask, a disconcerting experience as it reduces your vision to virtually nothing.

42

An average woman has a VO2 max of around 35 ml/kg/min, while an elite athlete might be as high as 70 ml/kg/min (for men the range is around 40–85). Mine is 54, which is respectable for a recreational runner. I also turn out to be a carb burner rather than a fat burner, which I'm taking as licence to eat more. Next up are a couple of cognitive tests to assess my reactions.

43

I don't do so well at the whole-body agility test – a frame with 12 lights at varying heights you have to leap or duck to extinguish – but Dr Carter reassures me that this matters less for endurance than for other sports.

44

You just pedal on a stationary bike, then accelerate madly for ten seconds, before trying to sustain that power for 30 seconds. Just? Add in increasing resistance and it feels as if you are cycling through treacle on a bike with two flat tyres into a headwind. And it hurts.

45

As I start to recover from this final challenge, it occurs to me that it's easy to imagine a future in which babies are screened at birth to join a super breed – or at least an elite training programme. Dr Carter mentions the film *Rocky IV* which has something similar in it. He is joking – but in truth, it's not so implausible.

46

There are, of course, things the tests can't show yet: the psychology of the athlete, tactics, nutrition. But the scientific data that can be recorded is very useful, and not just for professional athletes. I personally have learned a huge amount about what I could feasibly achieve in my next race, as well as specific steps to move up to my goal of a full marathon. And next time I come back, I'm determined to conquer that bike.

A The first of these uses a large board full of bulbs, which light up in a random sequence. You hit them to turn them off, while simultaneously shouting out the numbers that appear on a small screen. I do better than the average, which I put down to being used to dealing with two small children.

B For all the cutting edge equipment and carefully designed assessments, what Dr Carter is unable to evaluate, as he readily admits, are such crucial factors as 'pain tolerance, doing the training day in, day out and self-belief.'

C Looking at someone's genome to determine whether they're suited to team sports or individual endurance may be 'accessible in the next decade,' Dr Carter says. 'Say we've got a group of 15-year-olds who are genetically suited to certain sports, are we going to put them through special regimes for the next decade? That's where some of the research is going.'

D After measuring my handgrip strength (I'm delighted to be 'average', given my arms are like spaghetti), it's time for the final hurdle: the Wingate test. Or as I shall always think of it, the longest half minute of my life. It sounds relatively easy.

E Disappointingly, it turns out I've been kidding myself about my height for years. Weight, though, is less important than body composition and it's the latter that the first of a series of hi-tech tests will assess.

F So much so that hours later I can still feel the lactic acid, brought on by the extreme pedalling, burning in my legs. 'Sprinters, cyclists – this is their test,' explains Dr Carter. Top athletes 'need to be performing well on this or there's something wrong.'

G While I am doing this, Dr Carter records my data. One of the key indicators, he explains, is 'the respiratory exchange ratio, which is the combination or the ratio of oxygen consumed and carbon dioxide produced. When that ratio goes over one, that's when we know to increase the gradient.'

Essential tips

▶ Read through the main part of the text so that you know what it is generally about and how it is organised.

▶ Then look through the gapped paragraphs to see what the topic of each one is.

▶ Look for links between the main text and the gapped paragraphs. A gapped paragraph can have links with the previous paragraph, the following one, or both.

▶ Don't spend too long deciding which paragraph fits one of the gaps. If you have difficulty, move on to the next gap. You may be able to identify the solution for the problem gap by a process of elimination.

▶ Remember to check that the completed text makes sense by reading through it one final time.

Question 41: Look at the last sentence in the first paragraph of the main text. What are 'standard physical measurements' likely to be?

Question 42: In the last sentence of the second paragraph, the journalist describes running on a treadmill 'at increasing speed on an ever steeper incline'. An *incline* is a slope. Which gapped paragraph contains a phrase which has a similar meaning to 'ever steeper incline'? You may need to look at more than just the first sentence of each gapped paragraph.

Question 43: The last sentence of the paragraph before gap 43 tells us that the next tests she is going to take will assess her 'reactions'. Which gapped paragraph describes a test of reactions, rather than strength or stamina?

PAPER 1 Reading and
Use of English

PAPER 2 Writing

PAPER 3 Listening

PAPER 4 Speaking

Part 1
Part 2
Part 3
Part 4
Part 5
Part 6
Part 7
Part 8

You are going to read four people's thoughts about running your own record label. For questions **47–56**, choose from the people (**A–D**). The people may be chosen more than once.

Mark your answers **on the separate answer sheet**.

Which person

feels innovative approaches make sense in the current economic climate?	47
thinks time away from business is required to ensure good decision-making?	48
believes that making and selling music involves less risk than it used to?	49
values working with people who have different skills?	50
believes record labels should take on traditionally unfamiliar functions?	51
welcomes the variety of work that running a record label entails?	52
believes in delegating certain aspects of business to outside organisations?	53
thinks the future of the music industry is uncertain?	54
emphasises the importance of understanding consumers?	55
rejects the idea of producing music with commercial success as the main objective?	56

Essential tips

▶ Read the instructions and the title. If there is an introductory comment under the title, read this because it will give you an idea about the subject of the article.

▶ If you want to get faster at this task, try reading the questions first. As you read them, highlight the key words that indicate what to look for in the text.

▶ Then read the first section of the text. Each section is likely to have at least one and no more than four related questions.

▶ When you identify a sentence or phrase that you think answers one of the questions, highlight it and write the question number at the side of the text. This may save you time later if you find part of another section that you think may also answer the same question.

▶ Remember that similar points may be made in two or three sections, but there is only one correct answer. So, when you match a question with a section, make sure it says precisely what is in that section.

Question 47: First, find the sections that refer to the 'current economic climate'. Then, identify which of these refer to 'innovative approaches'.

Question 48: What is 'time away from business' likely to involve? Who is it likely to be spent with? Which of the sections referring to 'time away from work' includes a point about 'decision-making'? Remember that while the idea may be the same in the question and text, the words used in each are likely to be different.

Question 51: *Take on* here means 'start to do', and *functions* here are 'business activities'. Which section refers to business activities which may not 'traditionally' have been carried out by record labels?

What does it take to run a record label?

The internet and other developments in technology have had a major impact on the music industry. What are the implications for those wanting to run their own record label? Four people who have set up small, independent record labels share their insights.

A Ben Wolf

Fundamentally, I'm a music enthusiast. I started off as a DJ in dance clubs, and setting up a record label seemed like the logical next step. There are always unknown factors, but in my experience, the key to success in this business is putting yourself in the position of the other person involved and anticipating their needs or what makes them tick. Why does a DJ want to play a certain record? Who would sell or buy a record? With digital technology, establishing an independent label has become more manageable. The industry has a tendency to bemoan the fact that sales and income are massively down, but what is equally true is that the costs of producing, manufacturing and promoting music have been reduced, so if you're sensible, there's less to lose these days. Two other crucial points: you need to be a team player because no single person could handle everything, and while you need a balance between your professional and your family life, you need to be ready to dedicate yourself to the job 100% when necessary.

B Henry Stone

I'm co-founder of an independent record label. We've discovered some great musical artists, a few of whom have become very popular and have more than paid back what we invested in them, but we don't play the game of predicting which artists will fly or flop in the market. Our focus is on working with creative, inspiring songwriters or musicians, and how to further their message. The mutually supportive relationship I have with my co-founder, Mark, is fundamental to what we've achieved; neither of us could have survived on our own. We've been going for some years but it still doesn't feel like a job. No two days are the same, whether we're promoting an event, filming a documentary, releasing a record, or checking out a band in the studio. You have to be careful with burn-out, though. I'm often up at 7.00 a.m. and still emailing beyond midnight, but I ensure that when I'm with family and friends, work is blocked out entirely. Without perspective and space, your judgement can go to pieces.

C Kerry Murphy

If I was 21 years old, just out of college, and with the understanding of the music industry that I have now, I'm not sure I'd set up a record label. I can think of less time-consuming and more straightforward and lucrative businesses to get into, and it's not going to get any easier. But, if you feel compelled to do it – some of us do – then I would consider a partnership with somebody who has strengths in areas where you are weak, and vice-versa. That's worked for me. Also, I wouldn't get too enamoured with the things that others already do well. We're associated with distributors around the world that are just great at what they do, and we've learned not to interfere. We have even given up having an in-house sales team; outsourcing works fine. Our primary concern now is with the music; making sure our artists are on time, look great and are well funded.

D Riz Amal

I think now is a great time to start a label if that's your thing. With everything changing so rapidly, no one really knows what the landscape will be in two years' time, let alone 20. The old-school record label model has been dying out for years, and with sales and income falling, as they have been virtually everywhere, the smart thing to do is to try to break the mould. Being a pioneer always brings with it the danger of failure, and it's likely to require all-consuming commitment in terms of time and energy, but there may be no alternative. The lines between what an independent record label does and what the manager of a musician or band does will continue to blur. Labels will need to get involved in artists' tours, in their merchandising and even publishing – activities they have tended to stay away from. As long as the numbers balance, and the budgets and forecasts are realistic, then there's no reason why a new independent label can't work.

Essential tips

Question 1

▶ Remember the structure of a 'for and against' essay, and take a few minutes to plan your points and examples before you begin writing.

▶ The examiner wants to see that you can clearly present and support an argument. Try to consider arguments *both* for and against the proposal.

▶ It's not a good idea to bring your personal experience into the essay unless it's directly relevant and will usefully support a specific point.

▶ Because of the word limit, you need to make sure that your points are concise. Develop the habit of reducing long sentences so that they only include the key information. However, ensure that your sentences don't become too short; if they seem to be short, try to combine a couple. Try not to repeat yourself or use unnecessary words.

▶ When you reread your essay, check that it has a logical flow of ideas. Make sure it is not vague. Remember, the reader is unable to ask for clarification on any points, so ensure that you have been precise.

You **must** answer this question. Write your answer in **220–260** words in an appropriate style on the separate answer sheet.

1 Your class was in the audience of a panel discussion for a current affairs television programme, discussing a government proposal to make physical education and sport compulsory for five hours per week in all UK secondary schools, and for all year groups. You have made the notes below.

PE and sports in schools – 5-hour weekly minimum

- Sport and PE give students the opportunity to develop important skills outside the classroom, such as commitment and teamwork.
- Physical activity promotes overall well-being, and choices such as walking or cycling are also better for the environment.
- The number of overweight and obese young people has become alarming.

Various audience members expressed these opinions during the discussion:

"This may be OK for primary school, but students in secondary should be allowed to choose."

"Unfair; not everyone likes sport."

"How can we fit this into the school week? Will academic work suffer as a result?"

Write an essay for your tutor discussing **two** of the points in your notes. You should explain **how you think the government should proceed** and **provide reasons** to support your opinions.

You may, if you wish, make use of the opinions expressed in the discussion, but you should use your own words as far as possible.

PAPER 1 Reading and
          Use of English

PAPER 2 Writing ▶ Part 1
                      Part 2

PAPER 3 Listening

PAPER 4 Speaking

Write an answer to **one** of the questions **2–4** in this part. Write your answer in **220–260** words in an appropriate style on the separate answer sheet. Put the question number in the box at the top of the page.

2 You recently took a domestic flight which was badly delayed, and service from the crew was poor. Write a letter to the customer services manager and include the following information:

- plane sat on the runway for over two hours with no information from the crew
- one member of staff was particularly rude when two passengers asked if they could switch seats
- after take-off, it was announced that no food or drinks would be served, not even mineral water.

Write your **letter**.

3 Every student at your university received this email from the Vice Chancellor.

> Dear Student,
>
> We are deeply grateful to Mrs Iris Kerr, who has generously donated the sum of £20,000 to the university. Mrs Kerr specifically requested that the students be consulted on how these funds should be used. Please put your ideas into a proposal and submit it to my office by 15 March. Be sure to indicate why you believe your suggestion would be the very best use of this money.
>
> Yours sincerely,
>
> Dr Walter Greenleigh
>
> Vice Chancellor, Offords University

Write your **proposal**.

4 You have attended the first music festival ever held in your region, which ran for ten days with various events in different parts of the area. Write a review for your local newspaper. Be sure to say whether you felt the festival was a success and what, if anything, might be done differently next year.

Write your **review**.

Essential tips

Question 2:

▶ What kind of letter do you need to produce here? What register should you use?

▶ In letters of complaint it is acceptable to use strong words to convey your dissatisfaction but remain polite and avoid making accusations. You should never be rude.

▶ State the facts clearly and firmly.

▶ It is not explicitly stated in the instruction, but you should tell the Customer Services Manager what you expect from them. You can also state a time frame in which you require any follow-up or action.

▶ Remember to end the letter with a respectful closing phrase.

Question 3:

▶ Ask yourself if you have a solid proposal for how this money could be spent. You need to begin writing as quickly as possible so don't spend too long trying to think of ideas. Remember, however, that your idea does not have to be an excellent one. What is important to the examiner is how you present it in the proposal.

▶ The objective of a proposal is to convince somebody of something. Practise using persuasive language for this part of the test.

▶ You don't have to use headings when you write this piece, but include them if they will make your proposal clearer. You can also use numbered or bulleted lists.

▶ Remember to finish with a solid conclusion summarising the main points of your proposal.

Question 4:

▶ You have some scope in this task type. The input text does not give a great deal of information about the music festival, which means that you are free to invent your own details.

▶ Decide how you want to approach the task. Will you indicate that the event was mainly a big success or a complete failure, or somewhere in between?

▶ What kind of adjectives could you use? Try to avoid very general adjectives such as *good* or *nice*.

▶ Bear in mind that your review will be published in a newspaper. What register should you use?

▶ While a review is essentially an opinion piece, and your opinion needs to be stated, don't lose sight of providing facts and clear examples with each point.

▶ Note the final part of the instruction. Do you have a suggestion for the next music festival?

Essential tips

Question 1: Read the three answer options carefully. Does the man say anything about money or expenses? Does he mention dirt or filth, or any similar terms? Does he talk about the pace of life? What does *pace* mean?

Question 4: A very important listening skill is identifying feelings and attitudes, which you are required to do in this question. What does the woman actually say? How does she *sound*? Which adjective best describes how she feels? If you are not familiar with one of the words provided, focus on the ones you do understand and decide whether they answer the question correctly or not. Through a process of elimination, you can still arrive at the correct answer.

Question 5: In this part of the test, you may find that all of the answer options are items you have heard in the extract. It is vital that you pay close attention to the question and focus on what you are specifically asked.

Question 6: Listen carefully for a phrase of disagreement. What, specifically, is it in relation to?

Track 9

You will hear three different extracts. For questions **1–6**, choose the answer (**A**, **B** or **C**) which fits best according to what you hear. There are two questions for each extract.

Extract One

You hear two former college friends who bump into each other in London.

1 What did the man not like about London when he lived there?
   A the pace of the life
   B the dirt of the city
   C the cost of living

2 To make the man feel better, the woman says that
   A she really loves the countryside too.
   B she is also quite a boring person.
   C her feelings about London might change.

Extract Two

You hear a new employee chatting with a colleague about her first week at the company.

3 Why does the woman have to go to so many meetings?
   A Because it's her first week at the company.
   B It's a particularly busy time at the company.
   C It's a normal part of that company's culture.

4 How does the woman seem at the end of the conversation?
   A outraged
   B alarmed
   C reassured

Extract Three

You hear two friends discussing college applications.

5 Where will the woman go to university?
   A She's going to the college best known for her subject.
   B She is still trying to make her mind up about it.
   C She's going to a university which is very far away.

6 The woman doesn't agree that a bigger university would mean
   A better faculty members.
   B a better campus life.
   C a more fun experience.

Track 10

You will hear a community volunteer called Conor McManus talking about how he first got involved in this area, and describing the kind of projects he has worked on. For questions **7–14**, complete the sentences with a word or a short phrase.

Essential tips

Question 8: From the sentence structure, you should be able to identify what part of speech is missing here. What adjective does Conor use about his friend?

Question 10: Remember that the statement may paraphrase what was said by the speaker, but the missing information will always be the exact word or words they used. What does Conor describe as being 'limited'? He may have used another word with a similar meaning to *limited*.

Question 11: Food items are mentioned with regard to the garden project but, remember, the question is about a project Conor was involved in himself. Does he mention anything related to food? You have an additional clue in the statement: it was the project that meant the most to him.

Question 13: What verb is missing here? What does Conor say about other people getting involved in projects?

COMMUNITY AWARENESS

Conor's first community involvement was with a group that effectively stopped the building of a big (**7**) .... in the town centre.

Conor admits that, at first, he wasn't keen to get involved, but his friend was very (**8**) ....

He describes his original impression of community volunteers as (**9**) .... people.

Later, he explains, he realised that his (**10**) .... was quite limited.

Conor says the project that meant the most to him was providing food for (**11**) ....

Conor's friend told him about her community garden project in which (**12**) .... were given by an experienced gardener.

He mentions that anyone interested could contribute their talents to projects, or just (**13**) .... their time.

Conor finishes by pointing out that, for some people, this area could become their (**14**) ....

PAPER 1   Reading and
              Use of English

PAPER 2   Writing

PAPER 3   Listening   Part 1
                                 Part 2
                                 Part 3
                                 Part 4

PAPER 4   Speaking

Essential tips

Question 17: What does the word *obligatory* mean? If you are not sure, what do you think it could mean, given that only one answer option is correct?

Question 18: In his answer about the Councillor for International Relations role, Mr Meade also talks about the Sports Exchange Advisors. Listen carefully so that you do not confuse the information about each one. You need to identify what he says about the CIR role.

Question 19: Regarding the application process, Mr Meade mentions several phases and the periods in which they take place. What is another way of saying 'successful candidates'?

🎧 **Track 11**

You will hear a public meeting in which Dr Freya Davidson, the Dean of Studies of Caledonia College, is interviewing Malcolm Meade, the Administrative Officer from the Consulate-General of Japan, about the Japan Exchange and Teaching Programme. For questions **15–20**, choose the answer (**A, B, C** or **D**) which fits best according to what you hear.

15   The number of participants in the first JET Programme was around
   A   25.
   B   50.
   C   1,000.
   D   50,000.

16   What, according to Mr Meade, is 'team-teaching'?
   A   sharing cultural information about one's home country
   B   supporting students with language skills like pronunciation
   C   preparing materials and teaching with Japanese teachers
   D   joining students in after-school activities like English club

17   Which of the following is obligatory in order to apply for the JET Programme?
   A   Japanese language ability
   B   an undergraduate degree
   C   knowledge of Japanese culture
   D   previous teaching experience

18   What does Mr Meade say about the Councillor for International Relations (CIR) role?
   A   Only seven people are hired each year.
   B   Applications for it are not accepted.
   C   A good level of Japanese is required.
   D   Candidates must be nominated for it.

19   When are successful candidates informed that they've been accepted to the JET Programme?
   A   January
   B   April
   C   July
   D   October

20   Mr Meade says that some JET participants feel lonely because
   A   they didn't think very carefully about the commitment.
   B   they find that one year is a long time away from home.
   C   the placements are usually in fairly rural communities.
   D   they tend to find it difficult to adjust to Japanese culture.

PAPER 1 Reading and
Use of English

PAPER 2 Writing

PAPER 3 Listening ▶ Part 1
Part 2
PAPER 4 Speaking Part 3
Part 4

Essential tips

Questions 21–25:

Option A: What do we mean when we say 'a trade'? Is it different from a profession? Do any of the speakers talk about this?

Option C: Does anyone speak about expectations and a family business?

Option D: What relevance does *justice* have to a chosen career path? Does this fit with any of the extracts?

Option E: Don't lose sight of the original question which is about the specific reason they are in their careers. Does anyone say they chose that line of work *because of* the salary?

Questions 26–30:

Option A: Who, if anyone, makes reference to art or creativity or artistic interests?

Option D: What is another way of saying *early retirement*? Does anyone mention this idea?

Option E: Does anyone talk about starting their own business? They may not have used this exact term.

Option F: What is typically involved in publishing? Does anyone talk about their hopes for the future in this regard?

🎧 **Track 12**

You will hear five short extracts in which people talk about their careers.

While you listen you must complete both tasks.

TASK ONE

For questions **21–25**, choose from the list (**A–H**) what each speaker says about how they came to be in this career.

A	had a preference to work in a trade		
B	wanted to have a challenging career	Speaker 1	21
C	was expected to join the family business	Speaker 2	22
D	has always had a strong sense of justice	Speaker 3	23
E	was motivated by a high salary and prestige	Speaker 4	24
F	came to this industry by chance	Speaker 5	25
G	never had particularly high ambitions		
H	started at the bottom, climbed the ranks		

TASK TWO

For questions **26–30**, choose from the list (**A–H**) what each speaker says about their plans or hopes for the future.

A	would like to be an artist		
B	has an opportunity to teach	Speaker 1	26
C	wants to be a big executive	Speaker 2	27
D	plans to take early retirement	Speaker 3	28
E	hopes to start their own business	Speaker 4	29
F	would like to be in publishing	Speaker 5	30
G	wants to work for a big charity		
H	dreams of being famous one day		

PAPER 1   Reading and
          Use of English

PAPER 2   Writing

PAPER 3   Listening

PAPER 4   Speaking

Essential tips

Part 3

▶ In Part 3 of the Speaking paper you have to work with the other candidate to discuss an issue and reach a decision.

▶ The examiner will give you a mind map containing the issue for discussion and a few key points to help you. You have three minutes for the main discussion, so there is time to really explore the issue in detail. As well as giving your own opinion, you need to involve and interact with the other candidate.

▶ After the discussion, the examiner will ask you to reach a decision together about an aspect of the topic. Remember that there is no correct answer here, and that it is acceptable to disagree.

▶ Remember that this part of the test is for you to show the examiner how well you can express your views, discuss an issue, negotiate and come to an agreement with another person.

Part 4

▶ In this section you will need vocabulary related to careers. If you can't think of the name of a particular profession, don't worry, you can always describe that job instead.

▶ When you are asked how you might feel about something, remember to use speculative phrases such as, *I imagine I might feel ...* or *For me, I suppose it could be ...*

▶ If a question asks you to address a preference, try to comment on both options before stating which one you prefer, and why.

Part 1 (2 minutes)

The examiner will ask you a few questions about yourself and about a general topic. For example, the examiner may ask you:

- **How many people are there in your immediate family?**
- **What quality do you most like in other people?**
- **Do you think people should continue to study new things throughout their lives?**

Part 2 (4 minutes)

You will each be asked to talk on your own for about a minute. You will each be given three different pictures to talk about. After your partner has finished speaking, you will be asked a brief question connected with your partner's photographs.

Important occasions (compare, contrast and speculate)

Turn to pictures 1–3 on page **175**, which show different occasions.

(*Candidate A*), it's your turn first. Here are your pictures. They show **various important occasions**.

I'd like you to compare **two** of the pictures and say **how the people appear to be feeling and why**. They could also be experiencing some **negative emotions**. **What might these be?**

(*Candidate B*), **which of these do you think is the most important occasion? Why?**

Shopping experiences (compare, contrast and speculate)

Turn to pictures 1–3 on page **176**, which show different shopping experiences.

Now, (*Candidate B*), here are your pictures. They show **different shopping experiences**.

I'd like you to compare **two** of the pictures. Describe **how these shopping experiences differ and whether each method of shopping is suited to a different type of person. Why (not)?**

(*Candidate A*), **which method of shopping do you personally prefer? Why?**

Part 3 (4 minutes)

Look at page **177**, which shows some general points about employment status.

Employment categories (discuss, evaluate and negotiate)

Here are some points about working full-time for a company versus working for yourself for you to discuss. First, you have some time to look at the task.

(*Pause 15 seconds*)

Now talk to each other about **the benefits of each employment category and whether you think one is better than the other. Why?**

Now you have a minute to decide **what qualities a person would need in order to be successfully self-employed.**

Part 4 (5 minutes)

The examiner will encourage you to develop the topic of your discussion in Part 3 by asking questions such as:

- What kind of careers do you think are best suited to self-employment?
- There has been a growing trend of self-employment in the past ten years. Why do you think that is?

PAPER 1 Reading and
          Use of English ▶

PAPER 2 Writing

PAPER 3 Listening

PAPER 4 Speaking

Part 1
Part 2
Part 3
Part 4
Part 5
Part 6
Part 7
Part 8

For questions **1–8**, read the text below and decide which answer (**A**, **B**, **C** or **D**) best fits each gap. There is an example at the beginning (**0**).

Mark your answers **on the separate answer sheet**.

Example:

0   **A**   uncovering   **B**   excavating   **C**   unearthing   **D**   exposing

0	A	B	C	D
	—	**—**	—	—

The world's oldest pots

While (**0**) …….. in Xianrendong Cave in south-east China recently, archaeologists discovered the oldest fragments of pottery ever found. These pieces of clay pots have been (**1**) …….. back 20,000 years to a time when many parts of the earth were covered by huge ice sheets. At this time, food was relatively (**2**) ……… Fat, an important (**3**) …….. of energy was hard to (**4**) …….. by, so cooking was essential to (**5**) …….. energy from various food sources such as potatoes and meat. Marrow found in animal bones is very (**6**) …….. in fat, and archaeologists believe the cave dwellers may have cooked bones to obtain it. There is also some evidence that they cooked other food items like shellfish.

One important (**7**) …….. of the pottery found in Xianrendong Cave is that it was made several thousand years before the birth of agriculture. This discovery, along with other recent ones in east Asia, (**8**) …….. the long-held conventional theory that farming and permanent settlements had to be established before people could begin to make pottery.

1	**A** referred	**B** counted	**C** chased	**D** traced
2	**A** faint	**B** scarce	**C** seldom	**D** bare
3	**A** source	**B** cause	**C** base	**D** root
4	**A** stand	**B** go	**C** come	**D** get
5	**A** relieve	**B** release	**C** restore	**D** retain
6	**A** lavish	**B** ample	**C** deep	**D** rich
7	**A** outlook	**B** factor	**C** aspect	**D** form
8	**A** disproves	**B** denies	**C** defeats	**D** disposes

For questions **9–16**, read the text below and think of the word which best fits each gap. Use only one word in each gap. There is an example at the beginning (**0**).

Write your answers **IN CAPITAL LETTERS on the separate answer sheet**.

Example: | 0 | I | N | T | O | | | | | | | | | | | | | | | | | |

A computer called Baby

When the machine jokingly named Baby whirred (**0**) …….. life on 21 June 1948, it became the world's first modern computer. And nothing (**9**) …….. ever be the same again. Developed by Tom Kilburn and Freddie Williams, two scientists at Manchester University in the UK, Baby was the first device to have all the components now regarded (**10**) …….. characteristic of the basic computer. It could store (**11**) …….. only data, but also a short user programme in electronic memory and process it at electronic speed. In many respects, Baby, which was big enough to fill a room, was completely (**12**) …….. today's small, powerful computers. A smartphone can store several hundred million (**13**) …….. more bytes of data than Baby could. But it was a key breakthrough.

(**14**) …….. being a British invention, however, the original research was not fully exploited in the UK, and other countries soon raced ahead in harnessing the new technology. Both inventors had successful academic careers, but (**15**) …….. ever made the money of people like Bill Gates, the billionaire founder of Microsoft, who was as (**16**) …….. unborn when Baby first came to life.

For questions **17–24**, read the text below. Use the word given in capitals at the end of some of the lines to form a word that fits in the gap **in the same line**. There is an example at the beginning (**0**).

Write your answers **IN CAPITAL LETTERS on the separate answer sheet**.

Example: | 0 | A | N | N | O | Y | A | N | C | E | | | | | | | | | | |

Overhearing mobile phone conversations

For many people, unintentionally hearing a mobile phone conversation causes more (**0**) …….. and frustration than the general background noise of people talking to each other. Scientists from the University of San Diego recently carried out an interesting study with a group of (**17**) …….. to investigate this phenomenon in a controlled way. The (**18**) …….. were asked to solve a series of anagram puzzles while, (**19**) …….. to them, researchers conducted a scripted conversation in the background, either between two people in the room or between someone on a phone and a caller not in the room. (**20**) …….., subjects found the one-sided phone conversation more (**21**) …….. and distracting than the two-sided interaction. One of the researchers, Dr Rosa Vessal, suggested that two-way conversations are less distracting because they are easier to follow. 'The content of a phone conversation is (**22**) …….. ,' she said. 'Not knowing where it's heading is distracting.' What are the (**23**) …….. of the research? One might be that we should not (**24**) …….. how distracting overheard phone conversations can be for drivers.

ANNOY

VOLUNTARY
PARTICIPATE
KNOW

OVERWHELM
MEMORY

PREDICT

IMPLY
ESTIMATE

PAPER 1   Reading and
           Use of English ▶

PAPER 2   Writing

PAPER 3   Listening

PAPER 4   Speaking

Part 1
Part 2
Part 3
Part 4
Part 5
Part 6
Part 7
Part 8

For questions **25–30**, complete the second sentence so that it has a similar meaning to the first sentence, using the word given. **Do not change the word given**. You must use between **three** and **six** words, including the word given. Here is an example (**0**).

Example:

0   Chloe would only eat a pizza if she could have a mushroom topping.

ON

Chloe .... a mushroom topping when she had a pizza.

The gap can be filled with the words 'insisted on having', so you write:

Example: | **0** | INSISTED ON HAVING |

Write **only** the missing words **IN CAPITAL LETTERS on the separate answer sheet**.

---

25   I was really surprised to bump into Marianne at the airport.

LAST

Marianne .... to bump into at the airport.

26   I was amazed that John stopped eating meat completely in an attempt to improve his health.

GAVE

Much .... eating meat completely in an attempt to improve his health.

27   Like many students, Joe would find it very difficult to pay for everything he needs if his parents didn't help him.

ENDS

Like many students, Joe would have great .... the help of his parents.

28   My tutor says she's been too busy to read my essay, but she'll mark it by the end of the week.

ROUND

My tutor says she .... my essay yet, but she'll mark it by the end of the week.

29   You can understand why Andrew's comments upset Sofia so much.

BLAMED

Sofia can't .... at Andrew's comments.

30   'I promise I will never tell anyone about the missing files,' said Jenny.

WORD

Jenny .... never tell anyone about the missing files.

PAPER 1 Reading and ▸
        Use of English

PAPER 2 Writing

PAPER 3 Listening

PAPER 4 Speaking

Part 1
Part 2
Part 3
Part 4
Part 5
Part 6
Part 7
Part 8

You are going to read a magazine article. For questions **31–36**, choose the answer (**A**, **B**, **C** or **D**) which you think fits best according to the text.

Mark your answers **on the separate answer sheet**.

Australia's lost giants

Thousands of years ago, Australia had large populations of huge animals. What happened to them?

Across Australia, scientists have discovered thousands of fossils of ancient megafauna, huge animals that lived 100,000 to 40,000 years ago, during the Pleistocene era. The remains include those of giant snakes, huge flightless birds, two-and-a-half-metre-tall kangaroos, hippo-like beasts and six-metre-long lizards. These animals dominated their ecosystems, and then were gone in an extinction spasm that swept away nearly every animal weighing 50 kilogrammes or more. What happened exactly? Given how much ink has been spilled on the extinction of the dinosaurs 65 million years ago, it's a wonder that more hasn't been devoted to the fate of the Pleistocene megafauna, creatures that were both dramatically large and, for some time, co-existent with humans.

In the Americas, native megafauna died out relatively soon after the arrival of humans, about 13,000 years ago. In the 1960s, scientist Paul Martin developed what became known as the 'blitzkrieg hypothesis' to explain the extinction process: humans created havoc as they spread through the Americas, wielding stone-tipped spears to annihilate animal populations. But it wasn't comprehensive; North America kept its deer, bears, bison and moose, while South America retained jaguars and llamas.

What happened to Australia's megafauna is one of the planet's most baffling paleontological mysteries. Kangaroos – hardly giants – are the largest indigenous land animals to have survived on the continent. For years, scientists blamed climate change. Indeed, Australia has been drying out for a million years or more, and megafauna were faced with a continent that became increasingly parched and denuded of vegetation. Paleontologist Tim Flannery suggests, somewhat differently, that humans, who arrived on the continent around 50,000 years ago, used fire to hunt, which led to deforestation and a dramatic disruption of the water cycle. What's certain, Flannery says, is that something dramatic happened to Australia's large creatures – abruptly (how abruptly is a matter of debate) – around 46,000 years ago, strikingly soon after the invasion of a tool-wielding, intelligent predator. There does appear to be more than mere coincidence here.

Flannery advanced the Australian version of Martin's 'blitzkrieg hypothesis' in a book called *The Future Eaters*. He also put forward an even more ambitious thesis that human beings, generally, are prone to ruining ecosystems and destroying their own futures. The book proved highly controversial. Some viewed it as critical of the Aborigines, the first Australians, who pride themselves on living in harmony with nature. The more basic problem is that nothing has been found to prove that humans killed any megafauna – not one animal skeleton with a spear tip in it, for example. Such kill sites have been found in the Americas, but there's no archaeological analog in Australia. One scientist said: "If this were a murder trial, it wouldn't get past first base."

The debate about megafauna pivots, substantially, on dating old bones and sediments. If scientists can show that the animals disappeared within a few hundred years, or even a couple of thousand years, of the arrival of humans, there's a strong case that one thing was the direct result of the other. Flannery contends that islands hold another clue to the mystery. Some species of megafauna survived on Tasmania and other islands until 40,000 years ago, when falling sea levels allowed humans to finally reach them, Flannery says. This argument relies on the lack of fossil evidence for a prolonged human-megafauna overlap. If, however, we find evidence that human beings and megafauna co-existed for thousands of years, then the role of humans in the extinctions would become blurry at best. Certainly it would rule out a rapid, Martin-Flannery-style blitzkrieg.

Although the data currently available is limited and inconclusive, there would seem to be great value in investigating what happened. The blitzkrieg hypothesis paints an alarming picture of human beings rapidly wiping out a great number of animals. But there's an even more ominous scenario: the extinctions didn't happen because of overkill but rather through an incremental sequence of events, including climate change, during which the people involved could not fully discern what was happening to their environment. This brings us to today. 'The way we've lived and are living is destroying our future,' Flannery says. Yet we're only gradually figuring out how we're changing our world and the extent to which we're harming or even driving to extinction countless species.

31 What does the reviewer suggest in the first paragraph about the large animals of the Pleistocene period?

A They were historically less important than the dinosaurs.

B More is known about them than about dinosaurs.

C Relatively little has been written about them.

D They were larger than is often thought.

32 What does the word 'it' in line 11 refer to?

A the spread of humans in the Americas

B the disappearance of megafauna

C the human practice of hunting

D the theory Martin put forward

33 What point does the writer make about the extinction of ancient Australian megafauna in the third paragraph?

A The idea that humans contributed to it is plausible.

B It is likely to have been more gradual than previously thought.

C The theory that it resulted from climate change has been disproved.

D It is hard to understand why kangaroos survived while other species didn't.

34 The writer quotes a scientist in line 28 in order to emphasise that

A it is a mistake to compare different continents.

B humans are being unfairly characterised as criminals.

C there is no real evidence to support Flannery's theory.

D Australian Aborigines should be allowed to defend themselves.

35 According to the fifth paragraph, what is the key information dating techniques need to provide?

A how long humans have lived on various islands

B when humans became capable of long sea journeys

C when megafauna first appeared in a certain locations

D how long humans and megafauna lived alongside each other

36 What is the writer doing in the final paragraph?

A anticipating further research developments

B introducing an opposing point of view

C illustrating a point made previously

D raising some wider concerns

PAPER 1 Reading and ▶
         Use of English

PAPER 2 Writing

PAPER 3 Listening

PAPER 4 Speaking

Part 1
Part 2
Part 3
Part 4
Part 5
Part 6
Part 7
Part 8

You are going to read four comments by media analysts about the future of printed newspapers. For questions **37–40**, choose from the comments **A–D**. The comments may be chosen more than once.

Mark your answers **on the separate answer sheet**.

Does the printed newspaper have a future?

As more and more people use TV, the internet and various forms of social media as sources of news and information, the future of the traditional newspaper is the subject of much debate. Can the printed format survive? Four media analysts offer their thoughts.

A

The traditional newspaper clearly faces stiff competition from television and the internet, but reports of its terminal decline are greatly exaggerated. In China, India and much of Latin America, newspaper sales have actually risen in recent years, and if news organisations work in an intelligent way – combining print and digital operations as many already do – then the future of news on paper should be assured. The format has a lot going for it, not least that people generally trust newspapers as sources of reliable, detailed information. Print journalists have time to check facts carefully and are able to present stories in well-written, coherent forms. So much reporting on TV and online, on the other hand, is instant, speculative and lacks the bigger picture. The other key factor is that people like to touch and hold paper, and newsprint tends to be much easier on the eyes than text on a screen.

B

There is something very satisfying about turning the pages of a newspaper, glancing across the headlines, then settling down to read an article that catches your eye. It is a feeling many people miss when accessing news in a digital format, but for the generations who have grown up reading electronic media, it is not something they will have any great attachment to. For most younger people, printed newspapers make little sense. The entire contents of a newspaper, and so much more, can be found on the website of the same title. Some people have welcomed the replacement of newspapers with digital media for environmental reasons – fewer newspapers mean fewer trees cut down – but this is not a real issue as most newspapers nowadays are printed on recycled paper. The key point is that, with rapidly declining readership, printed newspapers represent an increasingly antiquated business model, which is unlikely ever to recover.

C

A respected media analyst recently looked at current trends in the American printed newspaper industry and calculated that within 30 years it would be extinct. And there is no reason to believe that the fate of newspapers elsewhere in the world would be very different. Those who champion the traditional format have some strong arguments to make: that newspapers are friendlier objects to handle than electronic gadgets, that forestry and paper production are no less sustainable as industries than those which manufacture and power digital technology, and that the content of newspapers tends to be of greater depth, accuracy and trustworthiness than in any other form of media. These are all fine points worth making, but the bottom line is that the traditional newspaper is an obsolete format and, as such, is destined to perish sooner or later.

D

The printed newspaper has had a long life: over 500 years since the invention of the printing press. Fundamentally, however, it is just a piece of technology, a device now approaching the end of its natural lifespan. Its successor, digital technology, can do everything the newspaper does and much more. The vastness of the internet means it can provide information in a great variety of ways. Long, detailed investigations can be found as easily as brief, ephemeral updates. Technological developments mean that digital devices are as easy to handle and read as newspapers, and give far wider and more flexible access to information. In terms of energy and material resources, digital technology is much more efficient, as you only use it when content is actually required, whereas newspapers are printed whether they are read or not. The demise of a historically significant piece of technology is bound to cause distress but it will happen, whether we like it or not.

Which analyst

has a different opinion from the others about the
physical experience of reading printed newspapers?

| 37 | |

takes a similar view to C regarding the quality of news
reporting in printed newspapers as compared with digital media?

| 38 | |

shares B's opinion about the environmental impact of
printed newspapers?

| 39 | |

takes a different view from the others regarding the long-term
viability of printed newspapers?

| 40 | |

PAPER 1 Reading and ▸	Part 1
Use of English	Part 2
PAPER 2 Writing	Part 3
	Part 4
PAPER 3 Listening	Part 5
	Part 6
PAPER 4 Speaking	**Part 7**
	Part 8

You are going to read a magazine article about wildlife reserves in Kenya. Six paragraphs have been removed from the article. Choose from the paragraphs **A–G** the one which fits each gap (**41–46**). There is one extra paragraph which you do not need to use.

Mark your answers **on the separate answer sheet**.

Kenya's great wildlife – exploring two nature reserves in east Africa

'Is that a black or white rhino?' Our guide Joseph tested how much attention we had been paying. We had seen a white rhino first, extremely close up, casually grazing while we took pictures. That's the first clue. Black rhino are much more nervous and aggressive, and you shouldn't get close. Second clue, the shape of its back. Finally, look at the mouth. It turns out 'white' was coined by happy accident many years ago, when the Afrikaans word for 'wide' was mistaken and the name stuck; in contrast, the black rhino has a thinner, beak-like lip.

41 [gap]

Our trip was organised by an organisation called Farside Africa, whose passionate support for conservation efforts enabled us to get right to the heart of projects in Kenya. First stop was Lewa House, part of Lewa Wildlife Conservancy, a private reserve north of Nairobi, with a small airstrip a short drive away.

42 [gap]

At the forefront of rhino conservation in Kenya, Lewa currently has 71 black and 56 white rhino, more than ten per cent of Kenya's total rhino population – counted daily by a team of rangers. Huge resources have been channelled into their protection, but unfortunately the illegal hunters still sometimes win the day, their reward guaranteed by a buoyant black market in which the price of black rhino horn exceeds that of gold.

43 [gap]

Lewa House itself is perched on a hill, secluded cottages with dramatic vistas across the rolling landscape:

mighty elephants trundling along the horizon, a zebra wandering through your garden. Guests gather for lunch by the pool or dinner in the house, where Calum and Sophie welcome them like extended family.

44 [gap]

The second half of our trip was a couple of hours' drive away, in Laikipia, at Ol Pejeta Conservancy, another reserve dedicated to the protection of rhino and the development of local communities. While Lewa relies heavily on donors, Ol Pejeta is striving to create a sustainable project and, together with revenue from tourism, uses innovative ventures in combining livestock and arable farming with wildlife.

45 [gap]

In Ol Pejeta Conservancy, we were hosted at Kicheche Camp by Andy and Sonja. By 'camp' you may read 'canvas', but the comparison with traditional camping ends there; they have designed a cosy retreat with all creature comforts and personal touches. The only reminder we were in a tent came from our obvious proximity to a variety of animal calls that pierced the night.

46 [gap]

Oh, and we ticked the big cat box too. Both by day and by night, we encountered lion, witnessing what incredible beasts they are as they sauntered majestically through their kingdom. Somewhat lazily, they gave chase to some baby warthog and resting ostriches, and came away without a catch, but our immediate proximity to each event was exhilarating.

A They have steadily built a fine base for exploring, and we saw more than we could have hoped: graceful giraffe, endangered Grevy's zebra, large families of elephant, no less than four species of eagle and, of course, the rhino. Alas, we were not to see a big cat as the grass was high after the rains, and they proved elusive.

B As the sun dipped behind the hills at the end of each fantastic day, however, we were able to enjoy the serenity of the wilderness, along with enthralling conversation about Kenyan wildlife and culture.

C It's so disturbing it hardly bears thinking about, but when we were offered the chance to talk to the security team about their work, we took it. They treated us to a demonstration: from the scent of a single footprint, a specially trained dog expertly tracked a 'poacher' through the scrub, an exercise that has helped the team make hundreds of arrests.

D We steadily approached, and as the animal treated our arrival calmly, we could work out

which it was. Sadly, the few of these remarkable creatures we were lucky enough to see are part of a declining population – though, fortunately, there are many people battling to save them.

E Perhaps because the landscape was drier and flatter, we saw even more wildlife here than in the previous reserve, more than making up for the interrupted sleep. Swathes of warthog were an obvious addition, along with many jackal and a solitary hyena.

F Joseph came to collect us there, and needlessly explained that we would see much more than rhino; either side of the runway gathered zebra, a couple of giraffe and an ostrich before our very eyes.

G Besides this income diversification, there is a successful campaign to demonstrate that grazing cattle can regenerate grasslands and give back to the wildlife. Among the animals here are four of only seven remaining northern white rhino worldwide. They are in an enclosed reserve with added security, their horns trimmed to be less enticing to poachers.

You are going to read an article in which four composers write about their own favourite modern composers. For questions **47–56**, choose from the composer (**A–D**). The writers may be chosen more than once.

Mark your answers **on the separate answer sheet**.

Which writer says the following about their favourite composer?

He works closely with the people who interpret his music.	47
All his compositions have a dramatic quality to them.	48
He composes music with specific locations in mind.	49
He creates music that defies analysis.	50
He may not be the ideal teacher.	51
His compositions tend to be difficult to play.	52
His artistic output will outlive that of many of his contemporaries.	53
His compositions vary considerably in style.	54
His compositions seem to be ahead of their time.	55
The music he composes is instantly recognisable as his.	56

Modern composers

A Mark-Anthony Turnage on Louis Andriessen

I marvel at the extreme individualism of Louis Andriessen. Every time you hear a piece of his music, you know it's by him. When I first heard his composition *De Staat*, I was struck by the fact that although it was minimalist music, it was so much more harmonically interesting and hard-edged than most works in that genre. He's influenced a lot by Stravinsky, who is probably my idol, and he has in turn greatly influenced me in his directness, bold colours and harmonic language. He has an emotional depth and a sense of magic that a lot of modern music lacks. A big part of me regrets not studying with him, although he's such an overwhelming figure I might have become merely a bad copy. Andriessen's rigour would have been good for me because he is a master of structure and planning, which I struggle with. He is one of the few composers working today whose music will survive, whereas many of the current big names will sink without trace.

B Michael Berkeley on Harrison Birtwistle

I like several modern composers, but the one who, for me, seems to build inexorably on his own intensely personal vision with consistent integrity, is Harrison Birtwistle. Take a piece such as *The Triumph of Time*, seemingly hewn from stone, yet a simple little melodic motif rises up and soon takes on a haunting and unforgettable quality, like the cry of some ancient creature. I seized the opportunity to create a cantata (*Love Cries*) based on the love music from Birtwistle's opera, *The Second Mrs Kong*, because I knew that in compiling it I would learn so much. And I did – Harry moves ideas around like children's building bricks. 'Try that passage upside-down,' he would say. A sense of theatre permeates not only the operas, but even chamber works such as *Ritual Fragment* and *Secret Theatre*. Ultimately, though, it's what I cannot quantify that transfixes me – as Pierre Boulez said of him: 'Where does it come from, this music?'

C Sally Beamish on Peter Maxwell Davies

What I love about Max is that he is constantly surprising – from the intense complexity of *Eight Songs For a Mad King*, to the unaffected simplicity of *Farewell to Stromness*, which I recently heard played by guitarist Allan Neave. His opera *Taverner* was my first introduction to the world of 'contemporary' music, at 16, and I was fascinated by it. I then discovered *St Thomas Wake*: the toughness of the musical language thrown into relief by foxtrots. I finally met Max in person when I joined the Scottish Chamber Orchestra as a viola player, and he was conducting. I was on the brink of taking the plunge as a composer, and he encouraged and advised me, inviting me to be his assistant on his composers' course. I felt unequal to the job and wished profoundly I had simply applied as a participant, but I learnt an immense amount, things I have never forgotten. His works still enthral me; every new piece brings fresh surprises and is always an interaction with his performers, and often with the community in Orkney, the Scottish island where he lives.

D David Sawer on Benedict Mason

Benedict Mason's pieces always seem to walk the tightrope between perfection and total chaos. They are fresh, playful and ridiculous, and usually of such impossible complexity that they threaten to self-destruct. *Animals* and *The Origins of Dance*, a sequence of 12 dance movements, each precisely 90 seconds long, has the ensemble playing jitterbugs and bossa novas at up to 12 different tempi, coordinated by 12 different click tracks. *Hinterstoisser Traverse* is a 12-minute piece based on one note. The series of pieces *Music for Concert Halls* plays with the acoustical properties of the venues for which they were written. They are more like installations for orchestra, elegantly evoking space and distance through the choreographed movements of the musicians in and around the whole building, while the audience remain in their seats. His experiments are extreme and uncompromising, but entirely logical. The pieces push at the boundaries and point to future possibilities for the concert-going experience.

You **must** answer this question. Write your answer in **220–260** words in an appropriate style on the separate answer sheet.

---

1 You attended a public lecture given by a visiting professor of economics who proposed that early retirement (age 55) be made compulsory in all EU countries. You have made the notes below.

> **A case for compulsory retirement at age 55**
>
> • Younger people can't enter the workforce if older people stay too long in their jobs – unfair.
>
> • Older people do not have the same energy they once did – younger workers will increase productivity.
>
> • Older people would be happier without the stress of a long working week, which would be better for them and better for society.

> **These opinions were expressed after the public lecture:**
>
> "With life expectancy over 80 now, how would people support themselves during such a long retirement?"
>
> "For many people, their career gives meaning to their life. If you take this away, what will become of them?"
>
> "Older workers have invaluable experience and skills, which benefits both companies and the national economy."

Write an essay for your own economics lecturer discussing **two** of the points from your notes. You should **explain whether you think the proposition is realistic** and **provide reasons** to support your opinions.

You may, if you wish, make use of the opinions expressed in the lecture, but you should use your own words as far as possible.

PAPER 1 Reading and
Use of English

PAPER 2 Writing ▶ Part 1

PAPER 3 Listening Part 2

PAPER 4 Speaking

Write an answer to **one** of the questions **2–4** in this part. Write your answer in **220–260** words in an appropriate style on the separate answer sheet. Put the question number in the box at the top of the page.

2 The 12-year-old daughter of a family friend has written to you asking for advice about studying English. Your reply should address these questions:

- I'm embarrassed because my accent is strong when I speak English. What can I do to change this?
- I hate English grammar. Can't I just skip it and focus on the other skills?
- I want to be fluent by next year. How many hours a day should I spend studying English?

Write your **letter**.

3 You see this notice in your university library:

> As part of a new information pack for students beginning their first year at Quarry College, we have decided to include some recommendations for the laptops or other electronic devices which are the most suitable for student purposes. We would like to hear your recommendations. Please submit a report covering the following points:
>
> item, brand and model
> how it meets student needs
> cost / value for money
> any disadvantages

Write your **report**.

4 On a radio arts programme, you hear the presenter say how bored he is with novels he reads and promptly forgets. He issues a challenge for listeners to submit a written review of a book that had a major impact on them, and why.

Write your **review**.

PAPER 1 Reading and
Use of English

PAPER 2 Writing

PAPER 3 Listening   ▸ Part 1
                               Part 2
                               Part 3
                               Part 4

PAPER 4 Speaking

Track 13

You will hear three different extracts. For questions **1–6**, choose the answer (**A**, **B** or **C**) which fits best according to what you hear. There are two questions for each extract.

Extract One

You hear two people discussing electronic book readers.

1 Why did the man get an e-reader?
    A He wanted it for travelling.
    B It was given to him as a gift.
    C He needed it for his job.

2 What does the man believe about the future of printed books?
    A They will definitely be replaced by e-books.
    B They will never be replaced by e-books.
    C They will continue to exist alongside e-books.

Extract Two

You hear two colleagues discussing how they get to the office.

3 What is the man's reaction when the woman discovers that he drives to work?
    A He is embarrassed about it.
    B He thinks it's quite funny.
    C He doesn't particularly care.

4 What does the woman suggest to the man?
    A She challenges him to try taking the bus again.
    B She advises him to start walking to the office.
    C She recommends that he go to work by bicycle.

Extract Three

You hear two friends discussing an essay for college.

5 When the man arrives the woman is
    A in tears.
    B in control.
    C in a panic.

6 What does the man offer to help the woman with?
    A writing her essay
    B planning her essay
    C researching her essay

Part 1
Part 2
Part 3
Part 4

🎧 **Track 14**

You will hear a student giving a class presentation on citizen journalism. For questions **7–14**, complete the sentences with a word or short phrase.

CITIZEN JOURNALISM

The student points out that professional journalists have traditionally included comments from local people to (**7**) .... and make it more meaningful to others.

It was when Web 2.0 tools were developed that citizen journalism really started to (**8**) ....

The speaker explains how internet-enabled mobile phones with (**9**) .... have made it easy and common for people to post material online.

While citizen journalism wasn't widely accepted at first, it has now (**10**) .... as a very useful tool.

Citizen journalism provides the rest of the world with almost instant access to photos and stories (**11**) .... online by locals.

A great advantage of citizen journalism is that it can give us (**12**) .... into how the lives of people are affected during major political crises.

The authorities have also been able to (**13**) .... faster thanks to the collaboration of citizen journalists.

These days the (**14**) .... and video reports made by citizen journalists are often used in professional news stories and documentaries.

PAPER 1 Reading and
            Use of English

PAPER 2 Writing

PAPER 3 Listening ►

PAPER 4 Speaking

Part 1
Part 2
Part 3
Part 4

Track 15

You will hear a conversation between the director of a national charity, Brandon Tate, and a psychologist, Dr Joan Wells, who is also an expert on the issue of unemployment. For questions **15–20**, choose the answer (**A**, **B**, **C** or **D**) which fits best according to what you hear.

15 What is Dr Wells referring to when she says 'It's incorrect and it's unhelpful.'?
    A the difficulty unemployed people have in coming to terms with their situation
    B the pressure put on unemployed people by their friends and family members
    C the notion some people hold that unemployment is solely a financial problem
    D the negative impact upon the outlook of people dealing with unemployment

16 Mr Tate says that a contributing factor to an unemployed person's sense of hopelessness is the fact that
    A their essential nature changes.
    B finding a job is such a struggle.
    C they eventually decide to give up.
    D they know there are too few jobs.

17 Dr Wells compares the range of emotions experienced by an unemployed person to
    A the process of regaining control.
    B dealing with the death of a loved one.
    C reluctant acceptance of a bad situation.
    D developing a strategy for moving on.

18 In terms of practical advice, what does Dr Wells say is essential for unemployed people to do?
    A remember that it's not personal
    B ensure they do not get depressed
    C set goals daily and keep moving
    D get enough sleep and eat well

19 According to Mr Tate, financial support may be available for
    A taking a skills course.
    B applying for new jobs.
    C doing volunteer work.
    D relocating to a new city.

20 In their closing remarks, what do both speakers emphasise?
    A relying on friends and family members
    B improving application and interview skills
    C treating unemployment like a full-time job
    D having an action plan and keeping spirits up

🎧 **Track 16**

You will hear five short extracts in which people talk about travel.

While you listen you must complete both tasks.

TASK ONE

For questions **21–25**, choose from the list (**A–H**) what each speaker says about their main experience of travelling.

A	came late to travelling		
B	had a career as a diplomat	Speaker 1	21
C	has to travel for a living	Speaker 2	22
D	never travelled anywhere	Speaker 3	23
E	went on trips with friends	Speaker 4	24
F	has a major fear of flying	Speaker 5	25
G	was brought up travelling		
H	had bad holiday experiences		

TASK TWO

For questions **26–30**, choose from the list (**A–H**) how each speaker feels about travel now.

A	likes how dramatic it is		
B	disrupts the home life	Speaker 1	26
C	thinks of it as glamorous	Speaker 2	27
D	it's enriching and exciting	Speaker 3	28
E	considers it a privilege	Speaker 4	29
F	feels uneasy about it	Speaker 5	30
G	finds travel terrifying		
H	can take it or leave it		

Part 1 (2 minutes)

The examiner will ask you a few questions about yourself and about a general topic. For example, the examiner may ask you:

- **Do you prefer the mountains or the sea? Why?**
- **What is your favourite dish from your country?**
- **How might your best friend describe you?**

Part 2 (4 minutes)

You will each be asked to talk on your own for about a minute. You will each be given three different pictures to talk about. After your partner has finished speaking, you will be asked a brief question connected with your partner's photographs.

> **Choice of drink** (compare, contrast and speculate)

Turn to pictures 1–3 on page **178**, which show people having different drinks.

(*Candidate A*), it's your turn first. Here are your pictures. They show **three women choosing three different drinks.**

I'd like you to compare **two** of the pictures and say **what type of person each one is and what their lifestyle is probably like.**

(*Candidate B*), **which of these drinks would you be most likely to choose? Why?**

> **Waiting** (compare, contrast and speculate)

Turn to pictures 1–3 on page **179**, which show people waiting.

Now, (*Candidate B*), here are your pictures. They show **people waiting.**

I'd like you to compare **two** of the pictures and say **what you imagine the circumstances are in each picture and how these people might be feeling.**

(*Candidate A*), **are you someone who finds waiting difficult? Why (not)?**

Part 3 (4 minutes)

Look at page **180**, which shows some aspects of social-networking.

Social-networking sites (discuss, evaluate and negotiate)

Here are some ways in which social-networking sites have an impact on our lives, and a question for you to discuss.

First, you have some time to look at the task.

(*Pause 15 seconds*)

Now talk to each other about **how relevant you think these points are, and whether social-networking sites are really improving our lives.**

Now you have a minute to decide on **the most important benefit of social-networking sites.**

Part 4 (5 minutes)

The examiner will encourage you to develop the topic of your discussion in Part 3 by asking questions such as:

- There is now a big presence of advertisements and marketing campaigns on social-networking sites. Do you think this is a good or bad thing? Why?
- How do you feel about issues of privacy with regard to social-networking sites?
- Some people believe that the use of social-networking sites in the workplace is reducing productivity. Do you think this is true?

For questions **1–8**, read the text below and decide which answer (**A**, **B**, **C** or **D**) best fits each gap. There is an example at the beginning (**0**).

Mark your answers **on the separate answer sheet**.

Example:

0 **A** meditation **B** perception **C** sensation **D** comprehension

| 0 | A | B | C | D |

Teenagers and digital technology

In many countries, there is a widespread (**0**) …….. that teenagers' lives nowadays are (**1**) …….. by technology. However, information (**2**) …….. in a recent study of Australian teenagers' use of and attitudes towards technology suggests that this view doesn't (**3**) …….. the reality of their everyday existence. The research by academics from the University of Canberra in Australia found that, while most teenagers had ready access to home computers, mobile phones and other electronic devices, they generally spent more time on traditional (**4**) …….. such as talking to family and friends, doing homework, and enjoying hobbies and sports than on using technology. Accessing social media and playing computer games (**5**) …….. as low as ninth and tenth (**6**) …….. among the ten most common after-school activities.

Fifteen-year-old Laura Edmonds is one of the teenagers surveyed. She admits to being very (**7**) …….. to her smartphone and makes full use of various apps, but if she needs to (**8**) …….. after a hard day at school, she tends to 'hang out with my friends, listen to music or chat with my mum and dad'.

1	**A** mastered	**B** dominated	**C** prevailed	**D** commanded
2	**A** amounted	**B** gained	**C** achieved	**D** gathered
3	**A** repeat	**B** reproduce	**C** reflect	**D** recreate
4	**A** pursuits	**B** events	**C** operations	**D** processes
5	**A** classed	**B** ranked	**C** valued	**D** graded
6	**A** subsequently	**B** separately	**C** correspondingly	**D** respectively
7	**A** related	**B** attached	**C** absorbed	**D** fastened
8	**A** unwind	**B** unfold	**C** unload	**D** unbend

For questions **9–16**, read the text below and think of the word which best fits each gap. Use only one word in each gap. There is an example at the beginning (**0**).

Write your answers **IN CAPITAL LETTERS on the separate answer sheet**.

Example: | 0 | I N | | | | | | | | | | | | | | | | | | | | |

Animals that migrate

Animal migration comes (**0**) …….. many different forms – long or short, seasonal or daily, predictable or seemingly random. But (**9**) …….. one thing unites all migratory species, it is the fight to survive. (**10**) …….. this means looking for food, finding mates or laying eggs, survival is the fundamental motivation. But how do animals travel huge distances to precise destinations (**11**) …….. a map or GPS? (**12**) …….. single answer to this is available. Monarch butterflies, for example, are believed to use the sun to navigate from North America to Mexico. Leatherback turtles, on the other (**13**) …….., which can migrate 20,000 kilometres across the ocean, are thought to be guided by the earth's magnetic field. A seabird called the sooty shearwater flies (**14**) …….. average of 64,000 kilometres yearly over the Pacific Ocean. In (**15**) …….. so, it executes a figure-of-eight between New Zealand, where it breeds, and stopovers in Japan, Alaska and California. This bird seemingly has a variety of tools (**16**) …….. its disposal, using the earth's magnetic field, the sun and the stars, and even sight and smell when flying over familiar territory.

For questions **17–24**, read the text below. Use the word given in capitals at the end of some of the lines to form a word that fits in the gap **in the same line**. There is an example at the beginning (**0**).

Write your answers **IN CAPITAL LETTERS on the separate answer sheet.**

Example: | 0 | S | U | C | C | E | S | S | | | | | | | | | | |

Note taking

Of all the skills you need to make a (**0**) …….. of your college or   **SUCCEED**
university studies, note taking is still one of the most important,
even in this digital age. Whether you do it by hand or on a laptop,
taking good notes will (**17**) …….. things greatly when you come   **SIMPLE**
to do revision and write (**18**) ……..   **ASSIGN**

Nowadays, lecture slides and handouts are often uploaded
onto the college or university intranet. The (**19**) …….. of this   **SIDE**
guaranteed availability is that there can be a (**20**) …….. to stop   **TEMPT**
listening carefully to the lecturer. The advantage, however, is that
you can focus on the difficult parts of what is said. Taking notes
can aid concentration, but you need to do it (**21**) ……….., recording   **SELECT**
only what is most useful to you.

Lecturers often cover a lot of material swiftly, and to (**22**) ……….   **SURE**
that you record everything you need, some form of shorthand
will help. Use abbreviations (e.g.) and symbols (→), and you
can (**23**) ……….. certain words ('btwn' for 'between'). It is also   **SHORT**
important to be systematic in recording information like sources
of quotes and other (**24**) ……….. details.   **BIBLIOGRAPHY**

PAPER 1	Reading and Use of English	▶
PAPER 2	Writing	
PAPER 3	Listening	
PAPER 4	Speaking	

| Part 1 |
| Part 2 |
| Part 3 |
| **Part 4** |
| Part 5 |
| Part 6 |
| Part 7 |
| Part 8 |

For questions **25–30**, complete the second sentence so that it has a similar meaning to the first sentence, using the word given. **Do not change the word given.** You must use between **three** and **six** words, including the word given. Here is an example (**0**).

Example:

0   Chloe would only eat a pizza if she could have a mushroom topping.

   ON

   Chloe .... a mushroom topping when she had a pizza.

The gap can be filled with the words 'insisted on having', so you write:

Example: | **0** | INSISTED ON HAVING |

Write **only** the missing words **IN CAPITAL LETTERS on the separate answer sheet.**

---

25   I'm sorry now that we didn't save a bit more money for the holidays.

   SET

   I wish .... a bit more money for the holidays.

26   When people treated Emily like a child, she didn't like it.

   RESENTED

   Emily .... she was a child.

27   Reducing the time we spend on boring paperwork would be good for all of us.

   INTEREST

   It would be in .... on the time we spend on boring paperwork.

28   My cousins, Joe and Ben, are identical twins and when they were small my dad could never work out who was who.

   DIFFERENCE

   My cousins, Joe and Ben, are identical twins and when they were small my dad could never .... of them.

29   Stefano thought that no one had done much to prepare for Alicia's farewell party.

   THAT

   Stefano was under .... done to prepare for Alicia's farewell party..

30   People usually need specific qualifications to get onto the nursing course, but they said they would treat Maria differently because of her practical experience.

   EXCEPTION

   People usually need specific qualifications to get onto the nursing course, but they agreed .... case because of her practical experience.

PAPER 1	Reading and Use of English	▸	Part 1
			Part 2
PAPER 2	Writing		Part 3
			Part 4
PAPER 3	Listening		**Part 5**
			Part 6
PAPER 4	Speaking		Part 7
			Part 8

You are going to read a magazine article. For questions **31–36**, choose the answer (**A**, **B**, **C** or **D**) which you think fits best according to the text.

Mark your answers **on the separate answer sheet**.

Artificial reefs

Rocks under the sea attract lots of marine life. The best-known of these reefs are the spectacular coral reefs, but artificial, man-made reefs are also significant, as Stephen Harrigan reports.

When the 160-metre-long Vandenberg was deliberately sunk in May 2009, it joined many other shipwrecks in the Gulf of Mexico, off the coast of Florida in the USA. People around the world have long known that shipwrecks are prime fishing sites, and in modern times reefs have been created out of all sorts of objects including old refrigerators, cars, train carriages and oil drilling rigs.

The process of how a man-made hulk like the Vandenberg becomes an undersea garden is governed by variables such as depth, water temperature, currents and the composition of the seabed. But most artificial reefs attract marine life in a more or less predictable sequence of events. First, water currents deposit plankton to provide a reliable feeding spot for small fish, which then draw in bigger predators like blue fin tuna and sharks. Next come the creatures seeking protection from the ocean's lethal openness – hole and crevice dwellers like eels. Opportunistic predators such as jack and barracuda are also quick to come, waiting for their prey to show themselves. In time – maybe months, maybe years, maybe a decade, depending on the ocean's moods – the steel will be encrusted with algae, hard and soft corals, sponges and other forms of sea life.

For decades, oil and gas platforms in the Gulf of Mexico have been prime sites for recreational fishing, since many species of fish seek shelter in their underwater structures. Michael Miglini, the captain of a charter boat called Orion that takes fishermen and divers out to rigs off Port Aransas – an area blessedly spared from the oil that spilled into the Gulf after the Deepwater Horizon catastrophe in 2010 – knows the attraction of artificial reefs for water sports enthusiasts, and the revenue and jobs thereby generated. He says: 'Creating habitat is akin to creating oases in the desert. An artificial reef is a way of boosting the ocean's capacity to create fish, to increase the life of the Gulf.' Biologists suggest, however, that artificial reefs may simply attract fish from natural reefs and become killing zones for certain species, such as red snapper, one of the Gulf's most sought-after game fish.

'When it comes to red snappers, artificial reefs are bait,' says James Cowan, a professor of oceanography and coastal sciences. 'If success is judged solely by an increase in harvest, then artificial reefs are pretty successful. But if those structures – usually deployed in shallow waters to make them more accessible to fishing – are pulling fish off natural reefs farther from the coast, they may actually be increasing the overfishing of species that are already under stress.'

Some artificial reefs have become hazards to navigation and a toxic threat to the waters in which they rest. The danger of pollution is the reason almost 70% of the Vandenberg's $8.4 million sinking budget went to clean-up efforts, including the removal of more than ten tons of asbestos and more than 250,000 metres of electrical wire. And for every metre of wire there was a metre of red tape, since artificial reefs must now be created in strict accordance with the US government's National Artificial Reef Plan.

Even scrupulously planned wrecks can go very wrong. When the Spiegel Grove went down in 2002, the ship landed upside down with one corner of her stern on the bottom and part of her bow above the waterline, ready to serve as a can opener to unsuspecting vessels using the marine sanctuary. It took a massive effort to get her over on her side and fully underwater, and it wasn't until three years later that Hurricane Dennis finally gave her the intended upright – and harmless to traffic – profile.

The notorious Osborne Tire Reef project off the Florida coast was initially thought to be a good idea in the early 1970s, a win-win scheme that would liberate the nation's landfills of up to two million discarded tires to create a thriving marine habitat. But it turned out that vulcanized rubber is actually a poor base for coral growth, and the bundled tires, instead of helping to augment two adjacent natural reefs, ended up smothering and bashing into their fragile organisms. When the bundles broke apart, the tires washed up on beaches. The hopeful Osborne Tire Reef initiative has now given way to its expensive remedy, the Osborne Reef Waste Tire Removal Project.

31 The main purpose of the second paragraph is to
- **A** highlight the length of time required for an artificial reef to work.
- **B** outline the different stages through which an artificial reef develops.
- **C** emphasise the range of sea creatures that are attracted to artificial reefs.
- **D** explain the diverse factors that determine how successful an artificial reef is.

32 What point does the writer make about artificial reefs in the third paragraph?
- **A** They can stimulate economic growth in coastal areas.
- **B** Their impact is appreciated by scientists and fishermen alike.
- **C** Their primary function is to improve the marine environment.
- **D** They have helped the Gulf of Mexico recover from an oil disaster.

33 What does James Cowan suggest about artificial reefs?
- **A** Certain species of fish are driven away by them.
- **B** People excited by fishing from them may move on to natural reefs.
- **C** They should be established in parts of the ocean that are very deep.
- **D** Consideration should be given to the criteria used to assess their value.

34 Which aspect of artificial reefs does the writer seek to underline with the words 'for every metre of wire there was a metre of red tape'?
- **A** the various dangers they can pose
- **B** the regulations governing their creation
- **C** the costs incurred in putting them in place
- **D** the laws determining what they should look like

35 What point does the writer make about the Spiegel Grove?
- **A** Boats and ships have to carefully avoid the sunken ship.
- **B** Extreme weather conditions caused the ship to sink.
- **C** The ship is an unsuitable shape to serve as a reef.
- **D** The ship initially settled in an unhelpful position.

36 What does the writer say about the Osborne Tire Reef?
- **A** It would have worked better in a different location.
- **B** It has provided the inspiration for a similar scheme.
- **C** It was meant to benefit the environment in two ways.
- **D** It shows how little people cared about the ocean in the past.

PAPER 1	Reading and ▸	Part 1
	Use of English	Part 2
PAPER 2	Writing	Part 3
		Part 4
PAPER 3	Listening	Part 5
PAPER 4	Speaking	**Part 6**
		Part 7
		Part 8

You are going to read four comments in an online discussion about reality TV. For questions **37–40**, choose from the comments **A–D**. The comments may be chosen more than once.

Mark your answers **on the separate answer sheet**.

Reality TV

Reality TV programmes such as **Big Brother***,* **Survivor** *and* X Factor *have come to dominate the schedules of many television stations in the past decade. Four social commentators offer their thoughts on the phenomenon.*

A

The bottom line is that reality TV programmes attract audiences of all ages and types. Viewers want to be entertained, but, at the same time, are often happy to learn something – from a show set in a restaurant kitchen or a fitness camp, for example. Criticisms that particular combinations of people are selected and placed in unrealistic settings, and so reality TV is not real, miss the point. Audiences know that shows like *Big Brother* do not replicate real life, but they do offer us opportunities to observe how people like us, or not like us, interact and deal with challenges. In these unusual situations the participants' behaviour may at times be strange, ill-considered or even offensive, but society is imperfect and audiences know this. People generally watch reality TV shows in an analytical, critical spirit, making judgements about what they see rather than simply wanting to copy it.

B

There are many different types of reality TV programmes, of course. Lots of them focus obsessively on appearance, consumerism and celebrity status, and imply that anyone can become famous without working hard or displaying a particular talent. The concern is that impressionable viewers, taking what they see to be real life, may absorb the message uncritically, overlooking the fact that the narrative is invariably manipulated by clever programme makers. Other programmes, however, are more positive and even instructive. One show, *Jamie's Kitchen*, offered jobless youngsters the chance to train as chefs and lead a campaign to improve the quality of school meals. The programme was a valuable learning experience for audiences and participants, and even had an impact on government policy. More programmes like *Jamie's Kitchen* would be welcome. The fact is, however, that the quality as well as the sheer quantity of reality programmes shown on our television screens reflects market demand.

C

There seems to be a huge appetite for reality TV, and it is hard to argue with programme makers who claim they are just producing shows their audiences want. The unfortunate thing is that most reality TV is of very poor quality. Not only is it fundamentally dishonest in pretending to show 'reality', when in fact it is a strange mix of fiction and fact, distorted to suit the programme makers' requirements, but it so often relies on humiliation and conflict to create excitement, sending a message that crude, self-centred, empty-headed behaviour is the norm and that celebrity is a worthy aspiration. There are a few reality shows which purport to do good by showing us something we can learn from, some insight perhaps into human behaviour, but even in these cases a straightforward documentary format would be far more informative and trustworthy than these odd fabricated social experiments.

D

The most interesting thing about reality TV is that it is not what its label implies and perhaps what many believe it to be. Typically, a group of people are filmed in unusual situations over a period of time – not reality for most us. Occasionally, some 'reality shows' are supposed to reveal something new about people – how they interact, change or deal with a problem, for example – but such revelations invariably turn out to be utterly banal. What is sometimes forgotten is that reality TV is a cheap means to ensure there is always something on TV in this age of multiple channels and 24-hour programming. The fact that it fills the gaps does not mean that audiences want it, however. In fact, many reality shows have extremely low viewing figures, and some TV stations, like the Italian state broadcaster RAI, have decided to remove all reality shows from their schedules.

Which comment

shares B's opinion regarding the educational content of some reality TV?

37 ▢

has a different opinion from the others about the authenticity of reality TV?

38 ▢

expresses a different view from the others about the popularity of reality TV?

39 ▢

takes a similar view to C regarding the values represented in many reality TV shows?

40 ▢

PAPER 1	Reading and Use of English	▶	Part 1
			Part 2
PAPER 2	Writing		Part 3
			Part 4
PAPER 3	Listening		Part 5
PAPER 4	Speaking		Part 6
			Part 7
			Part 8

You are going to read a newspaper article about the history of art. Six paragraphs have been removed from the article. Choose from the paragraphs **A–G** the one which fits each gap (**41–46**). There is one extra paragraph which you do not need to use.

Mark your answers **on the separate answer sheet**.

Studying art history

In many countries, doing a degree in the history of art is considered something of a minority choice. While no one would deny that art is a fascinating subject with a longer and more diverse history than, say, literature, history of art tends to exist on the margins at most universities, the preserve of a few dedicated students.

41 [ ]

As Janice Burton, a former student at the Courtauld Institute, a specialist university in the UK that focuses entirely on the subject, explains: 'History of art is more than simply the study of creativity and aesthetics. It incorporates all aspects of history, as well as philosophy, anthropology, politics and religion. Art represents an insight into the spirit of a particular period, as well as supplying some of history's most fascinating protagonists.'

42 [ ]

So it's clearly a very interesting subject to study, covering a huge slice of the human experience, but what can you do with it? History of art lecturer Natalia Mellor believes her subject is crucial for the development of public culture. 'Our degree courses produce the museum directors of the future,' she says.

43 [ ]

Not everyone who attains a degree in history of art is forced into the art world, however. Jerome Hasler, for instance, now works for a crisis management consultancy. 'It's not a directly vocational position,' he admits, but history of art has still been very beneficial. 'It taught me to be creative, to research thoroughly and

to appreciate that many factors can contribute to a final product, things I use and value every day in my job.'

44 [ ]

There is a perception, perhaps, that history of art is an elitist subject. Professor Joanna Woodall, who teaches at the Courtauld, is at pains to disagree. 'People often think of art history as elitist, but it's a subject in which everyone has something to contribute. People notice different things and ask different questions,' she says. When considering applications from potential students wanting to take her courses, she is interested in people who clearly have a passion for art and art history, rather than those who have traditional qualifications.

45 [ ]

And what, in practical terms, does studying history of art entail? How is the programme organised, particularly for newcomers to the subject as an academic discipline? Rebecca Murphy, who graduated from the Courtauld last year, enjoyed every minute of it.

46 [ ]

'As you progress,' she says, 'you cover all the different aspects of theory, and every term you get to learn about a different period. In the first couple of years you get to build up this knowledge and then in the third you get the opportunity to tackle more specialist topics of your choice.' Like many of her peers, she is convinced it was worth it. 'The degree enabled me to acquire a lot of knowledge about important subjects, some good transferrable skills and a great bunch of friends too.'

A Burton concurs: 'Had I wanted to work in an auction house, curate or write for an art magazine, then I would have been very well placed, especially if I'd continued on with a master's degree, and there were some tempting options at the Courtauld, such as art restoration. But history of art led me into writing, specifically journalism, and achieving a good degree from a prestigious university did my job prospects no harm at all.'

B However absorbing or enriching history of art may be, this view of it as being accessible to and useful for only a small and probably privileged group of people can deter many with a genuine interest in it.

C Although it has a limited following, it is anything but insignificant in scope or academic rigour, however. It's about art, of course, but it's by no means confined to staring at paintings and stroking one's chin.

D 'If you've never formally studied the subject before, you start with a leveller course,' she says. This introduction provides an overall perspective on the degree. 'You then move on to a more in-depth look, and the chance to learn about things you're personally interested in.'

E In fact, anyone who wants to be seriously involved in museum and gallery curation needs to ensure they have a solid academic grounding in the subject. You don't get to run a major gallery without a deep knowledge of the art world as a whole – one you can't just get from avidly attending exhibitions.

F Another recent history of art graduate agrees: 'It gave me the opportunity to explore the stories within works of art, addressing social, political or personal reasons behind their particular appearance or fame.'

G 'We try to look for someone who shows a demonstrable interest in the subject – but that doesn't mean they have to know reams about art history. Those coming to history of art from other disciplines bring something different and enliven the discipline for everyone.'

You are going to read an article about people who work in museums. For questions **47–56**, choose from the people (**A–D**). The people may be chosen more than once.

Mark your answers **on the separate answer sheet**.

Which person

mentions the difficulty of keeping her professional knowledge up to date?	47
points out the advantage of specialising in a particular type of work?	48
is reluctant to take on a managerial role?	49
claims that people in her field are realistic about their career prospects?	50
mentions a misconception about the field she is in?	51
is grateful for the skills she acquired in a previous, different career?	52
points out that her responsibilities differ from those of other people in similar jobs?	53
emphasises the importance of talking to a wide range of people in her work?	54
regrets the range of duties she has to undertake?	55
regrets the lack of formal training available for her job?	56

Museum work

A

Melanie Kershaw works as a museum curator in Scotland. Her typical day might involve working on the museum's computer documentation system, packing up an exhibition of local artists, dealing with security issues or taking guided tours round the galleries. 'It'd be nice if I could focus on the natural history collection, where I have real expertise,' she says. 'But it's only a small museum so I get roped into all sorts of things. We do lots of work with local children and I give talks to geology societies in the area.' Melanie took her first degree in biology and then went into teaching. 'Dealing with school kids for a few years taught me how to communicate with groups, which serves me well here.' She left teaching after doing a part-time museum studies course and has been in her current post for four years now. She feels no real desire to climb the career ladder. 'What appeals to me is researching, documenting and displaying objects, not being in charge of other people, but I'll probably move to a bigger museum eventually.'

B

There's no traditional route into fundraising for museums and galleries, according to Angela Garcia, the head of development for a museum of culture in the north of Spain. 'You figure things out as you go along. It's not ideal, but that's how it is,' says Angela. 'Lots of my colleagues have come to it in an ad hoc way through an arts degree, some voluntary work, maybe some marketing and then into fundraising.' She manages a team of two development officers and an assistant, oversees a corporate patrons' scheme, administers a development trust and raises other sponsorship for exhibitions throughout the year. 'Networking is crucial,' she says. 'Not just with potential donors, but also with museum visitors, the press and colleagues from my museum and other institutions – it's good to keep up with what's happening elsewhere.' She says the work is challenging with only average financial rewards, but it's far from dull. 'For some people, the idea of museum work still conjures up images of geeks in dusty archives detached from the real world,' she says. 'If they only knew!'

C

As registrar for a regional museum service, Laura Johansson is responsible for all information relating to the objects kept in eight public museums. 'It could be information about what the object is and where it's come from, or it could be movement records.' says Laura. 'I'm involved with things such as documentation procedures and collections management policies. And unlike some registrars, I'm in charge of the information management system.' With advances in digital technology, it is a fast-moving field. 'That makes it exciting,' she says. 'But I don't really have the time or resources to stay abreast of all the developments in the way I should.' Like many people working in museums and galleries, Laura's career path has not been wholly predictable. After graduating in history, she managed a clothes store for five years, before realising she wanted something different. She completed a diploma in heritage studies and then documented items in a toy museum for three years. That led to her current post.

D

Yasmin Kumar is a sculpture conservator. 'You've got to know what an object's made from, how long it's been in its environment, the aesthetics of it, and be able to work on it,' she explains. She started by volunteering in museums to get practical experience, but she also has a degree in fine art and an MA in historic artefacts conservation. She is now one of four permanent staff who restore objects and get them ready for display and for going out on loan. 'It's quite narrow,' she says. 'And it can be hard to switch to anything else – we're all aware of that. On the other hand, there aren't many people with our expertise, so we're in demand. I'm often away for several days at a time, travelling with objects or going to work on artefacts in other countries.' Yasmin feels fulfilled, despite the uninspiring pay scales. 'I'd like the chance to earn more, of course,' she says. 'But, like everyone who works in this sector, I know it's not going to happen.'

You **must** answer this question. Write your answer in **220–260** words in an appropriate style on the separate answer sheet.

---

1 You attended a philosophy seminar in which the tutor suggested that all exams in schools and colleges be abolished. You have made the notes below.

> **Abolish exams**
>
> - Students are denied the enriching experience of learning because they are under too much pressure to pass the exam.
> - Exams are not very effective because they test memory rather than intelligence.
> - It's not a fair process; exam stress affects some students more than others. Not everyone performs well in exams.

> **Other students in the seminar expressed their opinions:**
>
> "But working towards the final exam often gives us the motivation we need in order to study."
>
> "Exam-based assessment is a good way of figuring out whether a student has really understood what they have been taught."
>
> "Taking exams at school and university is actually a good life skill because it trains us to plan, prepare and deliver."

Write an essay for your tutor discussing **two** of the points from your notes. You should **explain whether you think abolishing exams is a good idea** and **provide reasons** to support your opinions.

You may, if you wish, make use of the opinions expressed in the lecture, but you should use your own words as far as possible.

Write an answer to **one** of the questions **2–4** in this part. Write your answer in **220–260** words in an appropriate style on the separate answer sheet. Put the question number in the box at the top of the page.

2   You see this advertisement in a local newspaper.

> Here at Blackshaw Books we have a vacancy for a part-time sales assistant. If you love books and would like to join our small team, please send a letter of application to the manager, Eileen James. The ideal candidate will be organised, reliable and available to work flexible hours.

Write your **letter**.

3   You see this notice inside the main door of the apartment complex where you live.

> The Management Committee's plan to build a bicycle shed at the back of the property has met with some resistance. Some residents feel it would be better to create a patio area with picnic benches, while others have requested a small playground for their children. You are invited to send the Management Committee a proposal outlining which of these you would like to see, and explaining why. You may also propose a new idea of your own.

Write your **proposal**.

4   You read this advertisement in a technology magazine.

> What mobile phone do you use? With so many models on the market, we are compiling a spreadsheet of mobiles for consumer comparison. We want to publish reviews that highlight the best and worst features and benefits of each phone. Send in a review describing your mobile and explaining why you would recommend it, or not.

Write your **review**.

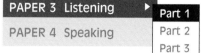
PAPER 1 Reading and
          Use of English

PAPER 2 Writing

PAPER 3 Listening ▸ **Part 1**
                           Part 2
                           Part 3
                           Part 4

PAPER 4 Speaking

🎧 **Track 17**

You will hear three different extracts. For questions **1–6**, choose the answer (**A**, **B** or **C**) which fits best according to what you hear. There are two questions for each extract.

Extract One

You hear two friends discussing plans for another friend's birthday.

1 Why does the woman not agree with any of the man's ideas?
   A They would be too difficult to organise.
   B They would cost too much money.
   C They wouldn't be appropriate for Ken.

2 The joke between the man and woman at the end was because their friend, Ken, doesn't
   A like birthday cake.
   B want any fuss.
   C get embarrassed.

Extract Two

You hear two college friends discussing their classmate, Phil.

3 The man thinks their classmate, Phil, is
   A strange.
   B self-important.
   C unhappy.

4 Why does the woman defend Phil's behaviour?
   A She's known him a long time; he's a close friend.
   B She knows about some problems he's been having.
   C She thinks he could be having some personal difficulty.

Extract Three

You hear a man telling his friend about some good news regarding his job.

5 What made the man so happy?
   A He secured a large order.
   B He got a salary increase.
   C He got a bonus.

6 Does he believe he'll get a promotion?
   A No, it's not company policy.
   B He thinks it's possible.
   C He's already been promoted.

Track 18

You will hear a young woman called Louise sharing her views with a group of schoolchildren about the impact of the internet on the music industry. For questions **7–14**, complete the sentences with a short word or phrase.

THE INTERNET AND THE MUSIC INDUSTRY

The speaker feels that her friend's view that the music industry has been destroyed by the internet is a (**7**) ....

Louise acknowledges how stopping people from copying CDs to their computers (**8**) .... at the time.

She points out that (**9**) .... became a significant issue once people started using MP3 players.

The consequences, if caught, usually involved (**10**) ....

Louise likes being able to buy (**11**) .... rather than entire albums.

The way music is distributed now (**12**) .... the role of the big executives.

Louise is encouraged to see that the music industry is still (**13**) ....

She likes the fact that musicians can (**14**) .... their work and reach new fans.

Track 19

You will hear a radio programme, *Wednesday Weekly*, in which blogging is the topic of discussion. For questions **15–20**, choose the answer (**A**, **B**, **C** or **D**) which fits best according to what you hear.

15 What type of programme is *Wednesday Weekly*?
   A a news show
   B a game show
   C a chat show
   D a tech show

16 Do the guests, Sophie and Joe, agree with Ann's general definition of blogging?
   A They think she's completely wrong.
   B They think she's more or less right.
   C They think she's completely right.
   D They think she only knows a little.

17 What does Joe refer to as the *blogosphere*?
   A the world of blogs
   B the first bloggers
   C personal bloggers
   D random blogs

18 What point is Sophie enthusiastic about?
   A that good blogging is now getting recognition
   B that the quality of bloggers' writing has improved
   C that everyone can now publish their own blog
   D that she has won several awards for her blog

19 According to Joe, who is getting an income from blogging?
   A all, or most, bloggers
   B some guest speakers
   C sellers of e-books
   D only the best bloggers

20 What does new research indicate about live-blogging?
   A that all news stories are now being live-blogged
   B that people prefer live blogs to traditional articles
   C that live-blogging is replacing sports reporting
   D that bloggers have now become more dynamic

Track 20

You will hear five short extracts in which people talk about giving money to charity.

While you listen you must complete both tasks.

TASK ONE

For questions **21–25**, choose from the list (**A–H**) what kind of charity, if any, each speaker supports.

A an animal shelter		
B human rights	Speaker 1	21
C doesn't donate at all	Speaker 2	22
D homeless people	Speaker 3	23
E a local charity	Speaker 4	24
F overseas aid	Speaker 5	25
G medical research		
H the environment		

TASK TWO

For questions **26–30**, choose from the list (**A–H**) what each speaker says about the reason for their choice.

A sees it as the government's role		
B improves others' job prospects	Speaker 1	26
C also had a learning disability	Speaker 2	27
D because of widespread corruption	Speaker 3	28
E considers it a responsibility	Speaker 4	29
F because of a family member	Speaker 5	30
G has plenty of money to spare		
H feels a personal duty to help		

Part 1 (2 minutes)

The examiner will ask you a few questions about yourself and about a general topic. For example, the examiner may ask you:

• **Where are you from?**
• **What do you like and dislike about your hometown?**
• **Who do you admire, living or dead, more than anyone else? Why?**

Part 2 (4 minutes)

You will each be asked to talk on your own for about a minute. You will each be given three different pictures to talk about. After your partner has finished speaking, you will be asked a brief question connected with your partner's photographs.

> **People and their pets** (compare, contrast and speculate)

Turn to pictures 1–3 on page **181**, which show people with different pets.

(*Candidate A*), it's your turn first. Here are your pictures. They show **three different people with their pets.**

I'd like you to compare **two** of the pictures and say **what kind of personality each of the people probably has and how you imagine their pet affects their life**.

(*Candidate B*), **which of these pets would you be most likely to have? Why?**

> **Extreme sports** (compare, contrast and speculate)

Turn to pictures 1–3 on page **182**, which show people doing extreme sports.

Now, (*Candidate B*), here are your pictures. They show **people doing various extreme sports.**

I'd like you to compare **two** of the pictures and say **why you think people do extreme sports and what kind of person might choose to do sports like these**.

(*Candidate A*), **is the risk associated with these sports worth it? Why (not)?**

Part 3 (4 minutes)

Look at page **183**, which shows some advantages and disadvantages of renting or buying a home.

> **Renting versus buying** (discuss, evaluate and negotiate)

Here are some advantages and disadvantages to renting a home and buying a home and a question for you to discuss.

First you have some time to look at the task.

(*Pause 15 seconds*)

Now talk to each other about **whether you think it's better to rent or to buy.**

Now you have a minute to decide **on the biggest disadvantage to renting and to owning a property.**

Part 4 (5 minutes)

The examiner will encourage you to develop the topic of your discussion in Part 3 by asking questions such as:

• Do you believe that life is less complicated for people who rent their home? How?

• Some people say that buying a home is more of a burden than an investment? Do you agree?

• Do you think there is too much pressure on people to buy property nowadays?

For questions **1–8**, read the text below and decide which answer (**A**, **B**, **C** or **D**) best fits each gap. There is an example at the beginning (**0**).

Mark your answers **on the separate answer sheet**.

Example:

| **0** | **A** result | **B** impact | **C** difference | **D** consequence |

| 0 | A | **B** | C | D |

The importance of a name

Have you ever thought about the (**0**) .... your name has on the way others perceive you? A recent study by Dr Simon Laham from the University of Melbourne and Dr Adam Alter from New York University Stern Business School reveals that people with 'easy-to-pronounce' names tend to be (**1**) .... more positively than those with 'difficult-to-pronounce' names. The researchers found that people with more easily pronounceable names were more likely to be (**2**) .... upon favourably for political office, and that lawyers with easier sounding names made their way up the career (**3**) .... faster. Surnames from a wide range of nationalities were used in the study, and researchers stressed that preferences were not (**4**) .... due to the length of a name or how unusual it was, but rather how easy it was to say.

Dr Laham believes the research highlights the kind of (**5**) .... that our everyday thinking is (**6**) .... to. The wider (**7**) .... is that our decisions are often shaped by preferences that are both trivial and subtle. An appreciation of this may lead to more impartial, fairer thinking and (**8**) .... of other people.

1	**A** evaluated	**B** reckoned	**C** figured	**D** determined
2	**A** put	**B** looked	**C** called	**D** come
3	**A** order	**B** stairs	**C** scale	**D** ladder
4	**A** barely	**B** hardly	**C** plainly	**D** merely
5	**A** angles	**B** biases	**C** weights	**D** turns
6	**A** subject	**B** obliged	**C** conditioned	**D** obedient
7	**A** connotation	**B** association	**C** implication	**D** manifestation
8	**A** attention	**B** regard	**C** treatment	**D** notice

For questions **9–16**, read the text below and think of the word which best fits each gap. Use only one word in each gap. There is an example at the beginning (**0**).

Write your answers **IN CAPITAL LETTERS on the separate answer sheet**.

Example: | 0 | N O T | | | | | | | | | | | | | | | | | | | |

A bird that can dance in time to music

It is (**0**) …….. often that a video posted online of a funny pet sparks a scientific breakthrough. Yet that is (**9**) …….. happened when scientist Aniruddh Patel saw a clip of a cockatoo called Snowball moving his body in time to a pop song. Scientists used to believe that no species (**10**) …….. from human beings could dance in time to music. Our closest cousins, chimpanzees, can't and (**11**) …….. can cats or dogs, in (**12**) …….. of the fact that they have lived alongside us for millennia.

Dr Patel contacted Snowball's owner and carried out various experiments with the bird, all of (**13**) …….. supported the notion that the cockatoo could genuinely follow different rhythms. Further studies have found that other species of songbird can do the same. (**14**) …….. to Dr Patel, something these birds and humans have in common, but most species don't, is that our brains are wired to hear and reproduce complex sounds. Dance, it is thought, emerged (**15**) …….. a by-product of our ability to imitate sound, and (**16**) …….. vocal imitation we wouldn't be able to keep a beat.

PAPER 1   Reading and
           Use of English

PAPER 2   Writing

PAPER 3   Listening

PAPER 4   Speaking

Part 1
Part 2
Part 3
Part 4
Part 5
Part 6
Part 7
Part 8

For questions **17–24**, read the text below. Use the word given in capitals at the end of some of the lines to form a word that fits in the gap **in the same line**. There is an example at the beginning (**0**).

Write your answers **IN CAPITAL LETTERS on the separate answer sheet.**

Example: | 0 | W | O | R | L | D | W | I | D | E | | | | | | | | |

Manchester – city of many languages

The city of Manchester in the north of England is famous

(**0**) .... for its industries, its rock bands and its football teams.   **WORLD**

But now Manchester has another claim to fame as one of the

world's most (**17**) .... varied cities. Researchers from the   **LINGUIST**

University of Manchester have discovered that at least 153

different languages are spoken among the city's half a million

(**18**) .... The researchers say that Manchester's language   **INHABIT**

(**19**) .... is greater than that of many countries.   **DIVERSE**

The city has been home to many ethnic (**20**) .... for a long time,   **MINOR**

but there has been a (**21**) .... change in the make-up of the   **NOTICE**

population in the last two decades, and with continuing

(**22**) .... into the city from various parts of the world and the   **IMMIGRATE**

arrival of many (**23**) .... students to study at Manchester's   **SEA**

colleges and universities, the number of languages is likely to

increase.

Currently, two-thirds of the city's schoolchildren are bilingual,

a very significant figure, and an indication that Manchester will

continue to be (**24**) .... by its great mix of languages and   **RICH**

cultures.

PAPER 1	Reading and Use of English	▸	Part 1
			Part 2
PAPER 2	Writing		Part 3
			Part 4
PAPER 3	Listening		Part 5
			Part 6
PAPER 4	Speaking		Part 7
			Part 8

For questions **25–30**, complete the second sentence so that it has a similar meaning to the first sentence, using the word given. **Do not change the word given.** You must use between **three** and **six** words, including the word given. Here is an example (**0**).

Example:

0   Chloe would only eat a pizza if she could have a mushroom topping.

ON

Chloe .... a mushroom topping when she had a pizza.

The gap can be filled with the words 'insisted on having', so you write:

Example: | **0** | INSISTED ON HAVING

Write **only** the missing words **IN CAPITAL LETTERS on the separate answer sheet.**

---

25   Enrico doesn't cook for himself in the evenings because he's too lazy.

BOTHERED

Enrico .... for himself in the evenings.

26   When questioned by journalists, the company director said he had never had any involvement in discussions about a merger with another organisation.

BEING

When questioned by journalists, the company director .... discussions about a merger with another organisation.

27   Why ever did it never occur to me to ask my grandmother if she knew when the picture had been taken?

EARTH

Why .... of asking my grandmother if she knew when the picture had been taken?

28   I'm sure that facing such an experienced opponent as Maria Suarez wasn't easy, but Ellie played very well.

COME

It can't .... against such an experienced opponent as Maria Suarez, but Ellie played very well.

29   'Please do whatever you can to persuade your colleagues to bring the date of the meeting forward,' Selina said to David.

UTMOST

Selina urged .... persuade his colleagues to bring the date of the meeting forward.

30   The new square has made the town centre nicer, but public transport could still be improved a lot.

ROOM

The new square has made the town centre nicer, but there's still plenty .... as public transport is concerned.

PAPER 1	Reading and ▶	Part 1
	Use of English	Part 2
PAPER 2	Writing	Part 3
		Part 4
PAPER 3	Listening	**Part 5**
PAPER 4	Speaking	Part 6
		Part 7
		Part 8

You are going to read a magazine article in which a psychologist describes a course he went on to learn how to be a comedian. For questions **31–36**, choose the answer (**A, B, C** or **D**) which you think fits best according to the text.

Mark your answers **on the separate answer sheet**.

Comedy and psychology

As an academic psychologist, Jamie Peters has investigated and written about humour. With the aim of exploring comedy from the perspective of a comedian, he attended a comedy course, as he describes here.

Earlier this year I did a part-time comedy course. The 18-strong class included people from many different walks of life and was taught by Ryan, a professional stand-up comedian. Of all of the participants, I think I'd probably gigged the most. For the last three years, I've performed a mind-reading show at an arts festival. It wasn't originally meant to be a comedy show – I thought I would cut a commanding, mysterious figure onstage, but on my debut, the audience laughed at my first joke, then continued to laugh throughout all the routines that were meant to be serious. Thankfully, they weren't laughing at me. Well, sometimes they were, but mostly they were with me. So it was the audience who told me I'm funny, but I haven't always understood why, or how to craft and control the comic moments. So, I joined the course to learn. And although, as a psychologist, I've published articles and books about humour, there was hardly a single joke in any of them, so I still felt like a beginner.

'Turn off your internal editor that makes you say the right thing. Find your inner idiot. Remember how to be a child,' explained Ryan. 'Don't try to be clever. Don't try too hard to be funny ... and knowing all about the theory of humour is unlikely to help you much. Just muck around. That's what people want to see on stage.' So we did. Ryan would help us loosen up by saying things like: 'Wander around talking to others in the room, but make sure that you're the lowest status person here.' Not to be outdone, I found myself conversing with others whilst lying prostrate on the floor.

I'd say that understanding the psychology of humour has actually helped a little. It was only last year that I stumbled across the book *Inside Jokes: Using Humor to Reverse-Engineer the Mind*, by Hurley, Dennett and Adams. As I read the introduction, I couldn't have grinned much wider if I'd put a coat hanger in my mouth. Past efforts to explain humour had never really cut it for me. For example, those theorists who simply thought that humour was a way of expressing anger, or of social control, or of proving intellect, or of attracting others seemed to have only explained some, incomplete, aspects of motivation, not the mechanics of humour. Here, finally was what felt like a true, unifying theory.

The crux of their thesis is that any self-directed intelligent system will need to correct its own bugs. Think of it in terms of the human mind running software to understand the world around it. As it makes sense of things, there's a risk that the occasional error will be made (a bug), which will have to be debugged before long. Now if this was tedious or onerous, we'd be less inclined to do it. However, evolution has conspired to make the process fun.

In more concrete terms, here's a joke cited in the book: Two fish are in a tank. One says to the other, 'Do you know how to drive this thing?' It works on the principle that we have started to imagine one thing – that the tank is the typical container people keep fish in – and, just in time, the punch-line tells us that our first assumption was wrong – it's the military vehicle. For correctly figuring out the contradiction (or bug), we are rewarded with a pleasurable feeling. The joke is an efficient way of stimulating this natural reaction, and comics have become experts in tickling this mental funny-bone in order to make us laugh.

So, was Ryan right when he said that knowing the theory of humour wouldn't help us that much as a stand up? I think he was. So much of what made our group laugh over our eight weeks of life-affirming mucking around would be very hard to script. During one exercise, four of us were told to perform an improvised opera. Whilst Susan and Caroline sang earnestly on either side of the stage, I spontaneously brought Henry to the floor, where we wrestled each other like out-of-control teenagers. The rest of the group, sitting in the audience, were in uncontrollable fits of laughter. As this moment was lost to the ether, and as a performer, I couldn't be an observer, I'll never appreciate just why it seemed so funny. But the point is, I would never have written this into a script. It was a joyous, found moment.

31 What does the writer say about himself in the first paragraph?
- **A** He was worried about how other people on the comedy course would find him.
- **B** He wanted to see how theories he had about comedy worked in practice.
- **C** He's had some unpleasant experiences when performing comedy.
- **D** He discovered by chance that he had some aptitude for comedy.

32 In one part of the course, the writer lay 'prostrate on the floor' because he wanted to
- **A** do what others in the group were doing.
- **B** show defiance of his tutor's instructions.
- **C** try to behave in a more playful manner.
- **D** make himself feel more comfortable.

33 The writer says 'I couldn't have grinned much wider if I'd put a coat hanger in my mouth' when reading the introduction to the book in order to
- **A** show his pleasure at discovering how it confirmed his own views.
- **B** underline his appreciation of the ideas expressed in it.
- **C** illustrate his sense of confusion at its contents.
- **D** emphasise how humorous he found it.

34 What does the word 'process' in line 26 refer to?
- **A** understanding the world
- **B** dealing with bugs
- **C** running software
- **D** making errors

35 What is the main purpose of the fifth paragraph?
- **A** to show why some people are funnier than others
- **B** to give an example of humour present in the book
- **C** to elaborate further on a theory about humour
- **D** to explain the point of a particular joke

36 What view does the writer put forward in the final paragraph?
- **A** What people find funny is often unpredictable.
- **B** Visual humour is what appeals to people most.
- **C** Theories explaining humour tend to be mistaken.
- **D** Observing comedy is a good way of learning comic skills.

PAPER 1	Reading and ►	Part 1
	Use of English	Part 2
PAPER 2	Writing	Part 3
		Part 4
PAPER 3	Listening	Part 5
PAPER 4	Speaking	**Part 6**
		Part 7
		Part 8

You are going to read four contributions to a debate about proposals to reintroduce wolves into Scotland. For questions **37–40**, choose from the contributions **A–D**. The contributions may be chosen more than once.

Mark your answers **on the separate answer sheet**.

Reintroducing wolves into Scotland

Wolves were last seen in the wild in Scotland in the seventeenth century but in recent times there have been proposals to reintroduce the animal to more remote highland areas of the country. Four scientists give their views on the idea.

A

The idea of reintroducing wolves into Scotland three centuries after they were eradicated has a romantic appeal, and if, as wolf reintroduction schemes in parts of the USA like Montana suggest would happen, they reduced red deer numbers and consequently stimulated greater biodiversity, this would be very positive. This potential ecological benefit is undeniable but comparisons with the USA are deceptive. Scotland is a small country and keeping wolves away from its many livestock farms would be difficult. Scotland also has limited economic resources, and the funds required to introduce and manage packs of wolves would be far better spent on maintaining and enhancing native species already present in the country. The few opinion polls that have been carried out on the subject reveal that most Scottish people, while attracted by the idea of wolves in their limited remaining wilderness areas, question the sense in pursuing the idea in the foreseeable future.

B

Scientists largely agree about reintroducing wolves into wilderness areas: by preying on deer and other vegetation-destroying animals, wolves help create conditions for various tree and plant species to prosper, which then attracts a greater variety of wildlife. All this happens at little expense. Even the cost of monitoring the wolves and compensating farmers for any livestock killed can be offset by growth in revenue from tourism as visitors are attracted by the opportunity to observe wolves in their wild habitat. The fact is, however, that Scotland is not ready for wolves. It is a relatively small country with many sheep farmers horrified by the idea that their flocks could be vulnerable to wolf attacks. The Scottish countryside is also heavily used by recreational walkers, climbers and fishing enthusiasts, most of whom would surely feel uncomfortable at the thought of carrying out their hobbies in the company of wolves.

C

Scotland is currently home to large numbers of red deer which over-graze and prevent native trees and other plants from growing. Each year, many deer have to be culled, but wolves, if re-introduced, would keep the deer population down naturally, leading to reforestation and greater biodiversity. We know this because of wolf reintroduction programmes in the USA. Comparative studies suggest that similar schemes would be eminently feasible in parts of Scotland. Monitoring wolf packs to ensure they were not a threat to farms and the general public would, of course, require funding, but there would almost certainly be a rise in tourism in areas with wolves, which would probably mean a net economic gain. Realistically, we will not see wolves reintroduced into Scotland any time soon, largely because of opposition from the powerful Scottish farming lobby, but surveys indicate a majority of Scottish citizens would actually be in favour.

D

The impression is sometimes given that wolves are a natural feature of the Scottish landscape and if reintroduced would restore the environment to some original, ideal condition. The fact is, however, that there have been no wolves in Scotland for 300 years and in that time, the country's ecosystem has been transformed. To introduce wolves would effectively mean bringing in an alien species. It is always difficult to know precisely what impact non-native species will have on a particular ecosystem, but in many instances – rats are a classic example in many parts of the world – huge damage has been caused, with considerable economic consequences. Why take a risk in Scotland where the farming sector is going through hard times as it is? It would be far more sensible to focus on looking after species we already have than to get involved in an over-ambitious project involving a potentially dangerous, though glamorous, animal.

Which writer

has a different opinion from the others about the
environmental impact of reintroducing wolves?

37 [ ]

takes a similar view to A regarding public attitudes
to the idea of reintroducing wolves?

38 [ ]

shares D's opinion about the economic implications
of reintroducing wolves?

39 [ ]

takes a different view from the others regarding
Scotland's suitability as a place for reintroducing wolves?

40 [ ]

PAPER 1	Reading and Use of English	▶	Part 1
			Part 2
			Part 3
PAPER 2	Writing		Part 4
			Part 5
PAPER 3	Listening		Part 6
			Part 7
PAPER 4	Speaking		Part 8

You are going to read a magazine article about one of the largest trees in the world. Six paragraphs have been removed from the article. Choose from the paragraphs **A–G** the one which fits each gap (**41–46**). There is one extra paragraph which you do not need to use.

Mark your answers **on the separate answer sheet**.

A giant tree

Sequoia National Park in southern California in the USA is the home of some of the largest trees in the world.

On a gentle slope in Sequoia National Park, over 2,000 metres above sea level, looms a very big tree. Its trunk is rusty red, thickened with deep layers of bark, and 8.25 metres in diameter at the base. It has a name, The President, bestowed about 90 years ago by admirers. This giant sequoia is one of several surviving species of redwoods. Recent research by scientist Steve Sillett of Humboldt State University and his colleagues has confirmed that The President ranks as the second largest among all big trees that have ever been measured.

41

Trees grow tall and wide-topped as a means of competing with other trees, racing upward, reaching outward for sunlight and water. And a tree doesn't stop getting larger – as a land mammal does, or a bird, their size constrained by gravity – once it's mature. A tree too is constrained by gravity, but not in the same way as a giraffe or a condor.

42

They achieve this longevity because they have survived all the threats that could have killed them. They're too strong to be knocked over by wind. Their heartwood and bark are infused with acids and other chemicals that protect against fungal rot. Wood-boring insects hardly bother them. Their thick bark is flame resistant.

43

Another factor that can end the lives of big trees, of course, is logging. Many giant sequoias fell to the axe during the late nineteenth and early twentieth

centuries. But the wood of the old giants was so brittle that trunks often shattered when they hit the ground, and what remained had little value as timber for construction work. It went into fence posts, stakes to support plants, and other scrappy products.

44

Among the striking discoveries made by Sillett's team is that even the rate of growth of a big tree, not just its height or total volume, can increase during old age. An elderly monster like The President actually lays down more new wood per year than a robust young tree. It puts that wood around the trunk, which grows wider, and into the limbs and the branches, which grow thicker.

45

They were given National Park Service permission to do this as part of a larger, long-term monitoring project on giant sequoias and coast redwoods called the Redwoods and Climate Change Initiative. Sillett's group put a line over The President's crown, rigged climbing ropes into position, donned harnesses and helmets, and started to climb.

46

That's how they came to know that The President contains at least 124,000 cubic metres of wood and bark. And that's how they detected that the old beast, at about the age of 3,200, is still growing quickly. It's still inhaling great breaths of carbon dioxide and converting the carbon in a growing season interrupted by six months of cold and snow. Not bad for an oldster.

A As they did so, they measured the trunk at different heights, limbs and branches; they counted cones; they took core samples. Then they fed the numbers through mathematical models informed by additional data from other giant sequoias.

B Ground fires, in fact, are good for sequoia populations, burning away competitors, opening sequoia cones and allowing seedlings to get started. Lightning hurts the big adults but usually doesn't kill them. So they grow older and bigger across the millennia.

C That's the remarkable thing, Sillett told me. 'Half the year, they're not growing. They're in the snow.' They grow bigger than their biggest cousins, the coast redwoods, even with a shorter growing season.

D It doesn't need to move around, unlike them, and fortifies itself by continually adding more wood. Given the constant imperative of seeking resources from the sky and the soil, and with sufficient time, a tree can become huge and keep growing. Giant sequoias are gigantic because they are extremely old.

E This finding contradicts a long-held premise in forest ecology – that wood production declines in the latter years of a tree's life. That premise may hold true for some trees, but not for sequoias. Sillett and his team have disproved it by doing something earlier forest ecologists didn't: climbing all over the trees and measuring every centimetre of them.

F Given the difficulties of dealing with six-metre-thick logs, broken or unbroken, the trees were hardly worth cutting. Sequoia National Park was established in 1890, and automobile tourism soon showed that giant sequoias were worth more alive.

G Sillett's team has surveyed quite a few. It isn't as tall as the tallest of coast redwoods or certain species of eucalyptus in Australia, but height isn't everything; it has greater mass than any coast redwood or eucalyptus. Its dead spire, blasted by lightning, rises to 75 metres. Its four great limbs, each as big as a sizeable tree, elbow outward from the trunk around halfway up, billowing into a thick crown. The President holds nearly two billion leaves.

You are going to read an article in which scientists talk about being inspired to take up science. For questions **47–56**, choose from the scientists (**A–D**). The scientists may be chosen more than once.

Mark your answers **on the separate answer sheet**.

Which scientist

appreciates the respect shown them by teachers?	**47**
claims to have studied science for the wrong reasons?	**48**
took a long time to understand an important aspect of their subject?	**49**
takes inspiration from the history of science?	**50**
regrets not having had a good science teacher as a young person?	**51**
was attracted by the idea that science can be used to do good?	**52**
suggests that learning science can require a lot of imagination?	**53**
sees the need to give students something missing in their own early education?	**54**
gave up a good job for the sake of scientific interests?	**55**
had to overcome disapproval to build a career in science?	**56**

Being inspired to take up science

A Dominique Laver

As a child, what most appealed to me was finding things out for myself through experimentation and observation. One of the most striking things about science at school, however, was having to suspend my disbelief; science lessons transported me and my friends from the everyday world to that of atoms, molecules, proteins and cells – a world in many ways more fantastical than works of fiction, yet one that could help explain why things are as they are. There's a mental leap to make there, and one I hope schools still inspire pupils to attempt. I qualified and worked as a vet, but, after a few years, I felt compelled to investigate the differences between animal brains and behaviour and those of humans. So, not without certain reservations, I left a thriving practice to pursue these questions. Part of the appeal of what I currently do is the ready access to scientific libraries. The idea that the books surrounding me contain the work of generations of scientists, collectively labouring to produce an ever better understanding of how the world works, fills me with awe and optimism.

B Graham Sterne

At primary school, one teacher mentioned the word *science* occasionally, but then at secondary school I studied the standard physics, chemistry and biology and immediately found them fascinating. I was particularly filled with amazement at the incredible complexity of biological systems. Where I came from, you left school at the first opportunity to earn a living, and when it became clear that, encouraged by a teacher who saw something in me, I was set on going to university and wouldn't be contributing to the family budget anytime soon, I faced considerable suspicion and resentment. In those days, science was largely taught as facts, and although I forged a successful career working in the pharmaceutical industry, it was years before something fundamental really sank in – that science is about a method as much as facts. This realisation came to me after an intensive period reading books by such contemporary scientific thinkers as Carl Sagan, Richard Feynman and Charles Medawar.

C Omar Said

I grew up in a time when the promise of science and technology was difficult to avoid. It offered a sense of certainty that the world can not only be understood, but also enhanced. Unfortunately, this general sense of optimism seems to have dissipated somewhat. At school, and then at university, I had tutors who treated me as though I could make sense of everything they knew about science – its past, present and future. There was never any sense of being talked down to, for which I am very grateful. The one thing I regret was that practical experimentation seldom featured, certainly at school. It may have been a simple question of resources, but, in my own work in physics, I have always tried to explain things from first principles, in the belief that I am giving people a chance to work physics out for themselves, and the one lesson I really try to get across is that scientific theory is nothing unless backed up by experimental evidence.

D Stefan Helder

I took sciences at school, not because I excelled at them, but because I was hopeless at the arts and humanities. Yet despite this rather dim view of my early years and the trigger for what I have ended up doing, I can now see that I was always a systemiser. I loved stripping down my motorbike to see how it worked and I also loved making things. But I did badly at school, – to the disappointment of my parents – didn't go to university and never really thought about science for years. Yet I always felt I could do more with my life than the unconventional series of jobs I found myself doing. Then, via a series of fortuitous events, I landed a research job at a hospital. From there, I eventually fought my way onto a PhD in radiology, and this was when I really began to grasp what science could be. Looking back, I feel that the spur for me going into science, rather than some inspirational educator – if only it had been, my route would have been less circuitous – or TV role model, was probably my own innate traits.

You **must** answer this question. Write your answer in **220–260** words in an appropriate style on the separate answer sheet.

---

1 During a recent class discussion about the world's worst inventions, the lecturer shared her own opinion with the class. She said that the mobile phone was the worst invention and she provided several reasons for this view. You have made the notes below.

The mobile phone: the world's worst invention

- A sense of courtesy has been lost as people continually conduct loud conversations in public places.

- People have forgotten how to experience the world and observe what's going on around them as they are constantly staring at their mobile phones.

- Some studies show that excessive use of mobile phones can be a hazard to our health.

Other students expressed these opinions:

"Mobile phones come in very handy when you're meeting people and need to let them know you'll be late."

"The GPS function on mobiles makes it easy to find your way around new towns and cities."

"The built-in camera allows us to take photos of interesting or important images everywhere we go."

Write an essay for your tutor discussing **two** of the points from your notes. You should **explain whether you think the mobile phone is a good or bad invention** and **provide reasons** to support your opinions.

You may, if you wish, make use of the opinions expressed in the lecture, but you should use your own words as far as possible.

Write an answer to **one** of the questions **2–4** in this part. Write your answer in **220–260** words in an appropriate style on the separate answer sheet. Put the question number in the box at the top of the page.

2   The vice president of a local IT firm agreed to show you around the company office. She introduced you to three of the managers, who each explained to you what their department does. The following day you decide to write a letter to the vice president to thank her.

Write your **letter**.

3   You see this pop-up ad on your local tourist information office website.

> Here at Happy Trails we are working on a new travel guide for visitors to your area. We need the latest information on all forms of entertainment currently on offer in your town. If you would like to contribute to this chapter, please send a report describing the options available.

Write your **report**.

4   You went to a new recently-opened restaurant with your family to celebrate your father's 50th birthday. Based on this visit, write a review of the restaurant

Write your **review**.

Track 21

You will hear three different extracts. For questions **1–6**, choose the answer (**A**, **B** or **C**) which fits best according to what you hear. There are two questions for each extract.

Extract One

You hear two friends discussing reality TV.

1 Why is the woman surprised that the man is watching reality TV?
    A She feels he should be studying for his psychology exams.
    B She thinks he's too intelligent to bother with reality TV.
    C She knows this reality TV programme gets on his nerves.

2 The man thinks that reality TV is
    A ridiculous.
    B irritating.
    C very funny.

Extract Two

You hear a conversation between two people who meet at a teachers' conference.

3 How long has the woman been a teacher?
    A less than a year
    B a few years
    C one full year

4 What difficulty is the woman having?
    A She thinks she may have picked the wrong career.
    B She finds the amount of preparation challenging.
    C She feels there are too many students in her classes.

Extract Three

You hear two college students discussing where they prefer to study.

5 The man is on his way to
    A the library.
    B meet his flatmates.
    C study at home.

6 Why doesn't the woman study at home?
    A She finds it too noisy there.
    B She'd find other things to do.
    C She doesn't trust her flatmates.

| Part 1 |
| Part 2 |
| Part 3 |
| Part 4 |

 Track 22

You will hear a speaker called Terry Carville informing a group of students about the *fair trade* movement. For questions **7–14**, complete the sentences with a word or short phrase.

THE FAIR TRADE MOVEMENT

The problem for small farmers in poorer countries is that importers can buy goods
more cheaply from (**7**) ....

The fair trade movement provides a more (**8**) .... way
of life for poor farmers and farm workers.

The speaker reassures the audience that, mostly, fair trade goods and those
produced in the UK are not in (**9**) ....

When UK (**10**) .... for a particular item are higher than
the local supply, fair trade goods make up the difference.

Terry Carville feels that the percentage of fair trade coffee consumed in the UK is
(**11**) ....

He brought leaflets for students to pass along to managers of supermarkets and
cafés that (**12**) .... fair trade goods.

Participants in the fair trade university and college project organise campaigns to
(**13**) .... of the movement.

They also put more (**14**) .... measures in place, such
as making sure that fair trade goods can be purchased at their university.

PAPER 1 Reading and
          Use of English

PAPER 2 Writing

PAPER 3 Listening

Part 1
Part 2
Part 3
Part 4

PAPER 4 Speaking

Track 23

You will hear a phone conversation between a successful actor called Annabel and a teenager called Maurice, who is considering studying drama. For questions **15–20**, choose the answer (**A**, **B**, **C** or **D**) which fits best according to what you hear.

---

15 Why is Maurice uncertain about applying to study drama at university?
    A He knows he wants to be very rich and famous.
    B He's not taking his college applications seriously.
    C He's worried about not having a regular income.
    D He's concerned that Annabel will be offended.

16 Why did Annabel stop studying art?
    A She didn't find it interesting or exciting enough.
    B She wanted to return home to Northern Ireland.
    C She felt very passionate about studying drama.
    D She was determined not to do anything risky.

17 How did Annabel feel about her application to the Royal Academy of Dramatic Art?
    A She fully expected to be accepted because she believed in herself.
    B She was sure she wouldn't be accepted but decided to try anyway.
    C She felt she had a good chance of being accepted, but wasn't certain.
    D She didn't expect to be accepted, but she was committed to trying.

18 Annabel says that her favourite kind of work is in
    A television.
    B films.
    C the theatre.
    D schools.

19 What is Annabel's main message to Maurice?
    A Working in theatre is the best job in the world.
    B Acting is hard work and only barely pays the bills.
    C It's wonderful, but be prepared for difficult times.
    D The career is very uncertain so try something else.

20 Based on what he says, is it likely that Maurice will apply to do theatre studies?
    A He doesn't say.
    B Yes, it's very likely.
    C It's not that unlikely.
    D He has no idea yet.

PAPER 1   Reading and
          Use of English

PAPER 2   Writing

PAPER 3   Listening ▶

PAPER 4   Speaking

Part 1
Part 2
Part 3
Part 4

🎧 **Track 24**

You will hear five short extracts in which people talk about their favourite subject when they were at school.

While you listen you must complete both tasks.

TASK ONE

For questions **21–25**, choose from the list (**A–H**) what each speaker enjoyed about that subject.

A	the analytical aspect of it		
B	all of the mysteries in it	Speaker 1	**21**
C	learning about our ancestors	Speaker 2	**22**
D	its creative use of language	Speaker 3	**23**
E	the sense of fun in it	Speaker 4	**24**
F	how reliable the subject is	Speaker 5	**25**
G	how complicated it is		
H	that it encourages self-expression		

TASK TWO

For questions **26–30**, choose from the list (**A–H**) what each speaker does or plans to do for a living.

A	secondary school teacher		
B	researcher	Speaker 1	**26**
C	archaeologist	Speaker 2	**27**
D	accountant	Speaker 3	**28**
E	author	Speaker 4	**29**
F	graphic designer	Speaker 5	**30**
G	professor of poetry		
H	fashion designer		

Part 1 (2 minutes)

The examiner will ask you a few questions about yourself and about a general topic. For example, the examiner may ask you:

- **Do you like cooking? Why (not)?**
- **What is your favourite kind of food?**
- **What type of climate do you like best? Why?**

Part 2 (4 minutes)

You will each be asked to talk on your own for about a minute. You will each be given three different pictures to talk about. After your partner has finished speaking, you will be asked a brief question connected with your partner's photographs.

> **Medical traditions** (compare, contrast and speculate)

Turn to pictures 1–3 on page **184**, which show different medical practices.

(*Candidate A*), it's your turn first. Here are your pictures. They show **different kinds of medical practitioners**.

I'd like you to compare **two** of the pictures and say **what kind of medical condition each one might treat and what cultural differences there are between these medical practices.**

(*Candidate B*), **what kind of character traits do you think a medical practitioner needs to have? Why?**

> **Places of learning** (compare, contrast and speculate)

Turn to pictures 1–3 on page **185**, which show different kinds of classrooms.

Now, (*Candidate B*), here are your pictures. They show **different places of learning**.

I'd like you to compare **two** of the pictures and say **how these places of learning are different and what they have in common.**

(*Candidate A*), **do you think people have a better learning experience if they have access to technology? Why (not)?**

Part 3 (4 minutes)

Look at page **186**, which shows some things people can do to cope with homesickness and culture shock.

> **Coping with homesickness and culture shock** (discuss, evaluate and negotiate)

Here are some things people can do to cope with homesickness and culture shock.

First, you have some time to look at the task.

(*Pause 15 seconds*)

Now talk to each other about **how these steps can help to cope with homesickness and culture shock.**

Now you have a minute to decide **what you think is the most effective thing people can do to combat homesickness and culture shock, and why.**

Part 4 (5 minutes)

The examiner will encourage you to develop the topic of your discussion in Part 3 by asking questions such as:

- Do you think that certain types of people are more likely to experience culture shock and feel homesick, or can anyone be affected by these conditions?
- Does the internet make it any easier to live far from your home country? How?

For questions **1–8**, read the text below and decide which answer (**A**, **B**, **C** or **D**) best fits each gap. There is an example at the beginning (**0**).

Mark your answers **on the separate answer sheet**.

Example:

0 **A** desire   **B** mood   **C** feel   **D** condition

0	A	B	C	D

Pop music – how does it make you feel?

Are you ever in the (**0**) …….. for a happy, up-tempo pop song? If you're American and happen to hear one on the radio, the (**1**) …….. are it was recorded quite a long time ago, according to a (**2**) …….. study carried out by scientists from universities in Canada and Germany. Glenn Schellenberg and Christian von Scheve (**3**) …….. to examine emotions conveyed by music in the American pop charts between 1965 and 2009. They classified songs according to pace and the key they were composed in.

People generally (**4**) …….. faster songs in a major key with happy feelings, and slower songs in a minor key with darker emotions. (**5**) …….. speaking, in the 1960s, the charts were dominated by upbeat music, but over the next five decades it (**6**) …….. to a more melancholic, complicated sound. Intriguingly, in the last decade, the (**7**) …….. of emotionally ambiguous songs (sad-sounding but fast, or happy-sounding but slow) has significantly increased.

The researchers believe these trends may give interesting (**8**) …….. into more general social changes. They speculate, for instance, that people may now engage with more varied emotions.

1	**A** prospects	**B** chances	**C** bets	**D** outlooks
2	**A** mutual	**B** tied	**C** joint	**D** coupled
3	**A** aimed on	**B** kicked off	**C** took up	**D** set out
4	**A** associate	**B** fit	**C** attach	**D** correspond
5	**A** Broadly	**B** Largely	**C** Primarily	**D** Widely
6	**A** translated	**B** swapped	**C** removed	**D** shifted
7	**A** degree	**B** proportion	**C** dimension	**D** measure
8	**A** regards	**B** revelations	**C** visions	**D** insights

For questions **9–16**, read the text below and think of the word which best fits each gap. Use only one word in each gap. There is an example at the beginning (**0**).

Write your answers **IN CAPITAL LETTERS on the separate answer sheet**.

Example: **0** | W | H | Y |

The sound of babies crying

Have you ever wondered (**0**) …….. it is so hard to ignore the sound of a crying baby? (**9**) …….. who has found themselves on a plane or train next to a baby in distress will recognise the feeling. Research by Dr Katie Young and Dr Christine Parsons from Oxford University suggests that our brains are programmed to respond strongly to the sound, no (**10**) …….. how hard we try to block it out.

The researchers subjected 30 people (**11**) …….. recordings of babies and adults crying as well as various animal distress noises, (**12**) …….. them dogs whining and cats mewing, and scanned the listeners' brains. The scans revealed that participants' brains responded quickly to all the noises, but only processed significant amounts of emotion in the (**13**) …….. of the babies' cries. Not a single (**14**) …….. of the participants was a parent, yet they all responded in the same way.

The researchers suggest that this brain activity is highly (**15**) …….. to be 'a fundamental response present in all of us', (**16**) …….. of parental status, something perhaps to consider when you are next trapped with a screaming infant.

For questions **17–24**, read the text below. Use the word given in capitals at the end of some of the lines to form a word that fits in the gap **in the same line**. There is an example at the beginning (**0**).

Write your answers **IN CAPITAL LETTERS on the separate answer sheet.**

Example: | 0 | R | E | A | S | O | N | A | B | L | E | | | | | | | | |

Can roads help nature?

It is (**0**) …….. to assume that roads, generally, are not very   **REASON**
good for nature, and there is good evidence to support
this assumption. Scientists William Laurance and Andrew
Balmford point out, for example, that '95% of (**17**) ………., fires   **FOREST**
and atmospheric carbon (**18**) …….. in the Brazilian Amazon   **EMIT**
occur within 50 kilometres of a road.' One hundred thousand
kilometres of roads now criss-cross the Amazon, and road-
building there continues, often (**19**) …….. contravening   **LEGAL**
environmental laws.

However, Laurance and Balmford believe that roads can
be environmentally (**20**) …….. . In agricultural areas where   **BENEFIT**
forests have already been cleared, good roads ease access
to markets, which improves the (**21**) …….. and profitability   **EFFICIENT**
of farms, and tends to encourage people to stay away from
vulnerable wilderness. Laurance and Balmford propose a
worldwide project to establish which areas should not have
roads and which areas governments should (**22**) …….. for   **PRIORITY**
road improvement. They believe a scheme of this kind could
(**23**) …….. the damage roads cause. It would be challenging,   **LESS**
but, in Laurance and Balmford's view, influencing road
development is (**24**) …….. more practical and cost-effective   **QUESTIONABLE**
than any other measure currently deployed to protect crucial
ecosystems.

ADVANCED
TEST 7

Exam Essentials

PAPER 1 Reading and
Use of English

Part 1
Part 2
Part 3
Part 4
Part 5
Part 6
Part 7
Part 8

PAPER 2 Writing

PAPER 3 Listening

PAPER 4 Speaking

For questions **25–30**, complete the second sentence so that it has a similar meaning to the first sentence, using the word given. **Do not change the word given.** You must use between **three** and **six** words, including the word given. Here is an example (**0**).

Example:

0   Chloe would only eat a pizza if she could have a mushroom topping.

   ON

   Chloe .... a mushroom topping when she had a pizza.

The gap can be filled with the words 'insisted on having', so you write:

Example: | **0** | INSISTED ON HAVING |

Write **only** the missing words **IN CAPITAL LETTERS on the separate answer sheet.**

---

25   My boss says he has no intention of making anyone redundant, even though the situation is difficult for the company right now.

   DREAM

   My boss says he .... off, even though the situation is difficult for the company right now.

26   They say New York was a rather aggressive city 20 years ago but it feels quite friendly these days.

   SUPPOSED

   New York .... a rather aggressive city 20 years ago but it feels quite friendly these days.

27   Jenny was the person who really didn't want to tidy up after the party.

   OBJECTED

   It .... up after the party.

28   The new software isn't the main point for discussion tomorrow, but should anyone raise the subject by any chance, I'll give my views.

   HAPPENS

   The new software isn't the main point for discussion tomorrow, but if the .... up by anyone, I'll give my views.

29   'As we climb higher, it gets harder to breathe,' our guide warned us at the start of the trek.

   THE

   Our guide warned us that the higher .... get.

30   Only when Yoshi was promoted to his new job did he realise how much he was appreciated by his colleagues.

   UNTIL

   It .... his new job that he realised how much he was appreciated by his colleagues.

You are going to read an article about music and mathematics. For questions **31–36**, choose the answer (**A**, **B**, **C** or **D**) which you think fits best according to the text.

Mark your answers **on the separate answer sheet**.

Maths and music

Mathematician Tim Gowers is also a keen musician.

An excellent way to kill a conversation is to say you are a mathematician. Tell your interlocutor you are also a musician, however, and they will be hooked. Even people who know nothing about mathematics have heard the counter-intuitive notion that mathematical ability is connected to musical ability. As a mathematician with strong musical interests, I have been asked about this many times. Bad news: although there are some obvious similarities between mathematical and musical activity, there is (as yet) no compelling evidence for the kind of mysterious, magical connection many people seem to believe in.

I'm partly referring here to the 'Mozart effect', where children who have been played Mozart compositions are supposedly more intelligent, including at mathematics, than other children. It is not hard to see why such a theory would be popular: we would all like to become better at maths without putting in any effort. But the actual conclusions of the experiment that originally prompted the belief in the Mozart effect were much more modest and remain grossly exaggerated. If you want your brain to work better, then you clearly have to put in hard graft.

But what about learning to play the piano? That takes effort. Could the rewards for that spill over into other areas of intellectual life? Is there any evidence that people who have worked hard at music are better at maths than people who are unmusical? And conversely, are mathematicians objectively better than average at music?

Firstly, there are plenty of innumerate musicians and tone-deaf mathematicians, so the best one could hope to identify would be a significant positive correlation between aptitudes. Then one would try to establish a statistical connection. So, if you want to show that professional mathematicians are on average better at music than other people, you have to decide quite carefully who those 'other people' are. You might expect that a professional mathematician is much more likely than average to come from a family where music was regarded as important, so for that reason alone one would expect at least some 'background correlation´ between the two. Therefore, not much will be proved if you compare professional mathematicians with the wider population.

But surely a connection is at least plausible. Both mathematics and music deal with abstract structures, so if you become good at one, then it is plausible that you become good at something more general – handling abstract structures – that helps you with the other. If this is correct, then it would show a connection between mathematical and musical ability, though not a mysterious one. It would be more like the connection between abilities at football and tennis. To become better at one of those you need to improve your fitness and coordination. That makes you better at sport and probably helps with the other.

Of course, abstract structures are not confined to mathematics and music. If you are learning a foreign language then you need to understand its grammar and syntax, prime examples of abstract structures. Yet we don't hear people asking about a mysterious connection between mathematical and linguistic ability. My guess is this is because grammar feels mathematical, so it would hardly be surprising to learn that mathematicians were better than average at learning grammar. Music, by contrast, is strongly tied up with emotions and can be enjoyed even by people who know very little about it. As such, it seems very different from mathematics, so any connection between the two is appealingly paradoxical.

To dispel this air of paradox, let's look at how we solve problems of the 'A is to B as C is to D' kind. These appear in intelligence tests (car is to garage as aircraft is to what?) but they are also central to both music and mathematics. Consider, for instance, the opening of Mozart's *Eine Kleine Nachtmusik*. The second phrase is a clear answer to the first. The listener thinks: 'The first phrase goes broadly upwards and uses the notes of a G major chord; what would be the corresponding phrase that goes broadly downwards and uses the notes of a D7?' Music is full of little puzzles like this. If you are good at them, when you listen to music, expectations will constantly be set up in your mind. Some of the best moments in music come when one's expectations are confounded, but we need the expectations in the first place.

31 What does the writer suggest in the first paragraph?

    A Musicians tend to be more popular than mathematicians.

    B Mathematicians have a reputation for being uncommunicative.

    C The attraction musicians often feel for mathematics is well-known.

    D The relationship between music and maths is a frequent source of fascination.

32 What does the writer say about the experiment referred to in the second paragraph?

    A The findings drawn from it have been misinterpreted.

    B The way it was carried out has been discredited.

    C The objectives set out for it were ill-considered.

    D The interest aroused by it was unexpected.

33 The writer's main intention in the fourth paragraph is to outline how connections between maths and music could be

    A exemplified by certain people.

    B explored most effectively.

    C difficult to demonstrate.

    D useful to investigate.

34 What is the writer emphasising with the reference to football and tennis in the fifth paragraph?

    A why the idea that music and maths have something in common is reasonable

    B how music and maths both have their practical sides

    C what is meant by the notion of abstract structures

    D how certain skills are developed through practice

35 What does the writer suggest in the sixth paragraph?

    A The structure of language is easier to understand than the structure of music.

    B Mathematicians have been proved to be good at language learning.

    C Languages generally hold less of an attraction than music.

    D Music may be no closer to maths than language is.

36 What is the writer's main intention in the seventh paragraph?

    A to illustrate how music ultimately differs from maths

    B to show how abstract thinking applies to both music and maths

    C to explain why Mozart is so highly considered by mathematicians

    D to describe the mathematical processes composers may engage in

PAPER 1 Reading and ▸ Part 1
        Use of English   Part 2
PAPER 2 Writing   Part 3
                        Part 4
PAPER 3 Listening   Part 5
PAPER 4 Speaking   **Part 6**
                        Part 7
                        Part 8

You are going to read four reviews of a book about teenagers. For questions **37–40**, choose from the reviews **A–D**. The reviews may be chosen more than once.

Mark your answers **on the separate answer sheet**.

Teenagers: A Natural History by David Bainbridge

We all go through adolescence. Four reviewers share their thoughts about scientist David Bainbridge's book exploring what goes on at this important stage of our lives, and why it is as it is.

A

To anybody exposed to teenagers swinging between extremes of energy and laziness, there is an obvious appeal in scientific explanations of their behaviour. The finely-judged tone of David Bainbridge's language – neither over-technical nor patronisingly simple – only adds to the attraction. Closer inspection, however, induces misgivings. Bainbridge traces the roots of much modern teenage behaviour to biological and psychological developments thousands of years ago. The notion that speculation about our distant origins can provide answers to questions about personal development and social relationships today is far too simplistic. Bainbridge dismisses the notion that the teenager is a modern social phenomenon, but some attention to the influences that have transformed adolescent experience over recent decades would be far more fruitful than trying to explain people in terms of pre-historic life. Popular psychology can be very worthwhile, but this book tells us little about how to raise young people or deal with their difficulties.

B

Humans take much longer to mature than any other animal, and David Bainbridge suggests this may be a crucial distinguishing feature because it gives our brains time to develop. This intriguing idea, together with accounts of how physiology and brain activity change as we go through adolescence, is communicated with enviable lucidity. Unfortunately, Bainbridge undermines the effect by repeatedly invoking hypotheses about pre-historic human development to understand specifics of teenagers today. The plausibility of various notions – for example, that risk-taking is 'built into' adolescence because of the survival requirements 300,000 years ago – relies more on wish-fulfilment than science. There is no attempt either to engage with the broader social, political and philosophical contexts within which teenagers develop; always crucial, surely. Despite such reservations, the insights provided into the chemical and physiological changes adolescents go through should definitely cause adults to think about how to respond to their moods and apparently chaotic behaviour.

C

Why will the average 15-year-old grumpily roll out of bed at two o'clock in the afternoon? David Bainbridge offers no-nonsense biological explanations to questions such as these: 'the terrible triangle of laziness, risk-taking and anger' reflects consistent reorganisations in the adolescent brain. What is more, Bainbridge draws on anthropology and psychology to show how many of the changes adolescent bodies and brains go through are the result of developments somewhere between 800,000 and three million years ago. Although Bainbridge can sometimes be irritatingly informal – the subject is inherently interesting and does not need any jazzing up or dumbing down – these explanations are coherent and persuasive. Where the book does fall down is in a failure to explore the external context within which modern teenagers move from childhood to adulthood. He is strangely silent, for example, on the impact on teenagers of new technologies such as computer games and the internet.

D

David Bainbridge believes that extended adolescence in humans may have been the spur 250,000 years ago to the final phase in the expansion of the human brain; adolescence gives us time to learn and increase our brain power. This fascinating idea, together with compelling explanations about how we can trace many of the transformations, physical and psychological, that modern teenagers go through back to human development in pre-history, are all delivered in fresh, amusing and intelligible prose. In some ways, it is reassuring to find out that certain patterns of behaviour are largely hardwired in teenagers, rather than determined by the way they are brought up, the relationships they have with the people around them and so on. Anyone who has witnessed how dramatically young people can change as they enter adolescence will appreciate how convincing this idea is, and worried parents should find comfort and inspiration in Bainbridge's central theme that supporting children and teenagers is what adults are really for.

Which reviewer

expresses a different view from the others about
the importance of social factors for understanding
teenage behaviour?

37

shares B's opinion on the use of ideas about ancient
human development to explain modern teenagers?

38

has a different opinion from the others about the style
of writing in the book?

39

takes a similar view to D regarding the book's value
for people responsible for teenagers?

40

You are going to read a magazine article about chimpanzees. Six paragraphs have been removed from the article. Choose from the paragraphs **A–G** the one which fits each gap (**41–46**). There is one extra paragraph which you do not need to use.

Mark your answers **on the separate answer sheet**.

Observing how wild chimpanzees behave

Joshu Foer visits a project in Congo in Africa where scientists can observe the behaviour of chimpanzees and other great apes which have had little or no contact with humans.

Dave Morgan and Crickette Sanz run an ape research site in the Goualougo Triangle, a remote jungle region of Congo, virtually untouched by humanity. On a sticky September morning, Morgan, Sanz, and I leave the Goualougo base with our tracker Bosco Mangoussou and head into the forest in search of chimpanzees. Our route regularly slaloms around heaps of rotting fruit, whose pungent aromas permeate the humid air.

41

Eventually, we spot a half dozen chimps lounging in a tree about 40 metres up. This community is well-known to Morgan and Sanz, who have even named each animal. We watch through binoculars as a young female, Dinah, plays with Owen, a juvenile. Finn, the group's most powerful male, looks on. Then something remarkable happens.

42

The thumping echoes off the surrounding trees. Then she rips a small twig off a nearby branch, dips it into the hive, and swirls it around. She pulls it out, realises there's no honey on it, throws it away, and starts pounding some more. After repeating the process several times, she finally plunges her finger into a crack and yanks out a bit of honey, which goes straight into her mouth.

43

The fact that this behaviour hasn't been observed at other sites outside central Africa suggests that it is not innate to the species, but rather is a learned skill that has been culturally transmitted. Part of what makes

Dinah's behaviour so intriguing is that she used a big club and a thin twig in sequence to accomplish her goal.

44

This is what happens: an older female arrives at the rock-hard structure. She rams a thick twig into a small hole and widens it by jiggling the stick vigorously. Then she grabs a thin, flexible stem, drags the end of it through her teeth to make it wet and frayed, like a paintbrush, and then pulls it through her closed fist to straighten out the bristles. She then threads it into the same hole, pulls it out, and nibbles off a couple of bugs that cling to the frayed edges.

45

'The Goualougo is probably the only place on earth where humans will ever have the chance to see what chimpanzee culture is really about,' conservationist Michael Fay tells me later. 'Ninety-five per cent of chimps on earth don't live like this because of humans.' Chimp study sites elsewhere are surrounded by people and often affected by logging and hunting.

46

It is known that even selective logging and casual hunting can throw chimp society into disarray if it pushes groups into conflict or decreases the number of termite mounds where they can fish. Morgan and Sanz have suggested that with fewer mounds and, therefore, fewer opportunities for young chimps to learn tool techniques from their elders, chimp culture may slowly decline, and complex learned behaviours may disappear.

A This is a powerful and troubling notion: what if everywhere scientists have thought they were observing chimps in their natural state, they've actually been studying behaviour distorted by the presence of humans?

B This is the signal for Finn to make a move, seemingly outraged that a young upstart is enjoying a sugary delicacy in his presence. He lunges at Dinah, who drops her club and flees to another limb.

C When wild chimps encounter humans, they typically flee in panic – understandable given that the relationship between our two species has often been one of prey and predator. This reticence is part of what makes wild chimp research so difficult. These ones, however, seem unperturbed by our presence.

D It is the immense variety of these more than two dozen edible species, ranging from pumpkin-size Treculia africana to rubbery, soft ball-size Chrysophyllum lacourtiana, that makes the Goualougo such an attractive habitat for chimps.

E What's so remarkable about this is not just that some clever chimp figured out it could break a plant and use it to fish for food; it's that some other chimp figured out a way to do it even better. Morgan and Sanz have themselves tried the process with both modified and unmodified sticks and found that they collected ten times more termites with the modified tool.

F Noticing a cloud of bees emerging from a hole near the main trunk of the tree, Dinah leaps to her feet and breaks off a branch about the size of a human arm. With the blunt end she begins whacking the bark. She knows that somewhere inside is a hive with honey.

G This isn't the only form of serial tool use common in the Goualougo. As we witness the beehive attack, a camera set up near a termite mound a kilometre mile away records another chimp engaging in what may be the most sophisticated form of serial tool use by any non-human animal.

You are going to read an article in which student nurses talk about courses they have taken online as part of their training. For questions **47–56**, choose from the people (**A–D**). The nurses may be chosen more than once.

Mark your answers **on the separate answer sheet**.

Which student nurse

gained a better understanding of an aspect of healthcare she had always disliked?	47
liked the way a complicated subject was made comprehensible?	48
was impressed by the varied approach on the course?	49
appreciated being encouraged to come up with new ideas?	50
was initially concerned about how much the course aimed to cover?	51
had been worried she might be too inexperienced for the course she was taking?	52
was helped to reflect on aspects of her performance as a nurse?	53
felt inspired by the course to take a practical initiative when on a work placement?	54
felt reassured about aspects of her nursing work she had concerns about?	55
feels the course she followed fulfilled its stated objectives?	56

Student nurses

Four student nurses talk about courses they have done online as part of their degrees.

A Alicia Denby

I'm in the second year of my nursing course and I recently took a module called *Leadership in Healthcare*. It was all done online, so an interesting contrast with my normal lectures, seminars and work placements. I was advised to do it by one of my lecturers, but I must admit I was initially apprehensive about it as the idea of leadership seemed more for people already in positions of responsibility and authority, rather than a student nurse. It turned out to be relevant to people across the health service, however. It was well designed with a range of activities including analysis scenarios in which leadership may play a key role; viewing short, interesting films which provided relief from the challenging reading; and regularly exchanging ideas, via different digital media, with other participants. I came away feeling much better equipped for dealing with work issues. In fact, the module gave me an idea for solving a real problem in the ward where I'm now doing a six-week practice stint.

B Maria dos Santos

The module I studied was called *Patient Safety* and it focused on procedural errors in the profession – why they occur and what strategies can be employed to avoid them. Impressively, the module manages to achieve its aims; it really does what it says on the tin! What I found particularly helpful was the understanding it brought about that while mistakes may be made by individuals, only the system as a whole can foster an environment where they are less likely to happen. It's precisely this environment that necessitates the number of policies and procedures that abound in the profession, which, in turn, results in the amount of dreaded paperwork we have to deal with – a need I hadn't really comprehended before. Now I approach all the documentation in a very different way. When I read the module overview, I was overwhelmed at first by the potential for problems to arise in healthcare, but by the end of the course I felt reassured that systems are in place to support staff and to provide patients with the safest healthcare possible.

C Maya Farsani

The module I did – *Introduction to the Culture of Safety* – explores real issues that new nurses are likely to come across. There are plenty of safety and professional guidelines we have to learn, but I'm not sure we know how to uphold them all in practice. As a third-year nursing student with several work placements under my belt, it made me consider the way I had worked and what my duty of care to the patient really is. I would hope that the attitudes of psychological safety, fairness and transparency dealt with on this course are acknowledged as standard across the clinical setting – and if they aren't, I would want to know why not. I would definitely recommend this course to any other healthcare students! The notion of a culture of safety is quite new in some ways and there's a lot to it, but I never had any sense of having to battle to get to grips with it, and I think that boils down to the quality of the module.

D Krystyna Blazek

I'm coming to the end of my degree now and I think what I did on the module *Quality Control in Healthcare* should prove very useful when I'm in my first proper nursing job. It highlighted the fact that the health service is a system, with many variables that affect patient outcomes, so that when an error happens, whether harm occurs or not, blame cannot be placed on an individual but is down to a failure of the system as a whole. This doesn't mean you can just pass the buck and ignore errors, but as a young nurse you have vulnerable people's well-being in your hands, and it is good to know that you're not on your own, that there is a system to monitor and support you. Apart from this, I think the course is also relevant because it shows you the importance of thinking out of the box and not becoming blinkered into believing there is only one way to do something, particularly if things are going wrong.

You **must** answer this question. Write your answer in **220–260** words in an appropriate style on the separate answer sheet.

1 During a college seminar one of your fellow students stated that the sciences are more important than the arts. You have made the notes below.

> **Science more important than art**
>
> - The creative arts are OK as a pastime, just for fun, but they are not necessary.
> - Scientific developments enable us to understand the world we live in.
> - Without the sciences we wouldn't have the knowledge required to treat medical conditions and cure diseases.

> **Other students in the seminar expressed these opinions:**
>
> "Artistic expression is what separates us from animals. Human beings have a talent and a need for art."
>
> "Through art we learn about ourselves in a way that doesn't feature in science."
>
> "Life can be stressful and difficult, but the beauty of art provides something special and vital."

Write an essay for your tutor discussing **two** of the points from your notes. You should **explain whether you think the sciences are more important** than the arts and **provide reasons** to support your opinions.

You may, if you wish, make use of the opinions expressed in the seminar, but you should use your own words as far as possible.

Write an answer to **one** of the questions **2–4** in this part. Write your answer in **220–260** words in an appropriate style on the separate answer sheet. Put the question number in the box at the top of the page.

2 You are spending the summer abroad. While you are away, your best friend from home emails you with some bad news. He has just learned that his application to the university he wanted to attend was not accepted. He is feeling very demotivated and unsure about what he will do instead. Write an encouraging and supportive email back to him.

Write your **email**.

3 A former colleague has set up her own catering business and has asked for your help in improving her website. Choose two or three points for improvement, focusing on design, ease of use and organisation. Write a proposal explaining how your recommended changes will make the website more attractive as well as easier for customers to navigate.

Write your **proposal**.

4 A history teacher at a local secondary school would like to show his students a film about an important historical event. He has invited people to send in reviews of films they feel would be appropriate for his final-year students. Write a review and include reasons for your choice of film.

Write your **review**.

Track 25

You will hear three different extracts. For questions **1–6**, choose the answer (**A**, **B** or **C**) which fits best according to what you hear. There are two questions for each extract.

Extract One

You hear two people discussing the royal family.

1   Why does the woman say she supports the royal family?
    A   She likes the romantic idea of royalty.
    B   Because she was born in Great Britain.
    C   She feels that it's part of her identity.

2   At the end, do the man and woman agree?
    A   Yes, they completely agree.
    B   No, they don't agree at all.
    C   They agree on some points.

Extract Two

You hear a conversation between two friends about a person called Paul.

3   The real reason the woman changes her mind about going to the beach is that
    A   the weather looks uncertain.
    B   she's actually extremely busy.
    C   someone she doesn't like is going.

4   What does the man explain about Paul?
    A   He actually doesn't have much confidence.
    B   He's just someone with a lot of confidence.
    C   The truth is that he has no confidence at all.

Extract Three

You hear a man and woman discussing the woman's younger brother.

5   The woman's principal concern is that her brother
    A   is unable to cope with his exams.
    B   is not focussing on his education.
    C   is going to play football professionally.

6   How is the man's attitude to the situation best described?
    A   He believes that the brother doesn't need an education.
    B   He fully expects the brother to be a professional footballer.
    C   He thinks the brother is going through a normal phase.

Track 26

You will hear a woman talking about a personality test called the *Myers-Briggs Type Indicator*. For questions **7–14**, complete the sentences with a word or short phrase.

THE MYERS-BRIGGS TYPE INDICATOR

During World War II Myers and Briggs first began developing the personality test, which (**7**) .... Carl Jung's work.

Intuition, as defined by the speaker, is a way of reaching an understanding of things that doesn't rely on (**8**) .... them.

The test is supposed to reveal whether you typically rely on your judgement or your perception of things, and it categorises people as being either reserved or (**9**) ....

Overall, the speaker doesn't object to the (**10**) .... of the Myers-Briggs test, but she doesn't really take it seriously.

She is concerned about having to take the Myers-Briggs test as part of her job application because of its (**11**) ....

Part of her problem with the test is that it fails to (**12**) .... situations in which a person doesn't fit into one category or the other, but somewhere between the two.

Eventually, the speaker contacted the Human Resources manager because she was (**13**) .... about having to take the Myers-Briggs test.

The manager at the company put her mind at ease by explaining that they just use the test as a loose (**14**) ....

🎧 **Track 27**

You will hear an interview with a successful novelist called Hilton Sims. For questions **15–20**, choose the answer (**A**, **B**, **C** or **D**) which fits best according to what you hear.

15 How long ago was Hilton Sims' first novel published?
    A two years
    B ten years
    C six years
    D 20 years

16 The author has a background in
    A literature.
    B psychology.
    C social work.
    D film-making.

17 When asked about genre, what does the author say about his novels?
    A They don't fit into a single category.
    B He says they're psychological thrillers.
    C They're best described as crime fiction.
    D He refuses to categorise his books.

18 How did Hilton Sims meet the agent who published his first novel?
    A It happened through contacting dozens of publishers.
    B His friends contacted the agent on his behalf.
    C They happened to meet through Hilton's day job.
    D The meeting was just a lucky coincidence.

19 According to the author, what is the main reason for the popularity of crime fiction?
    A People have always been fascinated by the 'good versus evil' battle.
    B Readers enjoy the challenge of trying to figure out what happened.
    C The sophisticated nature of criminal minds has great popular appeal.
    D Science and technology have made solving crimes more interesting.

20 When the author finds it difficult to write, he
    A goes out jogging.
    B breaks for lunch.
    C always sticks with it.
    D writes somewhere else.

PAPER 1 Reading and
         Use of English

PAPER 2 Writing

PAPER 3 Listening ▶

PAPER 4 Speaking

Part 1
Part 2
Part 3
Part 4

Track 28

You will hear five short extracts in which people talk about what they do to keep fit.

While you listen you must complete both tasks.

TASK ONE

For questions **21–25**, choose from the list (**A–H**) what brought each speaker to this form of exercise.

A	living overseas		
B	gym membership	Speaker 1	21
C	their partner	Speaker 2	22
D	co-workers	Speaker 3	23
E	a hospital stay	Speaker 4	24
F	their partner's friend	Speaker 5	25
G	a childhood activity		
H	a charity event		

TASK TWO

For questions **26–30**, choose from the list (**A–H**) what effect each speaker says this form of exercise has on them.

A	becomes very competitive		
B	has a sense of balance in life	Speaker 1	26
C	enjoys being close to nature	Speaker 2	27
D	likes feeling out of control	Speaker 3	28
E	feels grateful for good health	Speaker 4	29
F	is keen to live in the country	Speaker 5	30
G	loves how thrilling it is		
H	brings on a good mood		

Part 1 (2 minutes)

The examiner will ask you a few questions about yourself and about a general topic. For example, the examiner may ask you:

- **What would be your ideal job? Why?**
- **Who has had the greatest influence on you?**
- **Which world problem are you the most concerned about? Why?**

Part 2 (4 minutes)

You will each be asked to talk on your own for about a minute. You will each be given three different pictures to talk about. After your partner has finished speaking, you will be asked a brief question connected with your partner's photographs.

> **Modern inconveniences** (compare, contrast and speculate)

Turn to pictures 1–3 on page **187**, which show some modern stresses.

(*Candidate A*), it's your turn first. Here are your pictures. They show **different types of stress** which did not exist 100 years ago.

I'd like you to compare **two** of the pictures and say **what kind of impact each situation generally has on people and whether these situations can be avoided**.

(*Candidate B*), **do you think these are a necessary part of modern life? Why (not)?**

> **Professional occupations and gender** (compare, contrast and speculate)

Turn to pictures 1–3 on page **188**, which show three different occupations.

Now, (*Candidate B*), here are your pictures. They show **different occupations which, traditionally, might be considered to belong to one gender or the other.**

I'd like you to compare **two** of the pictures and say **what kinds of skills are needed to do each of these jobs well and whether men or women are better suited** to each occupation shown.

(*Candidate A*), do you think **society has changed enough to accept men and women working in whatever occupation they wish? Does this vary from culture to culture?**

Part 3 (4 minutes)

Look at page **189**, which shows what graduates can do to improve their employability.

> **Ways of improving employability** (discuss, evaluate and negotiate)

Here are some things graduates can do to improve their employability and a question for you to discuss. First, you have some time to look at the task.

(*Pause 15 seconds*)

Now talk to each other about **how useful these steps might be in improving a new graduate's chances of being hired.**

Now you have a minute to decide **which step would have the most positive impact on a new graduate's employability, and why.**

Part 4 (5 minutes)

The examiner will encourage you to develop the topic of your discussion in Part 3 by asking questions such as:

- What might make it difficult for a new graduate to be hired?
- Do you believe that a person's attitude is more important to employers than their education and experience? Why (not)?
- Does luck play a part in whether or not a person is hired? What do you think?

For questions **1–8**, read the text below and decide which answer (**A**, **B**, **C** or **D**) best fits each gap. There is an example at the beginning (**0**).

Mark your answers **on the separate answer sheet**.

Example:

| 0 | **A** | hang | **B** | stick | **C** | fix | **D** | insist |

| 0 | A | **B** | C | D |

Do we really want variety in life?

Do you seek variety or do you (**0**) …….. with what you know? Research by behavioural scientist Daniel Read suggests we generally think variety is good, but we are (**1**) …….. to avoid it when we actually consume things. In one experiment over several weeks, volunteers were asked to either (**2**) …….. up on snacks (chocolate, fruit and crisps) at the start or select a snack each week. The former went for variety, but those selecting on a weekly (**3**) …….. prior to eating invariably picked the same snack. Moreover, if allowed to rethink, those who had gone for variety often (**4**) …….. to a single snack type.

Professor Read believes we display this 'diversification bias' in many (**5**) …….. of life. A weekly trip to the supermarket, for instance, is likely to (**6**) …….. us to buy a variety of items, some of which are likely to remain uneaten. (**7**) …….., financial managers will spread their investments, even though focusing on certain markets would probably be more profitable. Professor Read himself tries to (**8**) …….. his discoveries into practice: he is now 'more willing to buy ten of the same thing.'

1	**A** liable	**B** prone	**C** feasible	**D** vulnerable
2	**A** store	**B** save	**C** shop	**D** stock
3	**A** norm	**B** pattern	**C** rule	**D** basis
4	**A** reverted	**B** resumed	**C** recurred	**D** revolved
5	**A** quarters	**B** circles	**C** spheres	**D** zones
6	**A** affect	**B** lead	**C** produce	**D** guide
7	**A** Closely	**B** Comparatively	**C** Correspondingly	**D** Similarly
8	**A** set	**B** put	**C** fit	**D** get

For questions **9–16**, read the text below and think of the word which best fits each gap. Use only one word in each gap. There is an example at the beginning (**0**).

Write your answers **IN CAPITAL LETTERS on the separate answer sheet**.

Example: | 0 | T | H | R | O | U | G | H | | | | | | | | | | | | |

Internships

In many countries going (**0**) .... difficult economic times, job openings for new graduates can be few and (**9**) .... between. In this competitive environment, relevant work experience can help job seekers stand (**10**) .... from the crowd, and many organisations now offer temporary placements, called internships. The problem with (**11**) .... great many internships, however, is that they are unpaid, and this often puts young people (**12**) .... applying for them.

Employers and interns sometimes come to mutually beneficial arrangements, however. Dinesh Pathan, applying for an internship with an IT company, negotiated a deal in (**13**) .... he would be given travel expenses only for two weeks, and then, as (**14**) .... as he could show his marketing work was adding value, he would be paid a wage. The arrangement worked well: Dinesh had an incentive to work hard, and he ended up feeling 'not so (**15**) .... an intern as a temporary staffer.' HR consultant Denise Baker says similar arrangements are common. What is more, 'if interns do well, employers would often (**16**) .... make them full employees than recruit people they don't know'.

For questions **17–24**, read the text below. Use the word given in capitals at the end of some of the lines to form a word that fits in the gap **in the same line**. There is an example at the beginning (**0**).

Write your answers **IN CAPITAL LETTERS on the separate answer sheet.**

Example: | 0 | G | L | O | B | A | L | | | | | | | | | | | | | | |

Environmental psychology

Most scientists now agree that human behaviour is	
causing (**0**) …….. climate change and a disastrous	**GLOBE**
(**17**) …….. of biodiversity. In order to deal with these problems	**LOSE**
which, in the long term, threaten devastation on a scale which	
is (**18**) ………, we need to find ways to change behaviour. This is	**THINK**
where environmental psychologists come in. 'As we know a lot	
about human behaviour, we can help figure out how to motivate	
people to do (**19**) …….. things,' says psychologist Amara Brook.	**SUSTAIN**
While jobs (**20**) …….. for environmental psychologists are still	**SPECIFIC**
fairly unusual, psychologists are very much involved in such	
disciplines as urban (**21**) …….., conservation and environmental	**PLAN**
health. Using their knowledge of behaviour, psychologists have	
helped design (**22**) …….. messages on signs and notices to	**PERSUADE**
encourage environmentally friendly behaviour in nature reserves	
and parks. Others have investigated the effects of sunlight	
and access to parks and gardens on employee (**23**) …….. and	**PRODUCE**
on children's academic performance. Clinical psychologists	
with environmental (**24**) …….. are also in demand because	**EXPERT**
environmental concerns can cause great anxiety. As environmental	
issues become ever more significant, psychologists working in this	
field will surely become increasingly prominent.	

For questions **25–30**, complete the second sentence so that it has a similar meaning to the first sentence, using the word given. **Do not change the word given.** You must use between **three** and **six** words, including the word given. Here is an example (**0**).

Example:

0   Chloe would only eat a pizza if she could have a mushroom topping.

    ON

    Chloe .... a mushroom topping when she had a pizza.

The gap can be filled with the words 'insisted on having', so you write:

Example: | **0** | INSISTED ON HAVING |

Write **only** the missing words **IN CAPITAL LETTERS on the separate answer sheet.**

---

25   Make sure you know what the time is, otherwise you'll miss the start of the play.

    TRACK

    Make sure you .... as not to miss the start of the play.

26   It didn't take Steven long to show his true character.

    MATTER

    It was .... Steven showed his true character.

27   If we take everything into account, the street party was a great success in the end.

    CONSIDERED

    All .... out to be a great success in the end.

28   Everyone was horrified when the new manager dropped Ripley from the first team and picked Conway instead.

    LEFT

    To .... of the first team by the new manager and he picked Conway instead.

29   The company's owners are quite radical because they've got rid of a whole layer of managers, and they've introduced flexible working time.

    DONE

    The company's owners are quite radical because not .... with a whole layer of managers, but they've also introduced flexible working time.

30   The police apologised a great deal for having completely failed to recognise the seriousness of the situation.

    COMPLETE

    The police were very .... to recognise the seriousness of the situation.

PAPER 1 Reading and ▸
         Use of English

PAPER 2 Writing
PAPER 3 Listening
PAPER 4 Speaking

Part 1
Part 2
Part 3
Part 4
Part 5
Part 6
Part 7
Part 8

You are going to read a review of a book written by an author named Nicholas Carr, about the internet. For questions **31–36**, choose the answer (**A**, **B**, **C** or **D**) which you think fits best according to the text.

Mark your answers **on the separate answer sheet**.

Review of *The Shallows* by Nicholas Carr

Internet use may be changing our brains for good, but is this all bad?
David Cox reviews Nicholas Carr's investigation of how the internet is affecting us.

In their early days, as they challenged the established medium of communication, newspapers, cinema and broadcasting, like writing, libraries and printing before them, all provoked anguish. Would the upstart medium replace what was good with what was bad? The internet was bound to ignite the same kind of disquiet. It has indeed, yet according to Nicholas Carr in his intriguing and controversial book *The Shallows*, it is not the change in what our minds consume that should most bother us. It is the change that is being wrought upon our brains.

He tells us he can no longer read a book without getting fidgety and losing the thread. Constant searching and surfing online have made him expect a scurrying stream of particles and this means that the only way he absorbs information is in quick, small doses. The internet has really done his head in and, what is more, his friends fear they have the same syndrome.

Carr describes research which suggests this is no mere metaphor. Studies show that web use alters brain cells, creating new neural pathways and weakening old ones. The brain of a newcomer to the internet starts rewiring itself after just six days of surfing the web. Because of this, according to Carr, our powers of concentration are atrophying. 'As we come to rely on computers to mediate our understanding of the world,' he writes, 'it is our own intelligence that flattens into artificial intelligence.'

His account is plausible but far from surprising. Our grey matter constantly reshapes itself in the face of changing demands and circumstances. About 2,400 years ago, the Greek philosopher Socrates feared that the spread of writing would change the way brains worked: by focusing them on outer symbols (words written down) rather than inner recollection (in the mind), it would undermine memory and trivialise thought, thereby jeopardising wisdom and happiness. There was probably some truth in what he said. Once people could jot down a laundry list, say, the relevant sections of their brains doubtless decommissioned redundant storage capacity. At the same time, however, they learned to process a much richer body of data.

Carr acknowledges that the reshaping of our brains by digital media is in some ways improving them. He accepts that they are growing better at focusing attention, analysing data, multi-tasking and making instant decisions. Yet, for him, these benefits come at too high a price: the ability to attend patiently to lengthy narratives and long arguments is very much more valuable. However, this claim is debateable, to say the least.

Instead of reading the 256 pages in which Carr sets out his case, you could pretty much get his point by looking at one of the many summaries available, like this one, or indeed those to be found in various locations on the internet. This is not to say that Carr's book is poorly written or uninteresting – far from it – but if you take this course, you will be able to use the time saved to absorb the gist of a lot of other ideas as well as his. This might well be the more productive option.

People used to read three-volume novels largely because there wasn't much else to do. If our brains, through internet use, are now being reprogrammed to trawl the shallows broadly rather than narrowly plumb the depths, we may end up, on balance, better off. If we do not, in due course we shall doubtless notice, because we tend to notice these things, and remedial action will be available. An organ that has managed to unravel centuries of conditioning in a mere six days ought to be able to reverse the feat. Either way it will be up to us.

Carr's punchline is: 'We are welcoming the frenziedness into our souls.' Exactly. We are welcoming it, just as we welcomed the ability to read, in spite of the damage it would inflict on our memories. Now our brains are adapting once again to our new-found desires. We ourselves, not our media, are determining the kind of creatures we want to be; and our wits will remain our servants, not our masters.

31 What point does the reviewer make in the first paragraph?

    A Carr's views closely echo those of people in earlier times.

    B Concerns about the impact of the internet are inevitable.

    C The content of all new media tends to be of dubious quality.

    D The internet can effectively take over from all other forms of media.

32 Which is the 'metaphor' referred to in line 10?

    A The internet has really done his head in.

    B His friends fear they have the same syndrome.

    C He can no longer read a book without getting fidgety.

    D The only way he absorbs information is in quick, small doses.

33 What point is made about the spread of writing in the fourth paragraph?

    A It made people reconsider the value of acquiring knowledge.

    B It led to life in ancient times becoming more complicated.

    C It weakened Socrates' position as a respected thinker.

    D It relieved people's minds of certain mental burdens.

34 What is the reviewer's main intention in the sixth paragraph?

    A to suggest how Carr's use of the internet could be more effective

    B to explain how Carr's ideas have been stimulated by the internet

    C to illustrate why an aspect of Carr's thinking may be misguided

    D to criticise the way Carr's book is constructed

35 What point does the reviewer make in the seventh paragraph?

    A People are already careful about how they use the internet.

    B Human beings are good at adapting to new circumstances.

    C Reading long works of fiction is a waste of time these days.

    D It may be too late to worry about the impact of the internet.

36 What does the reviewer suggest in the final paragraph?

    A People are responsible for the internet rather than the other way round.

    B The impact the internet is having on us is similar to that of reading.

    C Our enthusiasm for the internet is ultimately beyond our control.

    D Carr's sense of unease about the internet has some justification.

You are going to read four contributions made by students to a debate about whether university education should be free of charge. For questions **37–40**, choose from the contributions **A–D**. The contributions may be chosen more than once.

Mark your answers **on the separate answer sheet**.

Should university education be free of charge?

In most countries, students have to pay fees to study at university, but there are some countries where the state guarantees a free higher education to all citizens with appropriate qualifications. Should free university education be a universal right? Four students give their views.

A

Free university education should be a universal right, but it makes sense for other reasons too. It gives talented people, irrespective of background, the opportunity to gain the knowledge, skills and qualifications that countries need citizens to have if they are to compete in the modern global economy. It enables the less affluent to break out of the class they are born into, and keeps society dynamic and aspirational. The state funding that allows free access also lets universities focus on what they do best, research and teaching, rather than administering fee payment and searching for private sponsorship. Claims that governments are no longer able to pay for free higher education because of competing demands on public finances conveniently ignore the fact that universities are free in some successful countries. Any government with the will to do so – and surveys suggest they would be supported by the wider population – could shift spending away from unproductive sectors like defence and into higher education.

B

There is little doubt that degree programmes benefit from the level of state funding that is necessary to make higher education free for all. Where universities are largely self-financing, inordinate time, energy and talent is invested in attracting fee-paying students and research-supporting corporate investors. The fact that a number of countries around the world offer free university education of a very high standard proves that it is still a viable proposition, but it would undoubtedly be difficult for a country to change to such a system. Free higher education is ultimately paid for by taxes, and, in this day and age, taxpayers are generally unwilling to pay more, particularly if it is to enable young people, mostly from well-off backgrounds, to qualify for lucrative employment. The idea that free higher education benefits anyone apart from those who would attend fee-paying degree courses anyway is largely illusory.

C

State-funded, free university education is a fine idea in principle. Besides giving all individuals the opportunity to become more knowledgeable and cultured, it also frees universities from the messy, distracting business of having to find ways to finance their work and allows them to focus on enhancing the student experience and carrying out research. The reality, however, is that the cost of paying for higher education is ruinously high for the state. Public-sector debt in many countries is astronomical, and governments have no choice but to prioritise spending. Unfortunately, higher education comes low down on the list of priorities. Also, the evidence suggests that people who want to go to university will generally find a way to finance themselves, whatever their class or background. Fee-paying does not particularly encourage underprivileged youngsters into higher education but neither does free university access.

D

In most modern economies, free university education is an illusion. Governments find it hard to provide adequate funds for healthcare, let alone a non-essential service like universities, and trying to convince people they should pay more taxes to finance university students is doomed to failure. States need university-educated citizens, but graduates can afford to pay for themselves, either up-front because of family background or retrospectively by paying off loans. Fee-paying makes no substantial difference to the number of people attending universities, and the figures suggest that people from particular socio-economic backgrounds are neither put off university by having to pay for it nor motivated to attend by having free access. In those countries where university fees have recently been introduced, the impact on universities themselves has been striking. Free of state influence, they have realised that they will only stay in business if they provide an excellent service to their clients, the students.

Which expert

takes a similar view to A about whether the state
can afford to finance free higher education?

37

has a different opinion from the others about how
state funding might affect the quality of university education?

38

has a different view from the others regarding the
implications of free university education for social mobility?

39

shares D's opinion about public attitudes regarding
free university education?

40

PAPER 1 Reading and ▸
            Use of English

PAPER 2 Writing

PAPER 3 Listening

PAPER 4 Speaking

Part 1
Part 2
Part 3
Part 4
Part 5
Part 6
Part 7
Part 8

You are going to read a magazine article about emotional intelligence and work. Six paragraphs have been removed from the article. Choose from the paragraphs **A–G** the one which fits each gap (**41–46**). There is one extra paragraph which you do not need to use.

Mark your answers **on the separate answer sheet.**

Emotional intelligence: thinking and feeling at work

Psychologists say 'emotional intelligence' can help manage our thinking and improve our behaviour at work and in our personal lives. Jill Insley reports.

If you work in an economy which is going through difficulties, the chances are you're calling on your emotional intelligence (EI) less than you might like, according to research which shows that the art of identifying, understanding and managing your emotions to improve your performance appears to decline in tough economic times. A team of occupational psychologists led by John Cooper studied 12,400 workers, mainly from the UK managerial population between 2001 and 2010, and found that use of emotional intelligence increased steadily during the economically strong years of 2001 to 2007, but dropped sharply between 2008 and 2010 during a banking crisis and recession.

41

The term 'emotional intelligence' was first used in psychology in 1966, and although several different interpretations have developed since then it is still a relatively new field. Cooper's report describes it as an 'innate human attribute' which, if understood and used well, can help us manage our thinking and feeling to improve our behaviour and relationships.

42

Emotional intelligence is divided into two main areas: personal intelligence and interpersonal intelligence. These, in turn, are split into 16 measurable scales including self-regard and regard for others, self-awareness and awareness of others, emotional resilience, flexibility, trust and emotional expression.

43

Measuring emotional intelligence can also identify areas of development for employees in specific

positions. An awareness of where you sit on each scale can help determine whether you need extra training, or will excel in a particular industry or sector. Self-employed people score higher than any other occupational group, possibly because there is a greater need to be emotionally intelligent if you are mostly dependent upon yourself for your success.

44

The study found that senior managers and directors tend to score highly in all aspects, but especially in self-belief, emotional resilience, positive outlook, going after goals, conflict handling and independence. Low scores on some of these scales, however, can have a negative impact on others, especially if the low scorer holds a senior position.

45

Another executive, by contrast, approached a colleague about the performance of a manager he was responsible for with the words, 'I think I've put him into the wrong position because he is very good, but he's not thriving. What's your opinion?' This showed humility and openness, features of good emotional intelligence.

46

The consequence of this appears to be that employees feel liked, competent and significant, and the business has become more productive and profitable. The implication to be drawn from this would seem to be that unlike personality traits and IQ, emotional intelligence can be changed and developed, which, in turn, can have a positive impact on work and economic activity.

A Having observed both approaches, one senior manager decided his own firm would benefit from the incorporation of emotional intelligence into management methods. Training to this end was accordingly organised.

B Results for other work sectors also proved interesting. People with jobs in health, for example, scored significantly lower in self-regard, which may result in them putting the needs of others first, while those in the sales sector scored strongly on self-assuredness, not being easily put off and being able to connect with people without being overly caring.

C 'If we liken the mind to a high-performance engine,' it goes on to say, then this 'would be the oil that enables us to maintain and manage ourselves to perform to our full potential.'

D Despite this, those who feel their effectiveness generally – but especially at work – isn't up to scratch, need not despair. Emotional intelligence is not fixed and can be enhanced. In order to do this, however, you need to know what your EI rating is.

E Using these categories, the study came up with results which seem to confirm some commonly held presumptions. For instance, while there is no significant difference between men and women in overall scores, men have a more critical mindset with higher self-esteem and lower estimation of others. Women, by contrast, tend to have lower self-esteem and higher valuation of others. Also, emotional intelligence improves with age, as we develop a more balanced outlook and become less dependent on, but more trusting of, others.

F In an example of this, six managers were asked by a company director to present their views of why a particular problem had emerged in the business. After the first person had outlined what he thought the problem was, the director shouted, 'So you've been lying to me for a year.' Who around that table would now say what they thought the problem was?

G The likelihood is that when facing uncertainty people may feel threatened and switch into 'survival mode' to try to protect what they have. Moreover, 'this can make things worse as workers become less adaptive and responsive to change, and may miss business or personal opportunities.'

You are going to read an article in which critics talk about crime writers that they like. For questions **47–56**, choose from the critics (**A–D**). The critics may be chosen more than once.

Mark your answers **on the separate answer sheet**.

Which crime writer is described as

having discovered a way of staying fresh as a crime novelist?	47
appearing to mix different genres at times?	48
using personal experience to good effect ?	49
using the genre to explore wider social issues?	50
expressing authentic feelings through their writing?	51
possessing great command of conventional crime fiction techniques?	52
exploring a particular geographical setting in an interesting way?	53
having substantially raised the calibre of their work at a certain point?	54
being prepared to take artistic risks?	55
writing in a concise style?	56

Critics' choice of crime writers

A Peter Temple

I started reading Peter Temple's books about ten years ago, and at the time it was fairly orthodox crime fiction set in Australia, much of it involving horse-racing. Then suddenly, with *The Broken Shore*, he hit something quite different and moved up several notches. Since then he has been writing the kind of novels many authors spend a lifetime striving for. He comes out of a line of taut, tough crime fiction that starts with Dashiell Hammett, writing in America in the 1920s and 30s, and goes through the Swedish authors Sjöwall and Wahlöö to William McIlvanney in Scotland over the last 40 years. Crime fiction with them is not just about the story; it's also a vehicle for saying something about the contexts within which the action happens. Frequently using dialogue instead of description, and providing an object lesson in how to say a lot without unnecessary verbiage, Temple absolutely nails the connections between politics, the police and the media. If you want to know anything about the media invasion of privacy, say, it's there.

B Liza Cody

There is a lot of good, slick writing out there that turns me off because it's unfelt. If, like me, you look for writers with a gift for language and storytelling, and who possess a willingness to do the hard work of digging into the nitty-gritty of emotional life, Liza Cody is likely to appeal. She doesn't just do the easy thing to be recognised in the marketplace; she goes where the story and her curiosity take her. For instance, she had to self-publish one book, *Ballad of a Dead Nobody*, because no one in the industry was willing to. She had a successful series with a private eye called Anna Lee but she branched out and did some unusual books about a woman wrestler. These days, genre writers are told to create a brand or a series, a recognisable hook. Cody will often turn her back on that and focus on what her inner voice is telling her, which requires courage.

C Michael Connelly

The first Connelly book I read was *The Poet*, his first stand-alone novel and a big breakthrough for him. By then, he had written four books in his Harry Bosch series, which I went back to read. Connelly has maintained a level of quality through a long-running series – an incredibly difficult thing to pull off. He does it by stepping away for a while and writing books such as *The Poet* and *Blood Work*, and then he comes back to it fired up with renewed vitality. People talk about how you create suspense and use cliffhangers, reveals and so on, and Connelly is an admirable exponent of all that, but the real secret is to create characters the readers care about. Bosch, a detective in the Los Angeles Police Department, is a character who has grown and changed, who you come to know and empathise with. All that aside, he is a fantastic storyteller. I think his days as a crime reporter on *The Los Angeles Times* stood him in good stead because he never forgets the story.

D Johan Theorin

I read Theorin's novel, *Echoes from the Dead*, when judging a competition for a crime fiction prize. It's the first of a quartet of stories, all of which take place on an island in the Baltic Sea. They are very atmospheric. They have this interesting detective who is elderly and lives in a sheltered housing complex, so he can't be out there doing car chases. Theorin is very good on the unspoken secrets of small communities. The first book takes place in the summer and the second, *The Darkest Room*, in the winter. It's about this crumbling house by the shore and there seems to be a supernatural thread running through it. It's as if the narrative switches into the realms of fantasy now and then. It has the most wonderful climax, but Theorin is ready to take his time over the telling of the story, which is unusual these days. If you look at the bestsellers, they are quite pacey and macho. There is nothing wrong with that, but Theorin writes in a much more textured, literary way.

PAPER 1 Reading and
         Use of English

PAPER 2 Writing ▶ **Part 1**
                          Part 2

PAPER 3 Listening

PAPER 4 Speaking

You **must** answer this question. Write your answer in **220–260** words in an appropriate style on the separate answer sheet.

1   You are doing a Marketing course. As part of the module on advertising strategies, your tutor asks whether advertising is typically designed to exploit or inform, and opens it to a class debate. You have made the notes below.

> **Advertising: Exploitation or Information?**
>
> • Of course it's information-based, how else will consumers learn about the product?
> • Most companies care too much about their reputation to risk false or unclear advertising.
> • There's information *and* persuasion; intelligent people know the difference.

> **Other opinions expressed included:**
>
> "Advertising exploits; it makes people feel bad for not buying things they don't even need."
>
> "It deliberately targets children and vulnerable people, who are less able to discriminate."
>
> "It exaggerates certain things and makes misleading claims."

Write an essay for your tutor discussing **two** of the points from your notes. You should **explain whether you think advertising is typically designed to exploit or inform** and **provide reasons** to support your opinions.

You may, if you wish, make use of the opinions expressed in the seminar, but you should use your own words as far as possible.

Write an answer to **one** of the questions **2–4** in this part. Write your answer in **220–260** words in an appropriate style on the separate answer sheet. Put the question number in the box at the top of the page.

---

2 You see a poster at the train station announcing the arrival of a large circus in your town. As you are opposed to wild animals being kept in captivity, especially being confined and constantly transported, you decide to state your objections and lobby your local council to have the event cancelled.

Write your **letter**.

3 In recent months, the cafeteria at the company where you work has been consistently losing money. Fewer and fewer members of staff are choosing to have their lunch there, and the chances of the cafeteria closing down are high. The office manager has sent a company-wide email inviting employees to submit a report detailing the existing issues and making suggestions for improvements.

Write your **report**.

4 You see this notice on an events website based in your area.

> **WE NEED YOUR HELP**
>
> Here at the Riverfront Theatre we'd like to add to our database of event reviews. If you were at last night's concert given by the student band, *Atmosphere*, we'd love to hear from you. Please send your review of the concert to the email address below.

Write your **review**.

Track 29

You will hear three different extracts. For questions **1–6**, choose the answer (**A**, **B** or **C**) which fits best according to what you hear. There are two questions for each extract.

Extract One

You hear two friends discussing studying.

1 What fundamental point does the man disagree with?
   A having to spend so much time studying
   B having to value doing unpleasant things
   C having to enjoy the present moment

2 What point does the woman clarify?
   A that people needn't seek out difficult tasks
   B that no one can escape their responsibilities
   C that the magazine article was a reliable source

Extract Two

You hear a woman admitting that she told a lie.

3 What was the problem with Brooke's choice of song?
   A It wasn't a good tune.
   B It was a sad love song.
   C It didn't suit her voice.

4 The woman lied because
   A she and Brooke are not very close friends.
   B Brooke is passionate about music.
   C she wanted to protect Brooke's feelings.

Extract Three

You hear two people discussing Facebook.

5 Which statement best describes the woman's attitude?
   A The neighbour's opinion is correct.
   B The neighbour is entitled to his opinion.
   C The neighbour's opinion is not correct.

6 The man is irritated because his neighbour
   A laughed at his attempts to explain Facebook.
   B dismissed Facebook without having tried it.
   C easily won the argument about Facebook.

Track 30

You will hear a man talking about genetically-modified (GM) foods. For questions **7–14**, complete the sentences with a word or short phrase.

GENETICALLY-MODIFIED FOODS

The objective of genetically-modified foods is to **(7)** ....
crops and plants so that they perform better.

The speaker says his father feels sorry for UK farmers and their
(8) .... against climate change.

One effect of failed crops due to weather conditions is
(9) .... for some farmers.

The speaker's mother objects to genetic engineering and feels it is dangerous to
(10) .... with how plants naturally grow.

The speaker himself feels that GM foods should not be entirely
(11) .... by governments in Europe and the UK.

His view is that we should be careful not to declare GM foods safe until
(12) .... have been carried out.

His father feels that it shouldn't be a complicated matter to ensure that the correct
labelling of foodstuffs is **(13)** ....

The speaker concludes that his own family is a good
(14) .... of public opinion on the GM debate.

PAPER 1 Reading and
Use of English

PAPER 2 Writing

PAPER 3 Listening ▶

PAPER 4 Speaking

Part 1
Part 2
Part 3
Part 4

🎧 **Track 31**

You will hear three members of an interview panel discussing the two candidates,
John and Rebecca, who are finalists for the job. For questions **15–20**, choose the
answer (**A**, **B**, **C** or **D**) which fits best according to what you hear.

15 Based on the discussion, what kind of job do you think the candidates have
applied for?
A   marketing
B   sales
C   research
D   design

16 What point does the man mention in Rebecca's favour?
A   She seems like someone with good ideas.
B   She is much more of an introvert than John.
C   She made an effort to learn about the company.
D   Her professional background might be useful.

17 What concern was expressed about how John described his weak points?
A   his lack of consideration
B   his lack of confidence
C   his lack of responsibility
D   his lack of communication

18 Based on the comments from the panel, as an employee Rebecca would
probably be very
A   dynamic.
B   self-conscious.
C   pushy.
D   conscientious.

19 Based on the comments from the panel, as an employee John would probably
A   make a good impression.
B   not cope under pressure.
C   excel in the role.
D   trust his own instincts.

20 By the end of the discussion, the panel members seem to be
A   clear on who they will vote for.
B   unanimous about Rebecca.
C   unanimous about John.
D   undecided on who they'll vote for.

Track 32

You will hear five short extracts in which people talk about a challenging experience they have had.

While you listen you must complete both tasks.

TASK ONE

For questions **21–25**, choose from the list (**A–H**) how the incident affected each speaker when it happened.

A started having nightmares	
B got quite depressed	Speaker 1 ☐ 21
C wouldn't go outside	Speaker 2 ☐ 22
D lost all self-confidence	Speaker 3 ☐ 23
E stopped feeling safe	Speaker 4 ☐ 24
F developed a fear of dying	Speaker 5 ☐ 25
G experienced anxiety	
H became a little hysterical	

TASK TWO

For questions **26–30**, choose from the list (**A–H**) how each speaker feels about the experience now.

A has become quite obsessive	
B no longer has any patience	Speaker 1 ☐ 26
C is still trying to get over it	Speaker 2 ☐ 27
D is embarrassed about it	Speaker 3 ☐ 28
E exercises increased awareness	Speaker 4 ☐ 29
F has a more optimistic outlook	Speaker 5 ☐ 30
G doesn't ever think about it	
H has put it into perspective	

Part 1 (2 minutes)

The examiner will ask you a few questions about yourself and about a general topic. For example, the examiner may ask you:

- **What's your favourite thing about where you are from?**
- **What's the biggest change you've experienced in your life so far?**
- **Are you a 'morning person'? Explain why (not)**

Part 2 (4 minutes)

You will each be asked to talk on your own for about a minute. You will each be given three different pictures to talk about. After your partner has finished speaking, you will be asked a brief question connected with your partner's photographs.

> **In the spotlight** (compare, contrast and speculate)

Turn to pictures 1–3 on page **190**, which show people in the spotlight.

(*Candidate A*), it's your turn first. Here are your pictures. They show **situations in which people are in the spotlight**.

I'd like you to compare **two** of the pictures and say **what is happening in these photos and how you think the people might be feeling**.

(*Candidate B*), **do you enjoy being in the spotlight? Why (not)?**

> **Less than happy** (compare, contrast and speculate)

Turn to pictures 1–3 on page **191**, which show people who appear to be unhappy.

Now, (*Candidate B*), here are your pictures. They show **people who appear to be unhappy**. I'd like you to compare **two** of the pictures and say **which emotions each person is probably feeling and what probably made them feel this way**.

(*Candidate A*), **do you think that people have a responsibility to be happy in life? Why (not)?**

Part 3 (4 minutes)

Look at page **192**, which shows some things people can do to go green.

> **Ways of going green** (discuss, evaluate and negotiate)

Here are some things people can do to go green and help the planet.

First you have some time to look at the task.

(*Pause 15 seconds*)

Now talk to each other about **which of these things most people are likely to do, and why**.

Now you have a minute to decide **which step you feel people would have the most difficulty adopting**, and **what could be done to change that**.

Part 4 (5 minutes)

The examiner will encourage you to develop the topic of your discussion in Part 3 by asking questions such as:

- Generally speaking, do you feel most people are willing to sacrifice certain things for the greater good of the planet? Why (not)?

- Some people claim that experts have exaggerated climate change and that reports on global warming are mostly propaganda? What's your view on this?

- What would you say is the single biggest obstacle to making the earth greener?

CAMBRIDGE ENGLISH
Language Assessment
Part of the University of Cambridge

Do not write in this box

Candidate Name
If not already printed, write name
in CAPITALS and complete the
Candidate No. grid (in pencil).

Candidate Signature

Examination Title

Centre

Supervisor:
If the candidate is ABSENT or has WITHDRAWN shade here ▭

SAMPLE

Centre No.

Candidate No.

Examination
Details

0	0	0	0
1	1	1	1
2	2	2	2
3	3	3	3
4	4	4	4
5	5	5	5
6	6	6	6
7	7	7	7
8	8	8	8
9	9	9	9

Candidate Answer Sheet

Instructions
Use a PENCIL (B or HB). Rub out any answer you wish to change using an eraser.

Parts 1 and 5-8: Mark ONE letter for each question.

For example, if you think **B** is the right answer to the question, mark your answer sheet like this:

0　A　B　C　D

Parts 2, 3 and **4:** Write your answer clearly in CAPITAL LETTERS.

For Parts 2 and 3 write one letter in each box. For example:

0　EXAMPLE

Part 1

1	A	B	C	D
2	A	B	C	D
3	A	B	C	D
4	A	B	C	D
5	A	B	C	D
6	A	B	C	D
7	A	B	C	D
8	A	B	C	D

Part 2

Do not write below here

9   9 1 0 u

10   10 1 0 u

11   11 1 0 u

12   12 1 0 u

13   13 1 0 u

14   14 1 0 u

15   15 1 0 u

16   16 1 0 u

Continues over ➡

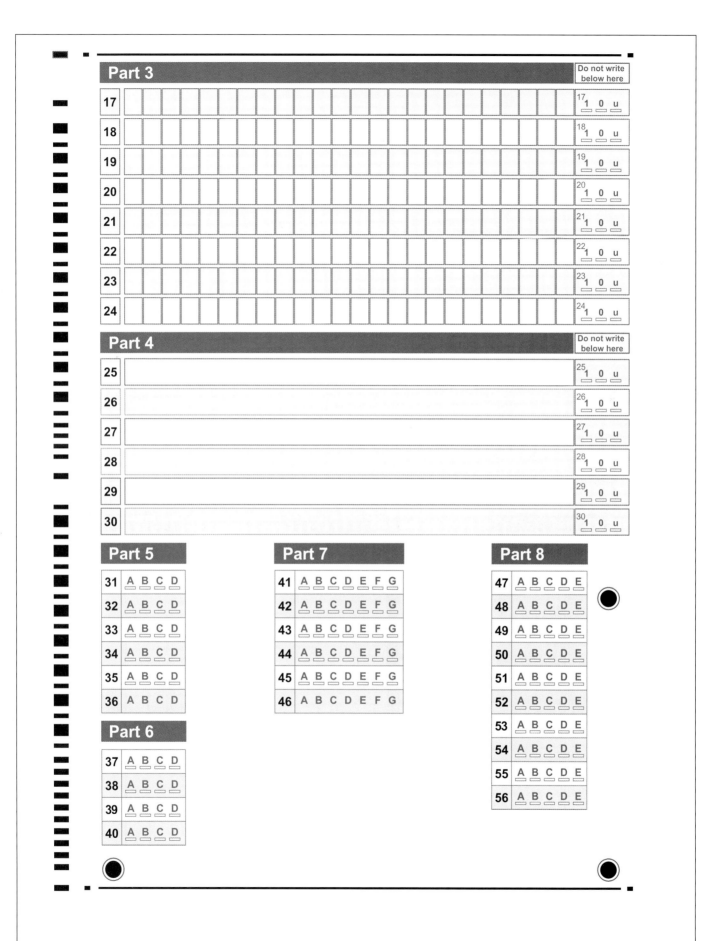

Part 3

		Do not write below here
17		17 1 0 u
18		18 1 0 u
19		19 1 0 u
20		20 1 0 u
21		21 1 0 u
22		22 1 0 u
23		23 1 0 u
24		24 1 0 u

Part 4

		Do not write below here
25		25 1 0 u
26		26 1 0 u
27		27 1 0 u
28		28 1 0 u
29		29 1 0 u
30		30 1 0 u

Part 5

31 A B C D
32 A B C D
33 A B C D
34 A B C D
35 A B C D
36 A B C D

Part 6

37 A B C D
38 A B C D
39 A B C D
40 A B C D

Part 7

41 A B C D E F G
42 A B C D E F G
43 A B C D E F G
44 A B C D E F G
45 A B C D E F G
46 A B C D E F G

Part 8

47 A B C D E
48 A B C D E
49 A B C D E
50 A B C D E
51 A B C D E
52 A B C D E
53 A B C D E
54 A B C D E
55 A B C D E
56 A B C D E

Paper 3 Listening

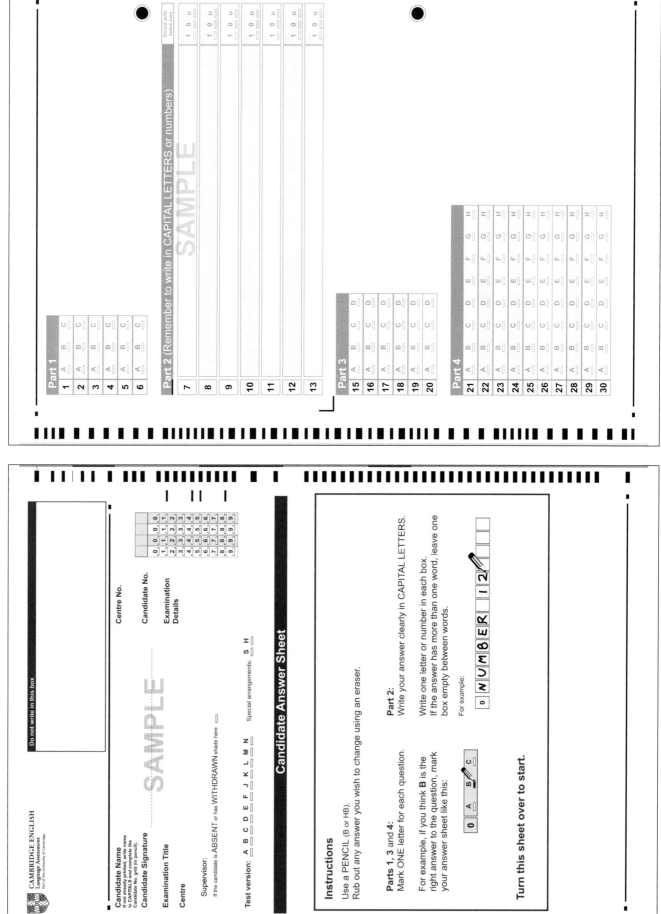

ADVANCED
TEST 1

▸▸ **PART 2**

Candidate A

Language bank

These people are likely …

They seem to be paying close attention.

They appear to be completely absorbed in what they are seeing and hearing.

This audience is probably …

The people in this picture look like they're being highly entertained.

I'm quite sure they're enjoying themselves.

I'd say these people are …

I'm not certain, but I think …

By the looks of things here …

There's a sense of anticipation in this picture.

In this one, however, there is clearly a great deal of tension.

The spectators look quite nervous here.

They can't bear to watch the match.

By contrast …

amused
anxious
auditorium
edge of their seat
entertainment
fascinated
football match
football supporters
lecture
listening intently
nervous
night out
presentation
screen
seminar
serious
sports event

- **What kind of event are the people attending?**
- **How are they responding to the event?**

▸ **1**

▸ **2**

▸ **3**

▶▶ **PART 2**

Candidate B

- **What kind of person would choose this job?**
- **What kind of challenges might the job present?**

Language bank

This looks like …

I imagine this is …

This person is almost certainly friendly and outgoing.

They would need to have …

They'd have to be …

This would be the sort of person who can work independently.

This role requires focus and attention to detail.

In this job, however …

This job needs a lot of patience.

As the picture shows, …

On the other hand, …

But in this role, …

It could be that …

attention to detail
department store
driving instructor
engaging
explain things clearly
hardware engineer
intense
keep the customer satisfied
patient
PC repair
people skills
personable
personal shopper
put people at their ease
sales assistant
technical skills
technician
unflappable
work alone

▶ 1

▶ 2

▶ 3

▶▶ **PART 3**
Candidates A and B

Language bank

Yes, I would definitely say it's important, and my main reason for that is …

I'm not completely against it; I just don't think it's all that important. What's your view?

While there certainly are some benefits, such as …

Don't you think teenagers are a little young to be burdened with saving?

At the same time, however …

Being prepared for emergencies is very important. Would you agree?

Do you really feel that saving money would make teenagers feel good about themselves? I'm not so sure.

The way I see it, saving brings a kind of independence, which can only be a good thing.

I'm a little concerned about the idea of teenagers having to worry about later life.

I must say, the idea that saving money will make their dreams come true is quite misleading; wouldn't you agree?

What would you say about the benefit of establishing financial security early?

avoid debt	pay into
bank statements	put towards
cash flow	run out
current account	save for a rainy day
deposit	save up
generate interest	set financial goals
learn the value of money	track your spending
make ends meet	(a) waste of money

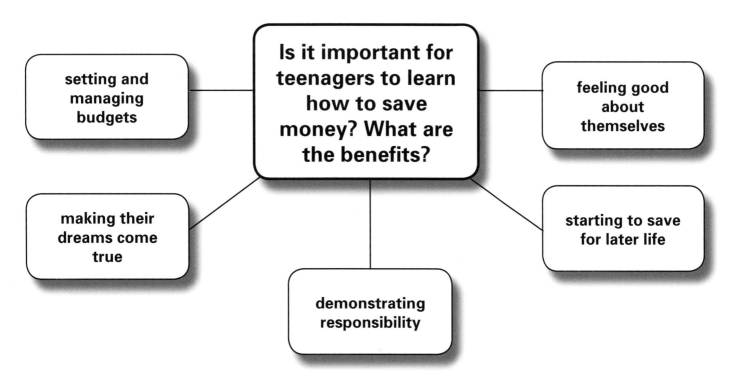

setting and managing budgets

Is it important for teenagers to learn how to save money? What are the benefits?

feeling good about themselves

making their dreams come true

starting to save for later life

demonstrating responsibility

▸▸ **PART 2**

Candidate A

Language bank

This one appears to be a nice corner café.

It's possibly in a university town.

It may be frequented by students.

It's clear that this one is more exclusive.

These restaurants are quite different …

By contrast, this one is …

Here, you'll notice …

I'm fairly sure that …

If you look at the furniture …

It seems a safe bet that this is a fast-food restaurant.

I can tell that …

I would say that this one …

Here, however …

affordable
casual dining
complex dishes
expensive
fine dining
inexpensive
junk food
moderately priced
pavement patio
popular
relaxed atmosphere
simple fare
special occasion
top of the line
unhealthy options
unusual ingredients
wealthy clientele

- What kinds of dishes are probably served in each restaurant?
- Who would typically dine here?

▶▶ **PART 2**
 Candidate B

Language bank

You could reasonably guess that …

This might be …

My assumption is …

This collector is almost certainly an older person.

I suppose you could say …

While it's important to avoid stereotypes …

They would need to have an interest in music.

It's just a guess, but …

I imagine that …

They'd have to be …

But it's also possible that …

This would probably be the sort of person who …

ambitious
an eye for pretty objects
ceramics
(a) collectible
comfortably off
delicate
desirable
for personal pleasure
hand-painted
(an) investment
middle aged
music fan
obsessed with
outward appearance
passionate about
pottery
rare
recognise quality
retired person
serious collector
sought-after
teapots
vast collection
vintage cars
vinyl / LPs
worth a fortune

- **What kind of person would collect these items?**
- **Why do people collect things?**

▶ 1

▶ 2

▶ 3

▶▶ **PART 3**

Candidates A and B

Language bank

From my point of view, online learning has more benefits than traditional classroom learning.

We've clearly seen real benefits for students since e-learning became popular. Do you agree?

Let's not forget some of the key disadvantages, however.

I see what you're saying, but I think you have to look at the overall picture.

Yes, I know what you mean. That is a concern.

At the end of the day, it's hard to see how a computer program can ever replace a real teacher.

But don't you think that this is simply the way of the future?

I feel it really depends on the individual student. What about you?

To be honest, I think the benefits for both types of learning are about equal.

access any time
case-by-case basis
chat rooms
consider all angles
dynamic
engaging
focus on your own needs
gives the learner more independence
immediate feedback
lack the confidence to work alone
online forums
online support
peer review
prefer a classroom setting
regular interaction
risk falling behind
study in a familiar environment
too much responsibility for some students
when you take into account …

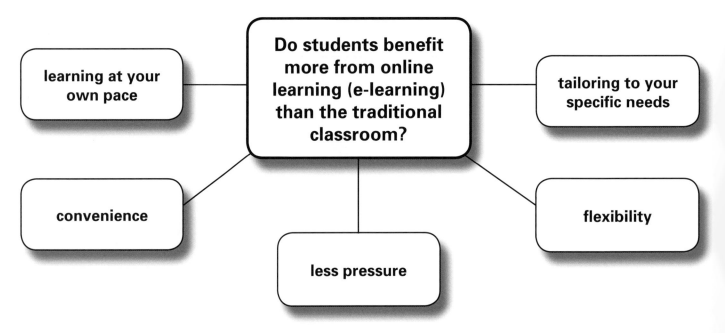

▸▸ **PART 2**

Candidate A

- How do these people appear to be feeling, and why?
- What kind of negative emotions do you think they might be feeling?

Language bank

By all appearances, these people are thrilled.

You can tell that they're incredibly happy.

The look on her face is pure delight.

Their happiness really shines through.

They're clearly overjoyed, and probably quite proud too.

Their delight is obvious.

It's possible that they also feel a little nervous.

They may be experiencing some anxiety as well.

These are big steps which can be quite overwhelming.

Deep down they could feel just a bit uneasy too.

best day of their lives
bride and groom
bundle of joy
celebration
deeply in love
first-time home-buyers
get on the property ladder
hand in hand
happy and healthy new baby
home is where the heart is
home sweet home
marital bliss
mortgage
parental responsibility
patter of tiny feet
place to call their own
tie the knot
wedding reception

▶▶ PART 2
Candidate B

• How do these shopping experiences differ?
• Is each method of shopping suited to a different type of person? Why?

Language bank

This one appears to be quite an expensive shop.

The woman shopping here is presumably very wealthy.

You can tell from the interior that it's quite an exclusive place.

Here we have an outdoor market with various stalls.

This one appears to be a more casual shopping experience.

All kinds of people enjoy browsing at markets like these.

You can find everything from antiques to junk.

You can shop online in the comfort of your own home.

Online shopping has become extremely popular.

I think this is probably the most convenient way to shop.

You can find some real bargains online.

at the touch of a button
bohemian
bric-a-brac
click of the mouse
crafts
credit card fraud
delivered to your door
designer goods
e-commerce
flea market
haggle
high-end store
interesting artefacts
opulence
personal service
quick and easy
shipping costs
something might catch your eye
street vendors

▶ 1

▶ 2

▶ 3

▶▶ **PART 3**
Candidates A and B

Language bank

When you're in a salaried job you have the benefit of a team environment, which is a good thing, I think.

That's true; you have the support of a manager and also of your colleagues.

It seems to me that employees have a more structured work day.

You can count on receiving a regular salary when you work for a company, can't you?

It's a valid point, and it helps with financial planning.

On the other hand, if you're self-employed you have much more flexibility.

Don't you think it's a lot of responsibility to stay on top of things?

But if it's your own business I imagine you would be motivated to run it well.

I expect it must get lonely sometimes, being self-employed.

Some people probably would feel lonely, but not necessarily everyone.

People who work for themselves can go out to lunch and do other social things.

be left to your own devices	freelancer
be your own boss	get burned out
bite off more than you can chew	goal-oriented
bureaucracy	independent
cash-flow problems	lack of commuter stress
climb the corporate ladder	manage all aspects of the business
common goals	management style
company policy	nine to five
corporate environment	office politics
disciplined	rat race
dress code	team player
driven	team spirit
endless meetings	toe the line
focus on what you enjoy	work to your strengths

fixed salary/ consistent income

Is it better to be employed full-time by a company, or to work for yourself (be self-employed)?

job security

time management and discipline

potential isolation

team environment

▶▶ **PART 2**

Candidate A

> • What type of person do you think each woman is?
> • Does their choice of beverage say anything about their lifestyle?

Language bank

It seems reasonable to assume that …

Looking at this, I would imagine …

My guess is that this person enjoys good coffee.

She probably likes relaxing with a coffee.

Her lifestyle could be a busy one, and coffee keeps her going.

This woman has gone with the healthy option.

Clearly, she has made an effort to blend fruit for a healthy drink.

She might be a fitness instructor, or a dance teacher.

It's possible that she's on a diet.

It looks like the young woman is enjoying a fizzy drink.

She may be enjoying a cold drink on a warm day.

Drinks like these often have a high sugar content and are quite unhealthy.

She seems quite relaxed and easy-going.

artificial sweetener
bubbly personality
caffeine fix
carbonated
chilling out
coffee addict
coffee break
detox
down-time
keep-fit enthusiast
milkshake
probably caffeinated
smoothie
soft drink
sugar high
super foods

▶ 1

▶ 2

▶ 3

▶▶ PART 2

Candidate B

- **What do you imagine are the circumstances in each picture?**
- **How might these people be feeling?**

Language bank

This man is obviously on a train platform.

He may have missed his train.

He could be there to meet his girlfriend off the train.

Who knows; maybe he just enjoys looking at trains!

He doesn't look very happy, but perhaps he's feeling pensive.

Maybe he's just arrived somewhere new.

He looks like a man with things on his mind.

This appears to be the waiting room at a dentist or doctor's office.

Some of the people could be there with a friend or partner.

It's likely that they're feeling unwell or apprehensive.

One of them seems to be quite preoccupied.

They could be at the clinic to get a vaccination, for example, a flu shot.

She's wearing a business suit. This could be a sales meeting for her job.

She might be attending a business meeting.

I would definitely say that she's there for an interview.

Her body language makes me think that she probably feels quite relaxed.

But she could be feeling quite anxious.

anticipation
apprehension
business clothes
fearing the worst
outside the meeting room
reception area
straight posture
the screech of brakes
time passes slowly
train timetable
trying to pass the time
waiting in vain
waiting to be called
watching the clock

Language bank

Well, whichever way you look at it, I think social-networking sites are here to stay.

I accept that these sites have certain disadvantages but, overall, I feel our lives are improved by them. And, don't forget, they're fun!

To tell you the truth, I think they're the worst thing that ever happened. They create a false sense of friendship.

I must say, I agree with that point. People are forgetting how to socialise normally.

On balance, though, it depends on how you use them. What do you think?

That's a fair point. Too much of anything is a bad thing!

I've noticed that people can be more cruel online than in person and this worries me.

Sometimes you hear amazing stories about how long-lost friends, and even family members, have reconnected through social-networking sites. I think that's wonderful.

My concern is that people don't seem to know where to draw the line and they share too much personal information.

I suppose we're still learning how to exist in the online world and in social-networking sites.

activity log	online chat
block friends	post comments
comments thread	privacy settings
deactivate your account	private message
direct message	professional recommendation
endorsement	profile picture
follow (celebrities and others)	registered user
followers	secret group
friend request	set up an event
game applications	share photos
hashtag	status update
microblogging	tweet
newsfeed	

```
                          ┌──────────────────┐
 ┌──────────────┐         │       Are        │         ┌──────────────────┐
 │new friendships│        │ social-networking│         │less face-to-face │
 │form / old friends│─────│sites improving   │─────────│communication     │
 │   reconnect   │        │   our lives?     │         │makes people      │
 └──────────────┘         └──────────────────┘         │more isolated     │
                                                        └──────────────────┘
 ┌──────────────┐              │                        ┌──────────────────┐
 │    more      │              │                        │  professional    │
 │opportunities to│            │                        │networking sites  │
 │express thoughts│         ┌──────────────┐            │improve job       │
 │and share news │         │cyber-bullying │            │prospects         │
 └──────────────┘          │has become a   │            └──────────────────┘
                           │serious problem│
                           └──────────────┘
```

▸▸ **PART 2**

Candidate A

- **What kind of personality do you think each of the people has?**
- **How do you imagine their pet affects their life?**

Language bank

You could guess that the man is quite sporty.

He seems like an outdoor type.

This man might be ...

The old lady appears to be very content.

I imagine she's very sweet and loving, and probably a grandmother.

You could probably say ...

This boy obviously has a gentle disposition.

He must be quite a brave boy. Not all children like snakes!

He appears to be ...

People say they find having a pet very rewarding.

Owning a pet is a lot of responsibility; you have to take good care of them.

Most pets are good companions.

People feel less lonely when they have a pet.

Pets can be a lot of work, but they can also be a lot of fun.

Animals can be fascinating, we can learn a lot from them.

animal kingdom
canine
cold-blooded
feeding time
feline friend
high maintenance
independent traits
indoor cat
intelligent creature
loyal companion
man's best friend
non-poisonous
outdoor lifestyle
reptile
vet's bills
walk the dog

▸ 1

▸ 2

▸ 3

▶▶ PART 2

Candidate B

- Why do you think people do extreme sports?
- What kind of person might choose to do sports like these?

▶ 1

Language bank

I suppose people like the excitement.

There's a big thrill associated with these sports.

The sense of adventure is probably what draws most people.

I think it's all about the speed!

While these sports can be dangerous, they all have safety mechanisms.

They say that people become addicted to the rush of it all.

This looks like a huge adrenalin rush.

Arguably, all sports contain an element of danger.

It's probably a release for anger or stress.

To me, this one looks terrifying!

I imagine they feel a great sense of accomplishment.

It's about challenging yourself, isn't it?

Some people want to push themselves to the limit.

I think they're having enormous fun.

adrenalin junkie
daredevil
determined to succeed
exhausting
fearless
feeling the elements
going the distance
letting off steam
overcoming fears
physical exertion
ready for action
taking a chance
thrill-seeker
trusting
working together

▶ 2

▶ 3

▶▶ PART 3
Candidates A and B

Language bank

It seems to me that renting is fine for a temporary period, but buying is better in the long term.

Many people rent on a long-term basis. I don't see anything wrong in that.

In many countries it's simply not affordable for most people to buy a home.

Exactly. It's a choice that can vary from culture to culture.

Personally, I think you have a lot more freedom when you rent.

Money isn't the only consideration in buying a house. What about the stress?

There's more security in buying a property than renting one.

OK, that's true, but it's only an advantage if you actually like the home you've purchased.

Buying means having to pay property taxes, but this doesn't apply to renting.

borrower	lease
building society	lender
deposit	long-term loan
depreciation	maintenance
financing	mortgage
fixed rates	mortgage broker
guarantor	property ladder
hidden costs	property rules
home owner	property tax
interest rates	tenancy agreement
landlord / landlady	tenant

Is it better to rent or to own your home? What are the advantages and disadvantages?

- relocating easier when you rent
- owning a home is an excellent investment
- painting and decorating may not be permitted in a rented property
- necessary repairs taken care of when renting
- possible decrease in value of a bought home while there's still a mortgage

▶▶ PART 2

Candidate A

- What kind of medical condition might each of these practitioners treat?
- What are the cultural differences between these medical practices?

Language bank

In this picture we see a doctor doing his rounds in a hospital.

People go to hospital for complaints from diseases to broken bones.

This one seems to be a more traditional kind of medical practitioner, perhaps in herbal medicine.

She might help local people with stomach complaints, skin problems and other issues.

Here, there appears to be a psychiatrist with a patient.

This could also be a psychologist.

People suffering from depression or anxiety might visit a psychiatrist.

Sometimes people go to counselling if they are finding life difficult to cope with.

Hospitals and mental health professionals are common in most countries.

Various forms of alternative medicine are becoming more popular in western countries.

I don't know very much about this ...

Some people are very sceptical about this form of medicine.

bedside manner
behavioural problems
clinical psychology
conventional medicine
counselling / counsellor
diagnose / diagnosis
healer
healing properties of plants
herbal remedies
herbalist
hospital ward
medical advice
medical chart
mental health issues
personality disorders
prescribe / prescription
ritual
stethoscope
study of the mind
therapist / therapy
traditional medical practitioner
visiting time

> 1

> 2

> 3

▸▸ **PART 2**

Candidate B

- How are these places of learning different?
- What do they have in common?

Language bank

This one shows a modern, brightly lit lecture theatre.

It's probably a university; they look like college students.

Several students are taking notes on their laptops.

On the other hand, these appear to be primary school children.

It looks as though they're having a lesson under the shade of a tree.

My guess is that this is a hot country.

It might be a poor country without proper classroom facilities.

It's possible they just decided to have a class outside to enjoy the nice weather.

By contrast, this is a cookery class.

I'd say it's an adult education course.

It might be at a local community centre.

In all these cases, we can see people learning.

There is one instructor in each picture.

The students are listening or observing.

They all appear to be paying close attention.

blackboard
continuing education
degree course
demonstration
diploma
evening class
learning for pleasure
learning the basics
lecture theatre
lifelong learning
module
outdoor classroom
Powerpoint presentation
rudimentary
tertiary education
training programme
vocational college

▸ 1

▸ 2

▸ 3

▶▶ **PART 3**

Candidates A and B

Language bank

People should be aware that it's normal to feel homesick when you're away from home.

That's a good point.

In some ways, knowing what to expect is half the battle.

Exactly, and remembering that it takes time is important too, wouldn't you say?

Being as positive as possible will also make a big difference.

In principle, getting involved in the local community is a good idea, but it might not be practical.

Yes, there could be a language barrier, for one thing.

I see what you mean. Perhaps the suggestion to make new friends is a better one.

Learning about the other culture is vital, I think. What's your view?

Oh, absolutely. When there's less mystery, there's less difficulty.

Having someone to talk to is an excellent idea. It's important to express your feelings and it also helps you to feel less isolated.

a different climate	new environment
assumptions and beliefs	regional accents
cultural differences	rules of behaviour
different values	separation anxiety
emotional state	snap judgements
etiquette	social norms
frustration	stereotyping
language barrier	take comfort in familiar things
local cuisine	take up a new hobby
loneliness and isolation	try to integrate
longing for home	unfamiliar surroundings
mood swings	well-being

What can people do to manage symptoms of homesickness and culture shock?

- talking about how you are feeling
- getting involved in the local community
- making an effort to understand cultural differences
- staying positive for the time it takes to adjust
- making new friends and participating in social events

▶ ▶ **PART 2**

Candidate A

• What kind of impact does each situation have on people?
• Can these situations be avoided or not?

Language bank

The impact of these situations can vary.

In the modern world, having to wait can bring about stress.

Traffic jams can sometimes be avoided by travelling on quieter roads.

If a traffic jam is caused by an accident, there isn't really any way to avoid it.

We can't see the people but it's likely that they're feeling stressed by the delays.

If you're flying, airport security is simply unavoidable.

People sometimes feel edgy and nervous going through airport security.

Getting frustrated doesn't help the situation.

The more organised people are, the quicker the process goes.

Identity theft can have a devastating impact, both financially and emotionally.

No one likes it when their privacy is violated.

These days, whether we like it or not, computer hackers and viruses are a fact of life.

We should install anti-virus software on our computers.

People should be careful about what information they share online.

backed up for miles
bumper to bumper
carry-on luggage
firewall
frayed nerves
hackers
high anxiety levels
highly stressful
identity theft
malware
metal detector
online security
password protection
permitted items
phishing
privacy settings
security guards
serious congestion
spyware
stuck in traffic
take the necessary precautions
total gridlock
traffic is at a standstill
virus writers
x-ray screening

▶ 1

▶ 2

▶ 3

http://www.

Virus Alert!
Warning! Threat detected!
A malicious item has been detected!

▸▸ PART 2

Candidate B

• What kinds of skills are needed to do each of these jobs well?
• Are men or women better suited to each occupation?

Language bank

People who work in construction need to be very aware of safety.

They also need stamina as the work can be heavy, and they have to be outside in all weathers.

I think it's becoming a more common career choice for women than it used to be.

To be a nurse or carer, a person needs to be reliable and patient.

It's a care profession, so it's important to have compassion and empathy too.

It's usually viewed as 'women's work' but the stereotype is changing and more men are choosing this profession.

Working as a plumber requires training and official qualifications.

As you work with the public, you also need to be personable.

There's been a huge increase in the number of women training in trades such as plumbing.

These days people are freer to choose whatever profession they want.

Personally, I don't believe that men are better suited to some roles and women to others.

From my point of view it's more about personality. Your character makes you more suited to one role or another, not your gender.

blockage
boiler repair
carer
construction site
dripping taps
efficient
fixing leaks
high-visibility jacket
nursing profession
pneumatic drill
safety equipment
scrubs
sensitive
sympathetic to a patient's needs
tool box

▸ 1

▸ 2

▸ 3

Language bank

There's no doubt that new graduates need to find ways of setting themselves apart from other candidates.

Learning a second language shows that you have discipline and determination.

I believe that doing work placements demonstrates commitment and provides experience.

As far as I'm concerned, a second language is always a plus, no matter what field you go into.

I also feel that making your CV stand out is vital because it's the first thing a prospective employer sees.

For most people, interviews are often nerve-wracking, so practising techniques and strategies can be very helpful.

In many ways, you're no one if you're not visible on the internet. Graduates should make sure that their posts on social networking sites don't show them in a bad light.

As a matter of fact, I think having a positive online presence is the most useful thing you can do. Employers can learn about you before they've even met you.

accomplishments	provide references
adaptability	qualifications and skills applicable to the job
being innovative	reach the interview stage
dress the part	recruitment
highlight your strengths	set apart
how you come across	showing initiative
improve your prospects	stand out
make an impression	team spirit
make the shortlist	transferable skills
objectives	willingness to learn

improving online presence with a website

What can new graduates do to improve their employability?

making sure their CV really stands out

practising interview techniques and strategies

learning a second language

doing a relevant work placement or internship

▶▶ **PART 2**

Candidate A

• **What do you think is happening in these pictures?**
• **How do you think these people might be feeling?**

Language bank

This picture shows a happy occasion, a birthday. The woman looks surprised and delighted, perhaps her friends surprised her with this birthday cake.

I imagine she's feeling loved and very grateful to have her friends around her.

This man is giving a speech. Judging by the number of microphones, it seems to be an important occasion.

He might be a politician giving a public address.

Perhaps this is an awards ceremony and the person is making an acceptance speech.

I suppose it's possible that he feels a little nervous, but I doubt that. He looks exhilarated.

He might be introducing another speaker.

In this picture, by contrast, the woman has dropped her groceries, which is unfortunate.

She's probably annoyed because she's lost some of her shopping.

People passing by can see what's happened, so she could also be feeling embarrassed.

annoyed
awkward
captivates the audience
centre of attention
comfortable with public speaking
cuts an important figure
doing too many things at once
elated, joyful
embarrassed
everyday accident
expression of love
group celebration
high-level businessman / politician
in control
in his element
in the limelight
in the public eye
in the spotlight
inconvenient
influential person
marking the occasion
multitasking
running errands
shared moment
unexpected treat

▶ 1

▶ 2

▶ 3

▶▶ **PART 2**

Candidate B

- • Which emotions are these people probably feeling?
- • What situation might have made them feel this way?

Language bank

The woman in this picture looks distinctly fed up.

Personally, I don't blame her; the person she's at the restaurant with is speaking on his mobile phone. That's just rude.

She's probably feeling neglected and upset. Maybe he makes a habit of ignoring her.

Then again, maybe it's just a quick call. Perhaps she's being unreasonable.

By all appearances, this businessman is very cross. He looks furious.

My guess is that a situation at the office has made him angry.

Maybe he has just lost a lot of money.

Perhaps someone made a mistake that has big consequences for the company.

He could be under a lot of pressure.

This child is crying; he looks so sad.

I'm guessing that his parents have been strict with him; they possibly refused to give him something.

Maybe a sibling, or one of his friends, was mean to him.

There could be any reason, really. Perhaps he's just fallen over.

agitated
blow a fuse
demanding
distressed
don't jump to conclusions
exasperated
finger-pointing
fuming
hard to please
incensed
indignant
over the top
overreaction
petulant
short-tempered
sulky
take a step back
tearful
there are two sides to every story
things are not always what they seem
throw a tantrum

▶ 1

▶ 2

▶ 3

Language bank

For the most part, I think these steps are easy enough for the general public to take on board.

It just means making relatively small changes in most cases, such as remembering to carry bags with you.

Awareness is an important aspect too. People need to be informed about where to recycle batteries and electronic goods, for example.

I would agree with that. It's really a question of changing the mindset, isn't it?

To be fair, not driving is simply not an option in some situations. It really depends on where you live, doesn't it?

It's basically about getting into the habit of doing – or not doing – certain things, like having quicker showers to save water, or stopping to think before you buy bottled water.

Maybe something can be done … neighbours carpooling for the school run, for example.

Sometimes I think people are too quick to take the convenient route without thinking about creative solutions.

alternative energy	environmentally friendly
biodegradable	global warming
biofuels	greenhouse gases
carbon footprint	organic
clean energy	pollution
climate change	recycling
conservationist	renewable energy
eco-tourism	social responsibility
energy efficient	sustainable
environmentalist	waste management

filtering tap water rather than buying bottled water

What things can people do to go green and help the planet?

reusing disposable shopping bags

recycling electronic goods responsibly

walking, cycling or using public transport rather than driving

taking a short shower instead of having a bath

Preparing, planning and checking

▶▶ Preparing for the Writing paper

Producing a piece of writing that fulfils a certain function is a difficult task for anybody, even in their native language. To prepare for the Writing paper, it goes without saying that you need to have read widely. Then, you need to have studied all the basic text types you may be asked to produce, and understood the basic features that characterise them: layout, organisation, style and register. You should also practise completing writing tasks in the time allowed in the exam. Remember the criteria the examiners will use in awarding marks:

- Has the candidate achieved the purpose stated in the instructions?
- Does the text have a positive general effect on the target reader?
- Does the text cover all the content points?
- Is the text well organised and are ideas linked appropriately?
- Has language been used accurately?
- Does the text exhibit a good range of vocabulary and grammatical structures?
- Is the register appropriate for the task?
- Is the layout appropriate?

Ideally, the pieces of writing you produce should be checked by an experienced teacher who can provide useful feedback. Such feedback can help you compile a list of useful expressions, such as the useful phrases you find with the model answers in this section. You can also learn what sort of mistakes you make habitually so you can avoid them. For instance, if you find that you frequently make mistakes with a certain tense, you should consult a good grammar guide to clear up your confusion.

▶▶ Planning your answer

Perhaps the most useful lesson that experienced writers learn is the importance of planning what to write before they actually begin writing. Most good writers usually write several drafts of a text before they are satisfied with the result. Unfortunately, in the exam you do not have

time to produce several drafts, and it would be a serious mistake to try: you only have time for a single draft. But you do have time to make a plan.

Always read the question carefully and make sure you understand the following:

- Who are you writing for?
- What are the points you must include in your answer?
- Does the text type have any particular layout requirements?
- Do you have the necessary vocabulary to answer the question?

Then prepare a plan or outline of what you are going to write. Its purpose is to help you, so it doesn't matter if you change it or cross things out – nobody else is going to read it. But it has to show clearly the different sections of your writing and what points you must include in which section. When you look at the plan closely, you might want to change it; for instance, something might be better in a different paragraph, or you might realise you will be repeating yourself. When you are satisfied with your outline, you will find it much easier to write your text. Planning takes time, so allow a minimum of 15 minutes for it.

▶▶ Checking

Most people make more mistakes than normal under exam conditions, so always allow at least ten minutes at the end to read through your work. Think of your task here as having two parts. First, check that you have answered the question correctly and that you have included all the information that was required. Secondly, check for mistakes in grammar, spelling, punctuation, etc. You should by now have had enough experience to know where you often make mistakes – the spelling of certain words, for instance, or a particular type of punctuation.

If you need to correct something, make the correction neatly and legibly. If you need to cross out something you have written, just put one line through the word or words.

1 Essay

▶ ▷ **Exam task – Part 1**

You attended a philosophy seminar in which the tutor suggested that all exams in schools and colleges be abolished. You have made the notes below.

> ### Abolish exams
>
> - Students are denied the enriching experience of learning because they are under too much pressure to pass the exam.
>
> - Exams are not very effective because they test memory rather than intelligence.
>
> - It's not a fair process; exam stress affects some students more than others. Not everyone performs well in exams.

> **Other students in the seminar expressed their opinions:**
>
> "But working towards the final exam often gives us the motivation we need in order to study."
>
> "Exam-based assessment is a good way of figuring out whether a student has really understood what they have been taught."
>
> "Taking exams at school and university is actually a good life skill because it trains us to plan, prepare and deliver."

Write an essay for your tutor discussing **two** of the points from your notes. You should **explain whether you think abolishing exams is a good idea** and **provide reasons** to support your opinions.

You may, if you wish, make use of the opinions expressed in the lecture, but you should use your own words as far as possible.

▶ ▷ **Approach**

▶ Pay careful attention to the structure you use for your essay. You can follow these guidelines:

Title: Always choose an appropriate title. A good essay title should leave the reader in no doubt as to the topic of the essay. The title should be relevant and, importantly, it should be concise.

Introduction: Your opening paragraph is your introduction. Begin by clearly stating the topic, then provide a brief outline letting the reader know what will be covered in the essay. Don't reveal your own opinions in the introduction; wait until the main body of your essay.

Main body: Remember, your task in this part of the exam is to discuss two of the points provided. You can certainly add to this as long as you do not exceed the limit of 260 words, but don't submit an essay with fewer than two points discussed. Depending on how many key points you wish to include, the main body of your essay can comprise two or three paragraphs but, ideally, not more. Dedicate one paragraph to each point.

Conclusion: Your final paragraph is your conclusion. This is where you should set out a balanced summary of the points you have made. In the essay, it's optional to present your own views on the topic, but this is where you should state or restate your opinions if you do decide to include them.

▶ The tone you adopt is important. Typically for an essay, it should be formal. An informal register is not appropriate for this part of the exam.

▶ Avoid losing focus in the pressurised environment of the exam by organising your thoughts before you begin writing. Having a plan in advance will ensure clarity and readability. Always keep the reader in mind as you write your essay.

Decide on a relevant and obvious title for your essay.

Should exams be abolished?

Your opening sentence should clearly spell out the topic.

The idea that exams should be abolished in schools and colleges is not a new one. In this essay, I will present some of the arguments for and against this suggestion, which regularly arises in education reviews, and consider the implications of each one.

In the introduction, establish the context of the essay and state what the reader can expect.

Feature a strong topic sentence early in each new paragraph.

First and foremost, many people feel that exams set learners at an unfair disadvantage. This is because some students – including excellent students – get very nervous and find it difficult to cope with the pressures of the exam situation. Their anxiety causes them to perform so poorly that the test is not a fair measure of their knowledge and hard work. In spite of this, it is generally agreed that exams are an important preparation for life, and we all need to manage stress.

Support your key points with examples or additional explanations.

Use passive reporting structures such as *It is thought/agreed/ argued that ...* for general opinions.

People also question the value of exams as an accurate measure of intelligence. It is argued that simply memorising information does not prove that a learner has meaningfully engaged with a subject. 'A monkey can be trained to memorise things,' is a sentiment often voiced. While this may be true, the question is what could effectively replace exams. The most common option put forward is that of continuous assessment based on coursework submitted throughout the year.

If possible, include statistics or quotes to bring your essay to life.

It's a good idea to offer counterpoints for balance.

Use your concluding paragraph to briefly summarise the essay and to record an outcome.

All in all, opinions are still divided about the value of exams as a form of assessment, but the majority opinion is in favour of retaining exams in schools and colleges. While the exam system certainly has flaws, summarily abolishing it is not a viable option.

Useful phrases

Introduction

Imagine if ... (all exams were abolished)

This essay will explore the idea of ...

In this essay, I am going to discuss whether ...

Main body

First of all, ...

The most important issue to consider is ...

In order to decide whether ...

Let us begin by ...

To begin with ...

This is illustrated by ...

A key point to note is ...

On the other hand ...

Another important point is ...

In contrast to this ...

However, it is also true to say ...

Conclusion

To sum up ...

Summing up ...

In conclusion, we have seen that ...

It seems clear that ...

As I have shown, ...

2 Formal letter

▶ ▷ **Exam task – Part 2**

You recently took a domestic flight which was badly delayed, and service from the crew was poor. Write a letter to the customer services manager and include the following information:

- plane sat on the runway for over two hours with no information from the crew

- one member of staff was particularly rude when two passengers asked if they could switch seats

- after take-off, it was announced that no food or drinks would be served, not even mineral water.

Write your **letter**.

▶ ▷ **Approach**

▶ Make sure you know how to structure a formal letter, e.g. a letter asking for information or a letter of complaint. You can follow these guidelines for a letter of complaint:

Opening: Use an appropriate salutation (greeting).

Main body: First paragraph: state what your complaint is about.

Second paragraph: explain exactly what happened, including where and when.

Next paragraph(s): mention any additional details and say how the problem affected you.

Final paragraph: state how you expect the problem to be resolved.

Closing: Use an appropriate ending.

▶ You should always write a formal letter in a formal register.

▶ Although the person writing the complaint letter may be unhappy, or even angry, it's very important to maintain a polite tone throughout.

Useful phrases

Opening
Dear Mr (or Mrs, Ms, Miss, etc.) Surname,
Dear Sir or Madam, (if you don't know their name or gender)

Main body
I am writing to complain about …
I would like to express my dissatisfaction with …
I wish to complain in the strongest terms about …
On (date) I purchased (product or service).
I was appalled to discover …
And as if that weren't bad enough, …
To add insult to injury, …

The experience was very distressing …
In the circumstances, I think a full refund is in order.
I expect to be fully compensated for …
Please let me know how you propose to rectify the situation.
I trust there will be a prompt resolution of …
I look forward to receiving your explanation of …

Closing
Yours sincerely, (if you have named the person in your opening greeting)
Yours faithfully, (if you have not named the person in your opening greeting)

▸ ▸ **Model answer**

Note the use of capitals and the use of a comma here.

Dear Sir or Madam,

Clearly state your reason for writing at the outset.

I am writing to express my deepest dissatisfaction with the unacceptable level of service I received from FlyLocal Airlines recently.

Continue with specific details of the problem.

I was booked on the 18.20 Glasgow to London flight last Wednesday, 17 February. Although we boarded on time, had the safety demonstration and taxied to the runway, the plane did not depart for several hours. While this was extremely frustrating in itself, far worse was the fact that we were given neither an explanation nor an apology for the delay.

Say how the experience made you feel.

Include additional details that compounded the problem.

When one passenger travelling with a small child made the reasonable request to switch seats so that she could sit with her husband, the flight attendant was unhelpful and extraordinarily rude. Overall, I found the crew to be inefficient and unfriendly. How a service industry – especially one like FlyLocal whose advertising campaigns are based on making travel hassle-free and pleasant – can expect people to tolerate such a poor level of customer service is beyond me.

The last straw, however, was the unavailability of any refreshments either before or on the flight. A perfunctory announcement after take-off informed us of this. Again, there was no attempt to apologise for the inconvenience to passengers, who could not even purchase bottled water. To deprive people for that long, at that time of the evening, of food or drink was a complete disgrace.

State what you expect to happen next.

Please process a full refund of my airfare immediately. I would also expect additional compensation or another gesture of goodwill. I look forward to receiving your reply as soon as possible.

Use an appropriate ending.

Keep the tone formal throughout and use a standard closing phrase.

Yours faithfully,

John Evans

3 Informal letter/email

▶ ▶ **Exam task – Part 2**

A couple of years ago you did a Volunteering Abroad programme in South Africa. Your 17-year-old cousin, Dan, is thinking of doing the same thing and has written to you asking about it.

Read the extract from Dan's email.

> The animal conservation work you did sounds interesting – can you tell me a bit more about it, for example, which animals did you work with? I definitely hope to do a lot of travelling while I'm there too. Can you suggest anywhere I can visit? I suppose what I'm wondering more than anything is whether you think I'll enjoy it.
>
> Thanks, Paul!
> Dan

▶ ▶ **Approach**

▶ The structure of an informal email is less prescribed than a formal email or letter. See the *Useful phrases* section below for appropriate opening and closing expressions. The main body of your email can be structured as you choose, but keep related points together, include linking words and phrases and use paragraphs to break up the text.

▶ Pay close attention to the points made in the input text as you will be expected to address each one in your reply.

▶ Since the question only shows an extract from Dan's email, you also have the option of 'inventing' additional points he may have addressed. However, make sure you don't exceed the permitted 260 word limit.

▶ As this is an informal communication your tone should be friendly and you can use contractions and colloquial expressions, but don't be tempted to slip into slang or text-speak; you are still expected to produce grammatically correct English. A good practice is to follow the tone used in the input text.

Useful phrases

Opening
Hi [first name],
Hello [first name],
Thanks for your email.
Great to hear from you!
I was delighted to get your email.
I was so glad to hear from you.
It sounds like things are going well.

Connectors
By the way, …
Oh, and one more thing, …
As I was saying earlier, …
To tell you the truth, …
Actually, …

About your question …
As far as [X] is concerned …
To your point about …

Closing
All the best,
Speak soon,
Take care,
Well, that's it for now …
Cheers,
Have to run,
Drop me a line soon.

Model answer

Use a casual, informal opening greeting.

Hi Dan,

Acknowledge the email you're replying to.

Thanks for your email; it was really great to hear from you yesterday! I'm so glad you're thinking about going to South Africa. I've just been reading through the travel diary I kept when I did that Volunteering Abroad programme and so many memories came flooding back.

Address the specific points you've been asked about.

Right, you wanted to know about the animal conservation work that I was involved in, so I'll start with that. I requested a placement on a lion reserve in the east of the country because I specifically wanted to work with lions. It was tough, but incredibly rewarding too. I worked with a brilliant team who tracked the animals in the bush. I was given thorough training in animal identification and data collection using the research equipment. Honestly, Dan, it's absolutely amazing to see these magnificent animals in their natural habitat. I really loved it, and I think you would too.

Include details that will help to paint a clear picture of the experience.

Using intensifying adverbs will make your email sound more authentic.

Don't be afraid to elaborate on what you've been asked; just keep an eye on your word count.

If you'd like to try the same project, let me know and I'll send you more details. The accommodation is shared and pretty basic, but it's fine. You'll have plenty of opportunities to travel and have fun. I can recommend the spectacular Drakensberg Mountains, which are nearby, and the Blyde River Canyon and beautiful Sodwana Bay. One of my friends even travelled to Mozambique. You should do it!

Bring the email to an end in a friendly way.

OK, I'll leave it at that for now. Drop me a line if you have any more questions or want any more information. Give my love to your Mum and Dad!

Make the offer to follow up with additional information, if needed.

Use an appropriate closing expression.

Cheers, Dan,

Paul

4 Proposal

▶▶ **Exam task – Part 2**

A former colleague has set up her own catering business and has asked for your help in improving her website. Choose two or three points for improvement, focussing on design, ease of use and organisation. Write a proposal explaining how your recommended changes will make the website more attractive as well as easier for customers to navigate.

Write your **proposal**.

▶▶ **Approach**

▶ A proposal is usually written in a formal register. Depending on the circumstances – in the scenario we are using here, for example – the tone could also be semi-formal because the people concerned know each other personally. A proposal would not typically be informal. Maintain a consistent tone throughout the proposal.

▶ In structure, a proposal should have a logical title, an introduction which provides some background, a main body made up of the suggestions you are proposing and a conclusion which summarises what you have already said. The main body can be structured any number of ways, using headings or bulleted lists, for example. You can always adapt the layout to suit the needs of a given proposal as long as your points are clearly separated, organised and easy for the reader to follow.

▶ A proposal is similar to a report but it is generally created in response to a problem, prompting action or further discussion. Its function is usually to convince somebody of something rather than just reporting facts and statistics. For this reason, make an effort to incorporate persuasive language into your report. It's also a good idea to have some business vocabulary to draw from in case the proposal is business-based.

▶ Even if you think of lots of ideas and suggestions for the proposal in the exam, resist the temptation to include too many. It's better to present a few well-developed suggestions than a long list of ideas.

▶ To make your proposal more effective, expound a little on your suggestions. Mention, for example, how they can be implemented and what they will accomplish.

▶ In some cases, you may wish to discuss finances and budgetary requirements in your proposal. This is optional unless expressly stated in the question.

Useful phrases

Introduction

This proposal will discuss …

As requested, I am submitting this proposal on …

The aim of this proposal is to …

In this proposal I will outline …

Main body

Based on this issue, I would suggest …

In terms of …

What I propose here is …

It would be advisable to …

The following steps need to be taken …

One way to counter this problem is to …

This issue could be resolved by …

The benefit of making this change would be …

I would strongly recommend …

Conclusion

In conclusion, the way forward appears to be …

Taking all these points into consideration, …

Having assessed the situation, I believe …

I trust you will give this proposal careful consideration.

▶ ▶ Model answer

The title should make the subject of the proposal obvious.

Use concise headings for clarity.

Explain what the issue is and how it can be addressed.

Proposal for improvements to the *Orderln* website

Introduction
As requested, I am submitting the following proposal to improve the website of your *Orderln* catering business.

Give a basic overview in your introduction.

Design
The existing design is adequate, but not compelling. The colour scheme is dull and would benefit from some brighter tones. It is also text heavy, which I suggest breaking up with various eye-catching images. I recommend including some shots of the dishes and platters you offer, and photos of catered events showing happy guests.

Make sure your suggestions and recommendations are easy for the reader to follow.

Ease of use
The whole point about ease of use is that every visitor to your site should have a positive user experience, and there are some basic steps you can take in this regard. For example, set the main menu across the top of the page; people do not enjoy scrolling down too far. The rule of thumb here is 'keep it simple'.

Organisation
Good organisation allows potential customers to find what they need quickly. Currently, the site lacks a clear structure; it is too cluttered and has too many tabs presented in no logical order. Making a list of the most important topics and deciding on a hierarchy for them will ensure that your key content is obvious at a glance. My advice would be to choose the most popular event types, such as weddings, parties, corporate events.

Tie the points of the proposal together in your conclusion.

Conclusion
To sum up, the issues with the site can be resolved by following the steps I have outlined above, all of which can be easily and inexpensively implemented.

5 Report

▶ ▶ **Exam task – Part 2**

You see this pop-up ad on your local tourist information office website.

> Here at Happy Trails we are working on a new travel guide for visitors to your area. We need the latest information on all forms of entertainment currently on offer in your town. If you would like to contribute to this chapter, please send a report describing the options available.

Write your **report**.

▶ ▶ **Approach**

▸ Reports are typically written in a formal or semi-formal register. Pay attention to the input text and keep the reader in mind as you create your report.

▸ Unlike a proposal, the purpose of a report is to inform rather than persuade. Information in a report should be presented in an organised format, making it easy for the reader to identify the facts. Use impersonal structures to present information, for example *It seems/appears that …, There seems to be …, It has been noted/suggested that …*

▸ The structure should feature a title, introduction, main body and conclusion. You are free to choose any style of layout for the main body but your goal should always be clarity.

▸ In your report, you can invent statistics, incidents, examples, place names and so on to support your ideas. Try to stick to plausible data so that the report does not sound too unrealistic.

▸ Most reports are entirely neutral, but some also feature the writer's opinion. Check the input text to see if it might be appropriate to include your own opinions.

Useful phrases

Introduction

The purpose of this report is to …

This report is based on …

Further to your request for a report on …

This report looks at …

Main body

With regard to …

Among the events on offer …

There appears to be widespread agreement that …

It has been noted that …

Moving on to …

It seems widely accepted that …

Opinions vary on the subject of …

As for …

What seems clear is that …

There seems to be a growing demand for …

… has proved to be extremely popular.

Due to the fact that …

Conclusion

It can therefore be concluded that …

The obvious conclusion to be drawn from this report …

For the reasons provided …

I trust this report will receive due consideration.

▶ ▶ Model answer

Think of a relevant
and concise title.

Visitor attractions in Oldtown

Introduction

The aim of this report is to illustrate the wide variety of
entertainment available in the Oldtown area for inclusion in a new
travel guide published by Happy Trails.

Break the report into
clear sections with
obvious headings.

Getting here

As location is a key consideration for tourists, the convenience of
Oldtown is a great advantage. A domestic airport is situated just
30 kilometres away and the train station connects with several major
routes.

What's on offer

Oldtown is a refreshing mix of old and new, combining sites of historical
interest with exciting new events. It has something for everyone, and
here are just some of the options.

Sub-headings help to
categorise different
types of information.

Culture and heritage

• Visit the castle on the outskirts of town for a stunning example of
  medieval architecture.

• Spend an afternoon in the museum on New Street which also
  features an award-winning range of exhibitions for children.

Bulleted lists draw the
reader's eye to your
key points.

• Enjoy a leisurely river walk, stopping for a picnic in the botanic
  gardens. Thirty-minute walking tours depart from the town hall
  every two hours. A fascinating literary tour is now on offer too.

Nightlife

• The Oldtown Theatre runs a compelling programme of plays
  showcasing local talent as well as visiting productions.

• Check out the line-up of bands playing at the Waterfront Hall; always
  book in advance for weekend performances.

• Laughter abounds at the comedy club on Oak Road, open to the
  public on Thursday and Friday nights.

Conclusion

A brief conclusion
summarises the
report.

From the information provided in this report, it is clear that Oldtown
is worthy of a dedicated chapter in the new travel guide.

6 Review

▸ ▸ **Exam task – Part 2**

You see this notice on an events website based in your area.

> ### WE NEED YOUR HELP
> Here at the Riverfront Theatre we'd like to add to our database of event reviews. If you were at last night's concert given by the student band, *Atmosphere*, we'd love to hear from you. Please send your review of the concert to the email address below.

Write your **review**.

▸ ▸ **Approach**

▸ Reviews are published to describe something, such as a book, film or performance, to the public and to indicate the quality of this product or event. Although a review is an opinion piece, it's a good idea to try to offer a balanced view rather than entirely positive or entirely negative comments.

▸ As always in the Writing paper, study the question and the input text carefully in order to establish exactly what you are being asked to produce and to decide which register you should use. Noting the audience here, an informal or semi-formal tone seems appropriate in this case.

▸ In structure, you can use headings and other formatting styles if you wish. You might decide to first describe the concert and then follow this with your opinions, or you could introduce your views in tandem with the points in your description. State the subject of the review at the beginning and make sure your opinion is stated (or restated) in the concluding paragraph.

▸ Use descriptive language. Include colourful adjectives and adverbs to really convey to the reader what the event was like.

▸ Be careful not to submit a basic list of criticisms and praise. It's important to develop your ideas and to support your points with examples in the review. In other words, don't simply comment that it was good or bad, say *why* it was good or bad.

Useful phrases

This event took place at ...

What made it a success was ...

Where it fell down was ...

In my opinion, ...

I found it rather ...

Unfortunately, ...

A particular weakness was ...

Slightly disappointing was ...

It was an incredible performance.

It seems to me that ...

You might think ...

... something of a let-down.

While I understand this criticism, I also feel ...

It's worth mentioning that ...

This would appeal to ...

What I particularly appreciated ...

However, overall ...

I highly recommend ...

On balance, ...

▶ ▶ **Model answer**

Choose a suitable title. Don't spend too long trying to think of something clever.

Enjoy the *Atmosphere*!

The Riverfront Theatre was the place to be last Thursday evening. Up-and-coming band, *Atmosphere*, played their hearts out for 95 electrifying minutes, at once delighting their already solid fan base while also gaining a multitude of new fans.

State early on exactly what it is that you are reviewing.

Try to open with a sentence that will immediately grab the reader's attention.

Atmosphere have been around for about a year now. Consisting of four permanent band members, they keep their sound fresh by regularly working with guest performers who contribute a variety of instruments and harmonies to the mix. Their main genre is high-energy rock, which is occasionally softened by pop beats and catchy lyrics.

Ideally, provide a little background to give the reader some context.

What made Thursday's concert such a resounding success was the choice of venue. Clearly this type of platform suits them best … a band with a big sound needs a big venue. Unfortunately, the sound quality was poor at the beginning of their set but this was quickly rectified.

Explain each point you make.

Like any good front man, lead singer Adam Elliott has a powerful stage presence. He connects with the crowd instantly, drawing them in through ballads and conducting them in several rousing choruses.

What *Atmosphere* might need to focus on a little more is rehearsal time. Some of the songs weren't as tight as they should have been and the bass player came in late a few times. Still, this did nothing to spoil the overall experience.

Try to balance your positive and negative comments.

Aim for a strong conclusion and make sure it represents your opinion of the event.

Your really should go and see this band at the first opportunity. They are destined for great things, no question, and I fully intend to catch them again the next time I have the chance.

TEST 1

PAPER 1 Reading and Use of English

▸▸ **PART 1**

eatery (n) informal word for a restaurant or café

Paleolithic (adj) from the early Stone Ages (2.6 million to 10,000 years ago)

hunter-gatherer (n) person whose food comes from wild plants and hunted animals, not agriculture

▸▸ **PART 2**

scepticism (n) being sceptical or doubting that something claimed to be true is really true

▸▸ **PART 3**

reside (v) to live in a particular place

truck in (phr v) to transport somewhere by truck or lorry

arid (adj) very dry

moist (adj) slightly wet

droplet (n) small drop of liquid

desertification (n) process of becoming a desert

▸▸ **PART 5**

lengthy (adj) continuing for a long time

guillemot (n) black and white seabird

symmetry (n) when two halves or sides of something are an exact match in size, shape, appearance, etc.

disprove (v) to show that something is wrong or false

nibble (v) to take small bites

cliché (n) idea that is used so often it becomes boring and loses meaning

preen (v) to spend a lot of time making yourself look attractive

steer clear of (phr) to stay away from

deviate (v) to do something differently from what is usually expected

hard-nosed (adj) not affected by feelings

incubate (v) to sit on eggs to keep them warm until they hatch (of birds)

fraught (with) (adj) filled with something difficult

physiology (n) all the processes and functions of a living organism (also the study of how living organisms function)

neurobiology (n) biology of the nervous system (also the study of the biology of the nervous system)

framework (n) set of beliefs and ideas used as the basis for making judgements and decisions

sensory (adj) connected with physical senses such as sight and smell

proportioned (adj) having parts that relate in size and shape to other parts

peacock (n) large bird with long blue and green tail feathers that open out in the shape of a fan

starling (n) common bird with dark, shiny feathers and loud call

▸▸ **PART 6**

implication (n) likely result of something

prosperity (n) economic success

spurn (v) to reject or refuse

subsidise (v) to give money to help pay for something

demographic (n) part of the population

perturbed (adj) worried

complacent (adj) too satisfied with the current situation and not making any effort to change

unenterprising (adj) uninterested in starting new projects

▸▸ **PART 7**

plague (n) serious contagious disease which kills a lot of people

boom (n) period of economic success

bust (n) economic collapse, often used in contrast to 'boom'

pandemic (n) disease that spreads across many regions or countries

stalagmite (n) rock pointing upwards from the floor of a cave, formed over a long period from drops of water containing minerals

proliferate (v) to grow fast in number

surge (n) rapid rise

anomaly (n) something different from what is normal or expected

pendulum (n) rod with weight at the end that swings from side to side, found in traditional clocks. 'The pendulum swings' is used as an image to describe something changing from one condition to another, and then back again.

drought (n) period with no rain and extreme dryness

conquistador (n) Spanish conquerors of the native populations of Central and South America in the sixteenth century

deforestation (n) destruction of forests

moisture (n) small drops of water

catastrophe (n) disaster

shape (v) to influence

sprout (v) to appear suddenly and in significant numbers

hallmark (n) typical feature

misconception (n) wrong belief or idea, often based on incorrect information

ride high (phr) to be successful

dire (adj) very bad

cautionary tale (phr) example that provides a warning

befall (v) when something unpleasant happens

divine (adj) coming from or connected to a god

commission (v) to pay for someone to create

intertwine (v) to connect closely

▶▶ **PART 8**

acknowledge (v) to accept to be true

precedent (n) action or decision that is used as an example for something similar to follow

exceed (v) to be more than

entrepreneur (n) someone who starts a new business

enterprising (adj) showing the ability to think of new ideas for projects, especially in business, and to carry them out

envisage (v) to imagine will happen

origami (n) Japanese art of folding paper to create shapes

cater (for) (v) to provide what is wanted

juggle (v) to do several things at the same time

dissertation (n) long essay as part of a university course

chance upon (phr v) to meet or find by chance

mentor (n) experienced person who gives advice and help

keep on track (phr) to keep doing the right thing

stand someone in good stead (phr) to be useful for the future

prototype (n) first design of something

file a patent (phr) to apply for the official right to be the only person legally entitled to make and sell a product

TEST 2

PAPER 1 Reading and Use of English

▶▶ **PART 1**

word of mouth (phr) informal spoken communication

viral (adj) something that circulates rapidly on the internet

▶▶ **PART 2**

coral (n) hard, colourful substance formed from the bones of very small sea creatures and found at the bottom of the sea

fjord (n) long, narrow strip of sea between high cliffs

numb (adj) without any feeling

▶▶ **PART 3**

expertise (n) expert knowledge

▶▶ **PART 5**

ADHD (abbrev) Attention Deficit Hyperactivity Disorder: a disorder, mainly affecting children, which makes it hard for them to be still and concentrate, and can affect their ability to learn.

deprive someone of something (v) to prevent someone from having something

Parkinson's disease (n) disease of the nervous system that gets progressively worse and causes the muscles to become weak and to shake

stationary (adj) not moving

incorporate (v) to become part of

life-enhancing (adj) life-improving

neurologist (n) doctor who studies and treats diseases of the nerves

induce (v) to cause something to happen

state of meditation (n) profound mental calmness

preceding (adj) previous

blissful (adj) very happy

blur (n) something you cannot see or remember clearly

grey matter (n) the brain, often referring to intelligence

jostle (v) to push roughly for position

Ritalin (n) medication used to treat disorders of the nervous system such as ADHD

aerobic (adj) exercising the heart and lungs

tandem (n) bicycle for two people

incrementally (adv) a little more each time and steadily

hop (v) to jump

discrepancy (n) difference between things that should be the same

rotate (v) to go round and round

cue (n) signal

hyperactive (adj) too active

notwithstanding (adv) in spite of

▶▶ **PART 6**

captivity (n) the state of being enclosed and not free

habitat (n) natural environment of an animal or plant

intervention (n) becoming involved to deal with a problem

enclosure (n) area of land surrounded by a fence or wall, where zoo animals are kept

primate (n) group of mammals including humans, apes and monkeys

odds (n) probability

revive (v) to bring back to life

endeavour (n) attempt to do something difficult

dissemination (n) spreading of information

divert (v) to entertain

acknowledge (v) to accept to be true

stave off (phr v) to prevent

replicate (v) to copy exactly

bear fruit (phr) to be successful

confinement (n) state of being enclosed and not free

enlighten (v) to help understand better

▶▶ PART 7

scatter (v) to throw to the ground in different directions

surge (v) to move quickly

thrive (v) to do very well

tranquility (n) peace and calm

peer (n) someone of the same age and position

therapeutic (adj) helping to treat an illness

sceptical (adj) doubting that something is true or useful

wholesome (adj) healthy

coriander (n) plant whose leaves and seeds are used in cooking

▶▶ PART 8

determine (v) to decide on

of note (phr) of importance

whimsical (adj) unusual and not serious

cute (adj) pretty

tome (n) book

heavy-hitting (adj) significant

stream of consciousness (n) continuous flow of ideas and feelings as they are experienced by someone

tidbit (n) small but interesting piece of information

creepy (adj) scary

harbour (v) to hide and protect

impetus (n) motivation or force that causes something to happen

hard-hitting (adj) very critical

muddled (adj) confused, unclear

monstrosity (n) something very ugly

refute (v) to reject

prose (n) style of writing

digestible (adj) easy to absorb

unearth (v) to discover

gem (n) something beautiful and precious

epoch (n) historical period

canonical (adj) belonging to a generally accepted list of the best work in its field

distilled (adj) summarised

caricature (n) a simplified exaggeration of something

put the record straight (phr) to establish the truth

quibble (v) to argue or complain about a small matter

 TEST 3

PAPER 1 Reading and Use of English

▶▶ PART 1

biodiversity (n) large number of different types of animals and plants in a particular environment

catfish (n) large fish with long hairs around its mouth which look like cats' whiskers

intervene (v) to become involved in a situation in order to improve it or to stop something happening

spine (n) sharp, pointed feature, usually to protect an animal

predator (n) animal that attacks and eats other animals

classify (v) to put things in groups according to type, size, etc.

▶▶ PART 2

organ (n) part of a human or other animal with a specific purpose, e.g. heart, lungs, liver

invariably (adv) always

▶▶ PART 3

adorn (v) to make someone or something attractive through the use of decorations

drought (n) period with no rain and extreme dryness

fuel (v) to stimulate or help something to develop

▶▶ PART 5

illustrate (v) to give information or examples to explain something

enhance (v) to improve

plausibly (adv) easily believed to be true

immersion (n) being completely involved in something

legacy (n) something that exists now because of what happened in the past

crew (v) to work on a boat

overlap (n) where two things cover the same area or subject

manuscript (n) the author's copy of a book before it is published

cut corners (phr) to do something in the easiest way by leaving something out

infantile (adj) like a small child

petulance (n) bad-tempered, unreasonable behaviour because you can't have what you want

remorse (n) feeling of regret for something wrong or bad that you have done

poignant (adj) having a strong impact on your feelings, usually to make you feel sad or moved

enlightening (adj) giving information to provide a better understanding

defy (v) to resist or obstruct

reservation (n) doubt

prose (n) style of writing

showily (adv) in an exaggerated way designed to attract attention (used to show disapproval)

tricksy (adj) cunning and intended to deceive

device (n) method designed to get a particular result

abound with (phr v) to have large quantities of

pompous (adj) formal in an exaggerated way and designed to show superiority

turn of phrase (phr) particular way of describing something

▶▶ **PART 6**

chronological (adj) in the order in which they happened in time

cartography (n) the process of making maps

(a) wealth of (n) large amount

painstaking (adj) very detailed and careful

rigorous (adj) well thought through and supported by detail

guiding principle (n) main idea which influences the overall way something is dealt with

pretension (n) ambition

enthralled (adj) fascinated

erroneous (adj) incorrect

GPS (n) (Global Positioning System) satellite-based navigation system

round off (phr v) to complete

anecdote (n) interesting personal story

trivia (n) unimportant information

gloss over (phr v) to avoid talking about something difficult by only briefly referring to it

compressed (adj) squeezed together into a smaller space

decipher (v) to interpret and understand

skip (v) to avoid or leave out

sample (v) to experience a small part of something

cram in (phr v) to force many things into a small space

▶▶ **PART 7**

recreational (adj) as a hobby or form of entertainment

treadmill (n) running machine found in gyms

puff (v) to breathe hard

disconcerting (adj) confusing

carb (n) carbohydrate

cognitive (adj) connected with metal processes

leap (v) to jump

duck (v) to move your head down quickly

sustain (v) to make something continue

treacle (n) thick, sticky liquid made by melting sugar

screen (v) to check or examine

implausible (adj) very unlikely to be true

cutting edge (phr) very modern and advanced

genome (n) complete set of genes in a living thing

hurdle (n) obstacle or challenge to deal with

lactic acid (n) acid produced in muscles during hard exercise

gradient (n) slope

▶▶ **PART 8**

record label (n) company which produces recorded music

innovative (adj) new and not used before

entail (v) to involve

delegate (v) to give responsibility for something to someone else

what makes someone tick (phr) what makes someone behave the way they normally do

bemoan (v) to complain about

flop (v) to fail

burn-out (n) being extremely tired as a result of having worked too much

perspective (n) the ability to think about problems in a reasonable way

lucrative (adj) producing lots of money

feel compelled to do something (phr) to feel you have to do something

enamoured (adj) in love with

outsourcing (n) business arrangement in which an outside individual or company does work for an organisation

let alone (phr) used to emphasise that one thing is even more impossible than the first thing mentioned

old-school (adj) traditional

break the mould (phr) to do something dramatically new

pioneer (n) one of the first people to do something

all-consuming (adj) total

blur (v) to become less clear

merchandising (n) selling goods

TEST 4

PAPER 1 Reading and Use of English

▶▶ **PART 1**

fragment (n) small, broken piece

marrow (n) soft substance inside bones

dweller (n) someone who lives in a particular place

▶▶ **PART 2**

whir (v) to make the noise of a machine

harness (v) to control and use something

▶▶ **PART 3**

anagram (n) puzzle in which the letters of a word or phrase are arranged in a different order

▶▶ **PART 5**

megafauna (n) large animals

characterise (v) to describe

fossil (n) remains of an animal or plant which have become hard and turned into rock

spasm (n) sudden, violent event

spill ink (phr) to write about – an idiom which is not very common

blitzkrieg (n) a German word that means a sudden violent attack

hypothesis (n) theory to explain something

havoc (n) destruction

annihilate (v) to destroy completely

bison (n) large hairy wild animal of the cow family, native to North America

moose (n) large deer native to North America

baffling (adj) difficult to understand

paleontological (adj) relating to paleontology, which is the study of fossils from prehistoric times

indigenous (adj) native to a particular place

parched (adj) extremely dry

denuded (adj) bare

water cycle (n) journey water takes as it circulates from land to the sky and back again

predator (n) animal that attacks and eats other animals

be prone to do something (adj) to have a tendency to do something

analog (n) something that is similar

pivot on (phr v) to centre or depend on

sediment (n) sand, stones and other substances that settle at the bottom of a lake, river or sea

refuge (n) a place of safety

blurry (adj) unclear

inconclusive (adj) not leading to a definite conclusion

ominous (adj) worrying

scenario (n) description of how things might have happened

incremental (adj) gradual or bit by bit

discern (v) to recognise or understand something that is not very obvious

▶▶ **PART 6**

viability (n) the possibility that something will succeed in future

terminal decline (phr) when something is certain to get worse and come to an end

speculative (adj) based on guessing or giving an opinion without having factual evidence

the bottom line (phr) the most important point

obsolete (adj) no longer in use

perish (v) to die

ephemeral (adj) lasting only for a short period of time

demise (n) the end or death of something

▶▶ **PART 7**

graze (v) to eat grass

ranger (n) person whose job is to look after a park, nature reserve or area of countryside

exceed (v) to be more than

donor (n) someone that gives money to a person or organisation that needs help

livestock (n) farm animals

arable (farming) (adj) growing crops like corn and wheat

proximity (n) being close to

pierce (v) to be suddenly heard

tick the box (phr) to put a mark on a list to show that something has been done

warthog (n) African wild pig

exhilarating (adj) very exciting

elusive (adj) difficult to find

serenity (n) calmness

poacher (n) person who illegally hunts animals

scrub (n) land in Africa covered with small bushes and trees

jackal (n) wild African animal similar to a dog

hyena (n) wild dog-like animal which has a cry that sounds like a human laugh

trim (v) to shorten

enticing (adj) attractive

▶▶ PART 8

defy (v) to make something impossible

output (n) production

contemporary (n) people living in the same period of time

minimalist (adj) made up of simple ideas and sounds

overwhelming (adj) extremely powerful

rigour (n) disciplined approach

integrity (n) honesty and being true to one's principles

motif (n) idea or phrase that is repeated

cantata (n) short piece of classical music for singers

permeate (v) to be present everywhere

chamber work (n) classical music for small group of instruments

quantify (v) to analyse

transfix (v) to capture someone's attention completely

throw into relief (phr) to make something more noticeable

foxtrot (n) music for a formal type of dance

take the plunge (phr) to decide to do something new and difficult

walk the tightrope (phr) to have to balance carefully

jitterbug (n) music for a fast style of dance

bossa nova (n) Brazilian style of music

tempi (n) plural of *tempo* – the speed at which music is played

acoustical (adj) relating to sound

property (n) quality or characteristic

venue (n) place where a performance takes place, e.g. a theatre

choreographed (adj) directed in the way that dancers' movements are directed

uncompromising (adj) sticking strongly to its character

ADVANCED TEST 5

PAPER 1 Reading and Use of English

▶▶ PART 1

app (n) software application, especially for mobile phones

▶▶ PART 2

migration (n) when animals or birds move in large numbers from one place to another, usually at particular times of the year

a figure of eight (phr) route which in shape is similar to the number 8

▶▶ PART 5

reef (n) natural reefs are rocks or sand mounds under the sea, often covered with corals

incur (costs) (v) to have to pay money for something done

shipwreck (n) ship that has been destroyed and has usually sunk to the bottom of the sea

oil rig (n) large structure and equipment used for taking oil from the ground or the seabed

plankton (n) very small forms of plant and animal life

lethal (adj) able to cause death

eel (n) long thin fish that looks like a snake

opportunistic (adj) ready to make use of an opportunity (usually used to express disapproval)

predator (n) animal that attacks and eats other animals

prey (n) animal that is hunted, killed and eaten by another animal

encrusted (adj) covered with a thin, hard layer of something

algae (n) very simple plants that grow in water

coral (n) hard, colourful substance formed from the bones of very small sea creatures and found at the bottom of the sea

recreational (adj) as a hobby or form of entertainment

spared (adj) saved or protected

catastrophe (n) disaster

akin (adj) similar

oasis (n) area in a desert where there is water and where plants grow

game fish (n) fish that people look for in recreational fishing rather than in commercial fishing

bait (n) food put on a hook or in nets to attract and catch fish

asbestos (n) material used in buildings and ships as protection against fire and to prevent heat loss. It is now known to be toxic and is used much less than in the past.

scrupulously (adv) extremely carefully

stern (n) back part of a ship

bow (n) front part of a ship

landfill (n) hole in the ground where waste materials are deposited

bundled (adj) tied together

augment (v) to add something to

adjacent (adj) nearby

smother (v) to cover thickly and kill

▶▶ PART 6

reality TV (n) television programmes in which ordinary people are continuously filmed, designed to be entertaining rather than informative

authenticity (n) how authentic or real something is

the bottom line (phr) the most important point

replicate (v) to copy exactly

invariably (adv) always

manipulate (v) to control or influence in a dishonest way

distort (v) to change so that something is no longer correct or true

humiliation (n) making someone feel ashamed or stupid

purport (v) to claim

banal (adj) very ordinary and lacking in interest

▶▶ **PART 7**

preserve (n) activity or job thought to be suitable only for one person or type of person

aesthetics (n) ideas about what is beautiful, especially in art

insight (n) an understanding of what something is like

protagonist (n) significant person who changes a situation

at pains to (phr) to make a lot of effort to do something

peer (n) someone of the same age and position

concur (v) to agree

auction house (n) company which organises auctions, where things of value are sold to the people who offer most money

curate (v) to organise an exhibition of art or other objects

absorbing (adj) very interesting

enriching (adj) raising the level of your knowledge or experience

deter (v) to make someone decide not to do something

scope (n) range of things that a subject deals with

avidly (adv) very keenly

enliven (v) to make more interesting and lively

▶▶ **PART 8**

reluctant (adj) unwilling, not wanting to do something

misconception (n) wrong belief or idea, often based on incorrect information

roped into (phr) persuaded to do something you don't really want to do

ad hoc (adj) not planned in advance

patron (n) person or organisation that gives money and support to artists, museums, etc.

trust (n) group of people that manages a fund to support a museum, a school, charity, etc.

networking (n) deliberately talking to a range of people who may be useful to your work

donor (n) person or organisation that gives money as support

geek (n) person who is obsessed with something that may seem boring to other people

archive (n) place where documents and records are stored

heritage (n) historical culture and traditions of a country or society

conservator (n) person whose job is to conserve and restore old works of art and other objects

artefact (n) object that is made by a person, usually of historical or cultural interest

 TEST 6

PAPER 1 Reading and Use of English

▶▶ **PART 1**

subtle (adj) not obvious

impartial (adj) unbiased, objective

▶▶ **PART 2**

cockatoo (n) bird belonging to the parrot family

millennia (n) thousands of years

wired (adj) organised or structured

keep a beat (phr) to stay in rhythm with music

▶▶ **PART 3**

ethnic (adj) relating to a particular race

▶▶ **PART 5**

aptitude (n) natural ability

prostrate (adj) facing downwards

defiance (n) refusal to obey

grin (v) to smile widely

coat hanger (n) curved piece of wood, plastic or wire with a hook on, used for hanging clothes

bug (n) problem in a computer program

gig (v) to perform in public

muck around (phr v) to behave in a silly way

outdo (v) to do better than someone else

stumble across (phr v) to find by chance

cut it (phr) to be convincing (idiomatic)

crux (n) most important part

onerous (adj) needing great effort

be inclined to (v) to feel like doing something

punchline (n) last few words of a joke that make it funny

script (v) to write in advance of a performance

wrestle (v) to fight someone by holding them and throwing them to the ground

lost to the ether (phr) disappeared for ever

PART 6

implications (n) possible consequences

eradicate (v) to get rid of completely

red deer (n) a type of deer common in Scotland

deceptive (adj) misleading

wilderness (n) area of land that has never been developed or used for agriculture

monitor (v) to watch carefully and record results

offset (v) to use one payment to cancel another cost

flock (n) group of sheep

graze (v) to eat grass

cull (v) to kill a number of animals of a group to prevent the group becoming too large

feasible (adj) possible to do

lobby (n) group of people who try to influence politicians on a particular issue

PART 7

bark (n) hard outside part of a tree

sequoia (n) type of tree which is very large and found in North America

redwood (n) very large species of trees. The sequoia is part of the redwood family.

longevity (n) long life

fungal rot (n) process by which wood decays and falls apart as a result of being attacked by fungus

flame-resistant (adj) able to survive a fire

logging (n) cutting down of trees for commercial purposes

brittle (adj) hard but easy to break – like some glass

shatter (v) to break into small pieces

timber (n) wood for use in building

robust (adj) strong and healthy

limb (n) large branch on a tree

crown (n) rounded top part of a tree

harness (n) set of straps attached to ropes to stop someone falling

cone (n) hard dry fruit of many species of tree, e.g. of the sequoia

seedling (n) young plant that has grown from a seed

millennia (n) thousands of years

premise (n) idea that forms the basis of an argument or way of thinking

eucalyptus (n) a species of tree, particularly common in Australia

mass (n) quantity of material that something contains

spire (n) tall pointed part at top of tree

billow (v) to move up and spread out like a cloud of smoke

PART 8

for the sake of (phr) in order to do something

disapproval (n) when someone thinks something is wrong

suspend your disbelief (phr) to believe temporarily that something imaginary or invented is real

reservation (n) doubt

awe (n) feeling of being very impressed

resentment (n) feeling of anger or unhappiness about something you think is unfair

dissipate (v) to gradually become weaker

talk down to someone (phr v) to speak to someone as if they are less important or intelligent

first principles (n) the most basic rules

trigger (n) original cause of a particular development

fortuitous (adj) by chance

radiology (n) study of radiation in medicine

spur (n) fact or event that makes you want to do something

innate (adj) born with

trait (n) characteristic

 TEST 7

PAPER 1 Reading and Use of English

PART 1

up-tempo (adj) with a fast rhythm

pace (n) speed

key (n) set of related musical notes based on a particular note. Some keys are major and some minor depending on the types of notes they are based on.

upbeat (adj) positive and enthusiastic

melancholic (adj) sad

ambiguous (adj) having more than one possible meaning or feeling

PART 2

whine (v) to complain with an annoying high sound

mew (v) to cry with a soft high noise, like a cat

scan (v) to use special equipment to take images of something

PART 3

contravene (v) to do something that is not allowed by law

wilderness (n) area of land that has never been developed or used for agriculture

PART 5

discredit (v) to make people stop believing something is true

ill-considered (adj) badly planned

abstract (adj) involving ideas rather than facts

hooked (adj) fascinated

counter-intuitive (adj) the opposite of what you would probably feel to be true

graft (n) work

innumerate (adj) very bad at mathematics

tone-deaf (adj) unable to hear the difference between musical notes

correlation (n) connection between two things in which one thing changes as the other does

aptitude (n) natural ability

plausible (adj) could be true

confined (adj) restricted

syntax (n) the way words and phrases are put together to form sentences

paradoxical (adj) and **paradox** (n) a paradox is a situation that has two opposite features and therefore seems strange. For example, music is to do with emotions and mathematics is to do with reason and logic, so it might seem paradoxical for someone to be good at both.

dispel (v) to get rid of

confound (v) to confuse and surprise

PART 6

adolescence (n) time in a person's life when he or she develops from being a child to being an adult

patronisingly (adv) if someone is patronising they show you they think they are better than you

induce (v) to cause something to happen

misgiving (n) feeling of doubt

speculation (n) forming opinions about something without having much evidence

physiology (n) way a living body functions

lucidity (n) in a clear way

undermine (v) to make something weaker

invoke (v) to mention or refer to

hypothesis (n) theory

plausibility (n) how likely something is to be true

wish fulfilment (n) hoping that an idea is true

grumpily (adv) in a bad-tempered way

inherently (adv) in itself, naturally

jazz up (phr v) to make something seem more exciting

dumb down (phr v) to make something seem easier than it really is

spur (n) cause of a change

prose (n) style of writing

hardwired (adj) naturally part of a person's physical development, not caused by external influences

PART 7

tracker (n) person who can find wild animals by following the marks they leave

pungent (adj) strong smelling

thumping (n) banging noise

twig (n) very small, thin branch

hive (n) structure where bees live

pound (v) to hit hard

innate (adj) born with

jiggle (v) to make something move up and down or side to side with quick movements

stem (n) long, thin, flexible part of a plant

bristles (n) short stiff hairs of a brush

nibble (v) to take small bites

cling (v) to hold on to

logging (n) cutting down of trees for commercial purposes

disarray (n) extreme confusion

termite (n) insect that lives in large groups, found in hot countries, looks similar to white ants

mound (n) large pile of earth

distort (v) to change so that something is no longer correct or true

delicacy (n) nice thing to eat

lunge (v) to make a sudden forward movement in order to attack

prey (n) animal that is hunted, killed and eaten by another animal

predator (n) animal that attacks and eats other animals

reticence (n) shyness, unwillingness to show yourself

whack (v) to hit hard

PART 8

trepidation (n) worry or fear that something unpleasant will happen

relief (n) something different that is easier or more enjoyable than what you have been doing

proactively (adv) preparing for problems before they happen

ward (n) department in a hospital

daunted (adj) anxious, worried

pitfall (n) danger or difficulty that might arise, especially one that is hidden or not obvious at first

averse (to) (adj) not liking, opposed to

eradicate (v) to get rid of completely

uphold (v) to apply, follow or support rules

under my belt (phr) if you have something under your belt, you have experienced or achieved it

transparency (n) when a situation – a policy, for example – can be understood clearly and easily

get to grips with (phr) to understand properly

boil down to (phr v) to be a result of

outcome (n) result of an action or event

pass the buck (phr) to make someone else responsible for something

think out of the box (phr) to think in a different, unconventional way in order to be creative

blinkered (adj) restricted in thinking, narrow-minded

TEST 8

PAPER 1 Reading and Use of English

▶▶ **PART 1**

prior to (adj) before

diversification (n) development of a wider variety of things

bias (n) personal preference for something, not based on logical reasons

▶▶ **PART 2**

work placement (n) temporary job, often part of a course of study, which provides work experience

HR (n) Human Resources, i.e. personnel

▶▶ **PART 3**

biodiversity (n) large number of different types of animals and plants in a particular environment

devastation (n) serious damage

▶▶ **PART 5**

echo (v) to express similar ideas

dubious (adj) uncertain, probably not very good

metaphor (n) way of describing something by comparing it with something else

do your head in (phr) to make you feel confused, upset, annoyed (informal expression)

syndrome (n) set of physical symptoms showing you have a particular medical problem

fidgety (adj) unable to remain still or quiet

relieve (v) to take something away

burden (n) something difficult or unpleasant you have to deal with

illustrate (v) to give information or examples to explain something

misguided (adj) wrong because you have understood or judged something badly

unease (n) feeling of being worried or unhappy

anguish (n) extreme unhappiness

ignite (v) to make something start or cause something

disquiet (n) feelings of worry and unhappiness

wrought (v) caused to happen (past and past participle form of *to wreak* – very formal)

lose the thread (phr) to no longer follow an argument or story

scurrying (adj) moving quickly

particle (n) very small piece of something

neural pathways (adj + n) connections between different areas of the brain or nervous system

rewire (v) to change the connections in the brain

atrophy (v) to become weak

mediate (v) to help deal with

grey matter (n) the brain, often referring to intelligence

trivialise (v) to focus on unimportant things

jeopardise (v) to put in danger

decommission (v) to stop using

redundant (adj) no longer needed

trawl (v) to search through a large amount of information

the shallows (n) here refers to information that does not require serious or deep thought

plumb the depths (v) to go deeply into something

in due course (phr) at the right time in the future

remedial (adj) aimed at solving a problem

unravel (v) to take apart, break up

conditioning (n) experience that makes people behave the way they do

feat (n) action or piece of work that needs skill, strength or effort

punchline (n) here refers to the words that express the main point

frenziedness (n) involving a lot of activity and strong emotions, and probably out of control

wits (n) intelligence

▶▶ **PART 6**

irrespective of (prep) without considering or being influenced by

aspirational (adj) wanting to do better

inordinate (adj) more than is expected or sensible

viable (adj) having the conditions to be successful

lucrative (adj) producing lots of money

illusory (adj) not real although it might seem to be

astronomical (adj) extremely high

underprivileged (adj) having less money and fewer opportunities than most people

illusion (n) idea that is not true

doomed (adj) certain to fail

retrospectively (adv) connected with something that happened in the past

▶▶ **PART 7**

attribute (n) quality or feature

resilience (n) ability to recover from a difficult or unpleasant experience

humility (n) quality of not thinking you are better than other people

trait (n) characteristic

IQ (n) intelligence quotient, a way of assessing intelligence through certain tests which largely focus on problem-solving, reasoning, memory and mathematics

liken (v) to compare

not up to scratch (phr) not as good as it should be

▶▶ **PART 8**

calibre (n) quality

concise (adj) using few words

orthodox (adj) conventional

verbiage (n) use of too many words

nail (v) to get exactly right

slick (adj) clever and smooth (used to express disapproval)

the nitty gritty (n) the basic or most important details

private eye (n) private detective

pull off (phr v) to be successful at

cliffhanger (n) very exciting moment in a story because you cannot guess what will happen next

reveal (n) point in a mystery story when you find out the truth

exponent (n) person able to perform a particular activity

empathise (v) to understand another person's feelings and experiences

sheltered housing (n) special housing for old people

crumbling (adj) falling down

pacey (adj) fast moving